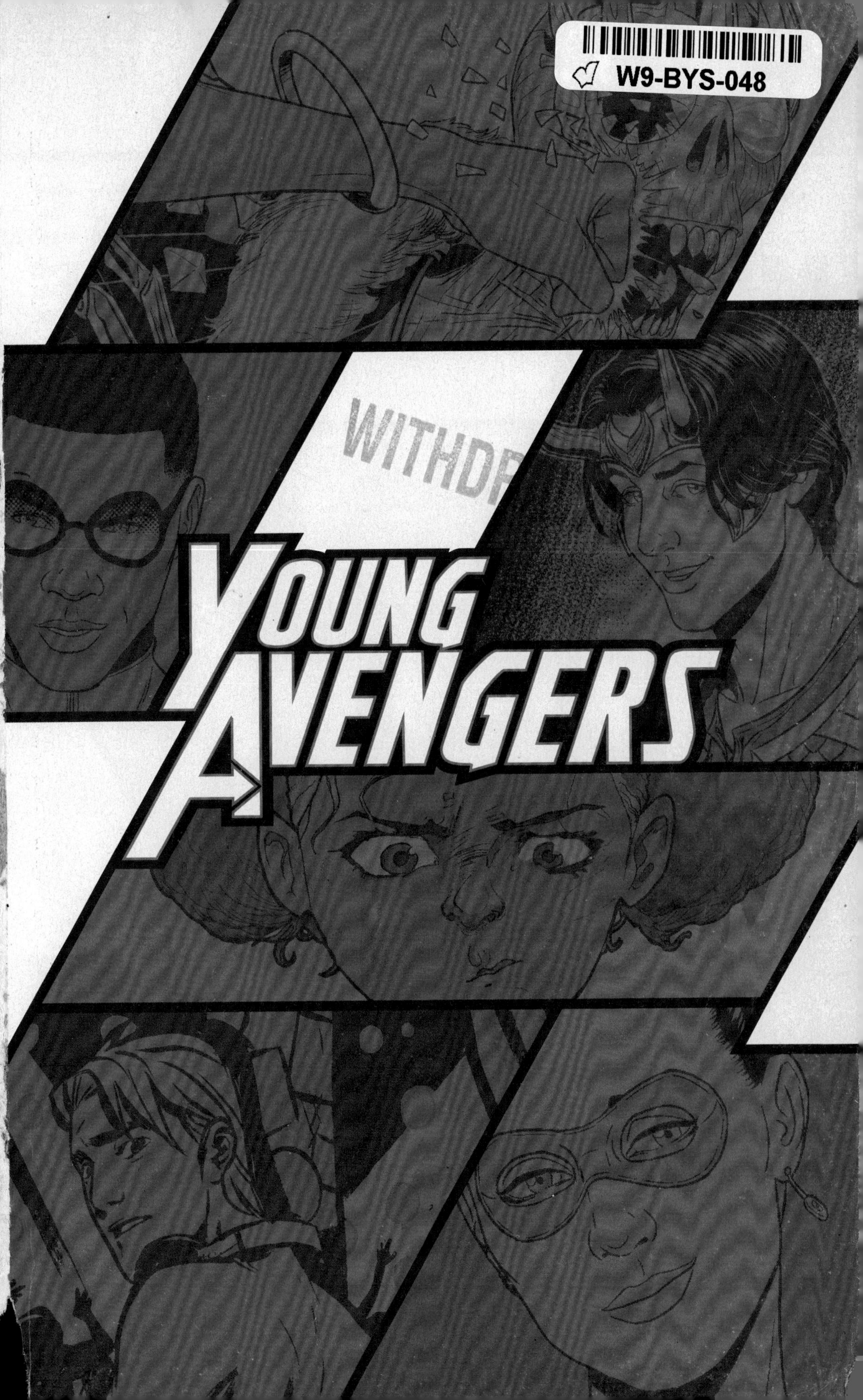
YOUNG
AVENGERS

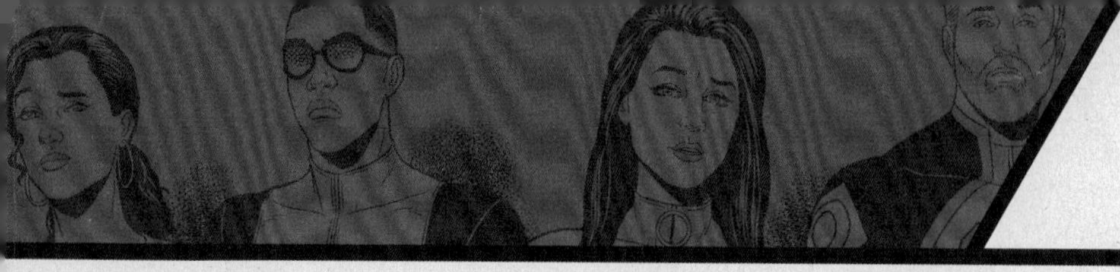

YOUNG AVENGERS:
MIC-DROP AT THE
EDGE C

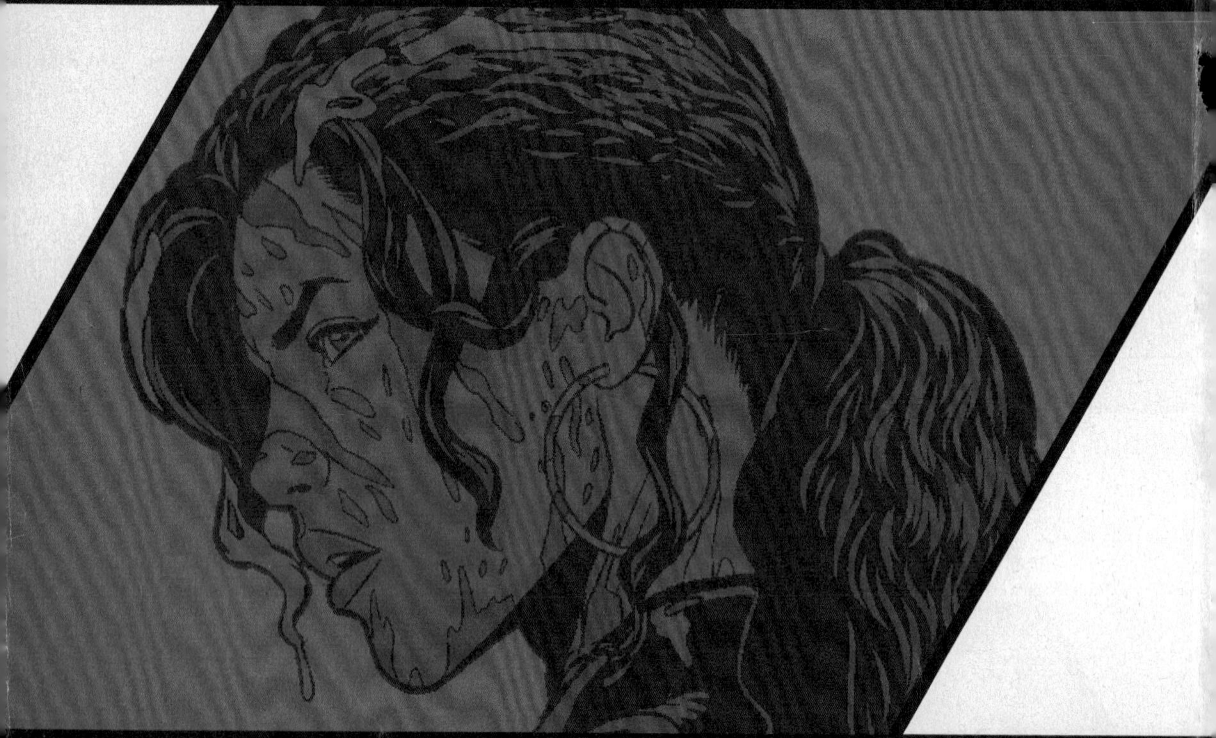

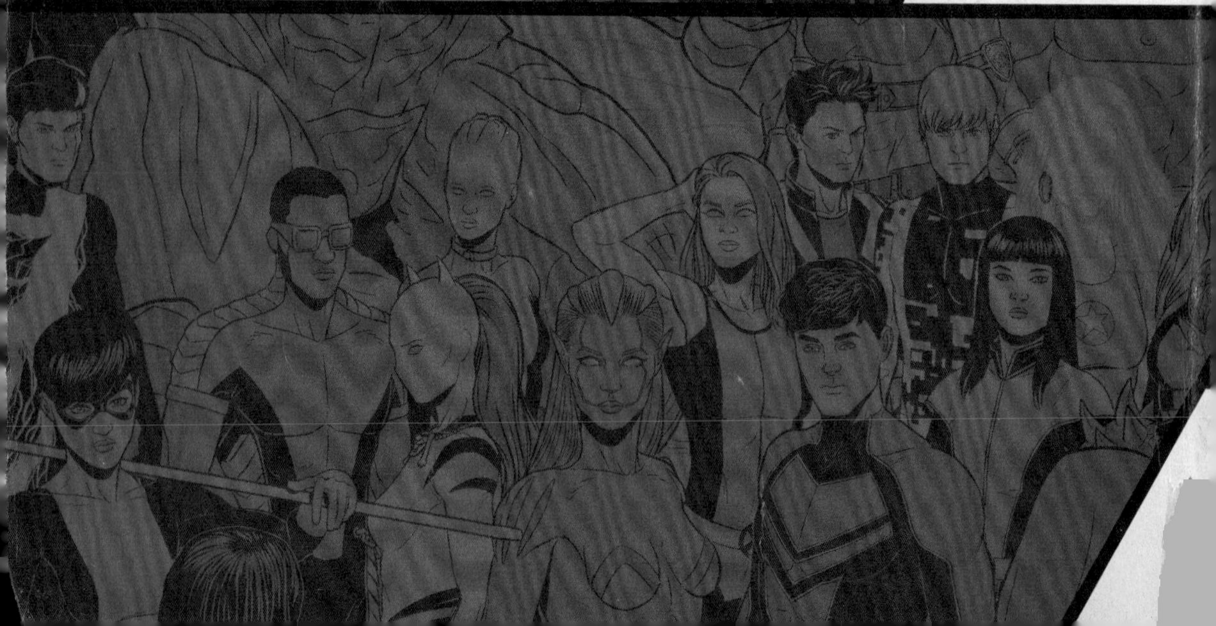

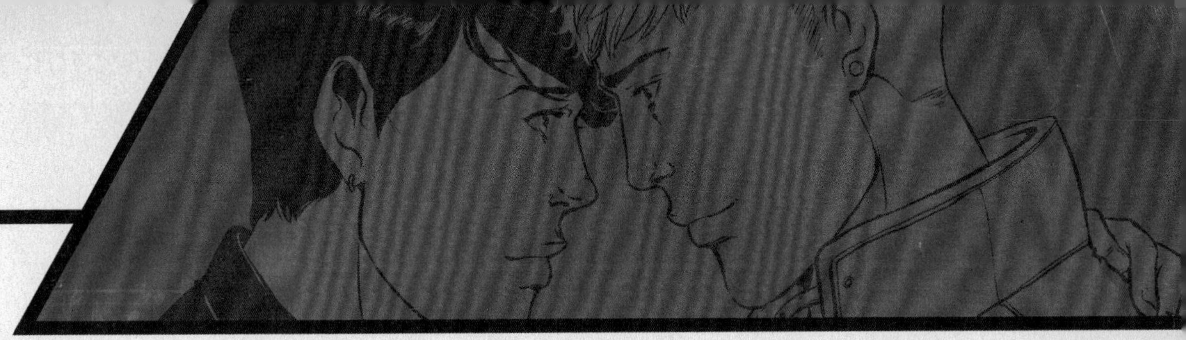

F TIME AND SPACE

writer: **KIERON GILLEN**
penciler: **JAMIE McKELVIE**
color artist: **MATTHEW WILSON**
additional artists, #14: **EMMA VIECELI & LEE LOUGHRIDGE** (pp. 6-10), **CHRISTIAN WARD** (pp. 11-15) **AND ANNIE WU & JORDIE BELLAIRE** (pp. 16-20)
additional artists, #15: **BECKY CLOONAN & JORDIE BELLAIRE** (pp. 1-5), **MING DOYLE & MARIS WICKS** (#6-10) **AND JOE QUINONES & MARIS WICKS** (pp. 11-15) letterer: **VC'S CLAYTON COWLES**
cover art: **JAMIE McKELVIE & MATTHEW WILSON**
assistant editor: **JON MOISAN** editor: **LAUREN SANKOVITCH**

collection editor: JENNIFER GRÜNWALD
associate managing editor: ALEX STARBUCK
editor, special projects: MARK D. BEAZLEY
senior editor, special projects: JEFF YOUNGQUIST
svp print, sales & marketing: DAVID GABRIEL
book design: JEFF POWELL
editor in chief: AXEL ALONSO
chief creative officer: JOE QUESADA
publisher: DAN BUCKLEY
executive producer: ALAN FINE

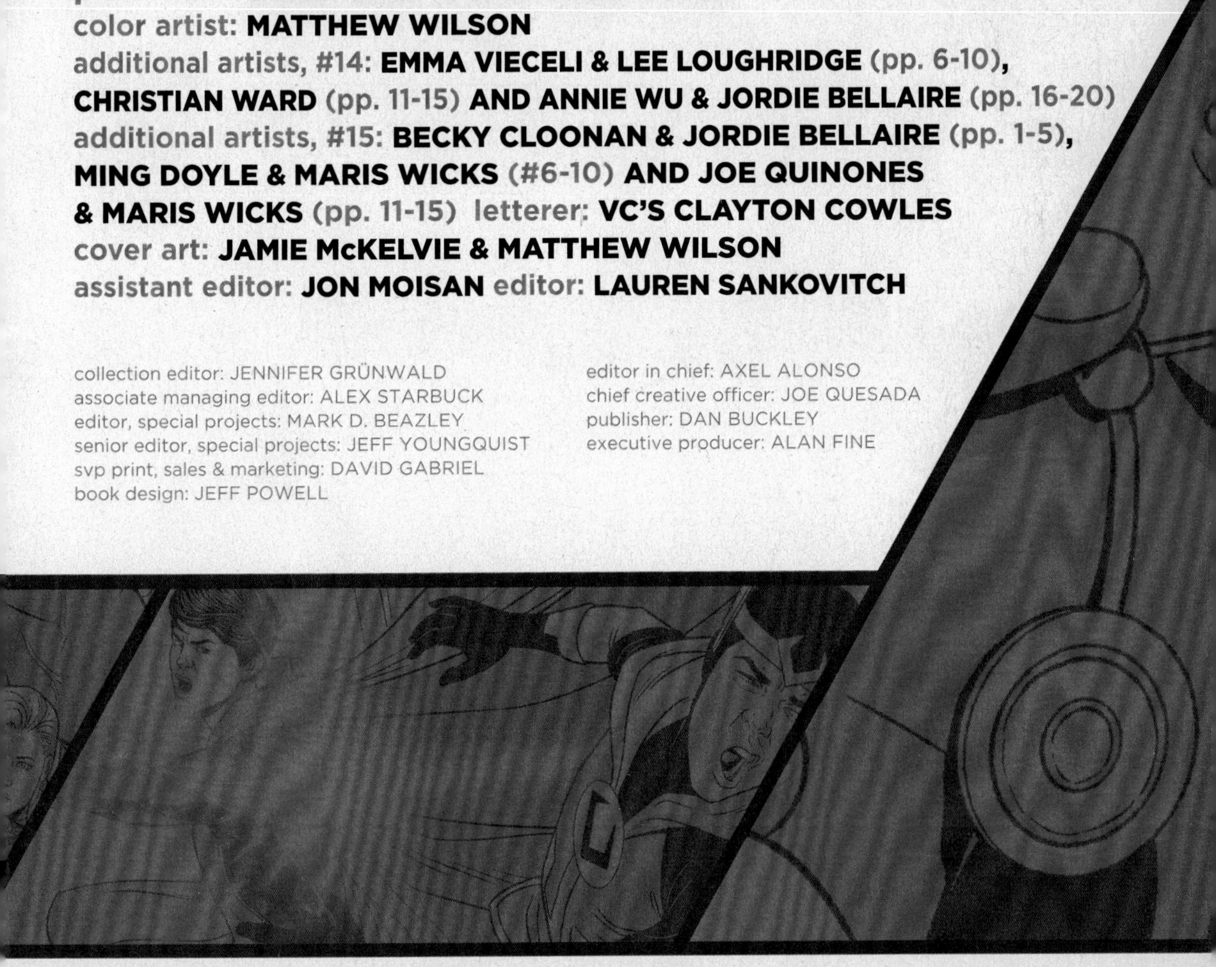

YOUNG AVENGERS VOL. 3: MIC-DROP AT THE EDGE OF TIME AND SPACE. Contains material originally published in magazine form as YOUNG AVENGERS #11-15. First printing 2014. ISBN# 978-0-7851-8530-7. Published by MARVEL WORLDWIDE, INC., a subsidiary of MARVEL ENTERTAINMENT, LLC. OFFICE OF PUBLICATION: 135 West 50th Street, New York, NY 10020. **Printed in Canada.** ALAN FINE, EVP - Office of the President, Marvel Worldwide, Inc. and EVP & CMO Marvel Characters B.V.; DAN BUCKLEY, Publisher & President - Print, Animation & Digital Divisions; JOE QUESADA, Chief Creative Officer; TOM BREVOORT, SVP of Publishing; DAVID BOGART, SVP of Operations & Procurement, Publishing; C.B. CEBULSKI, SVP of Creator & Content Development; DAVID GABRIEL, SVP Print, Sales & Marketing; JIM O'KEEFE, VP of Operations & Logistics; DAN CARR, Executive Director of Publishing Technology; SUSAN CRESPI, Editorial Operations Manager; ALEX MORALES, Publishing Operations Manager; STAN LEE, Chairman Emeritus. For information regarding advertising in Marvel Comics or on Marvel.com, please contact Niza Disla, Director of Marvel Partnerships, at ndisla@marvel.com. For Marvel subscription inquiries, please call 800-217-9158. **Manufactured between 1/24/2014 and 3/3/2014 by SOLISCO PRINTERS, SCOTT, QC, CANADA.**

10 9 8 7 6 5 4 3 2 1

11

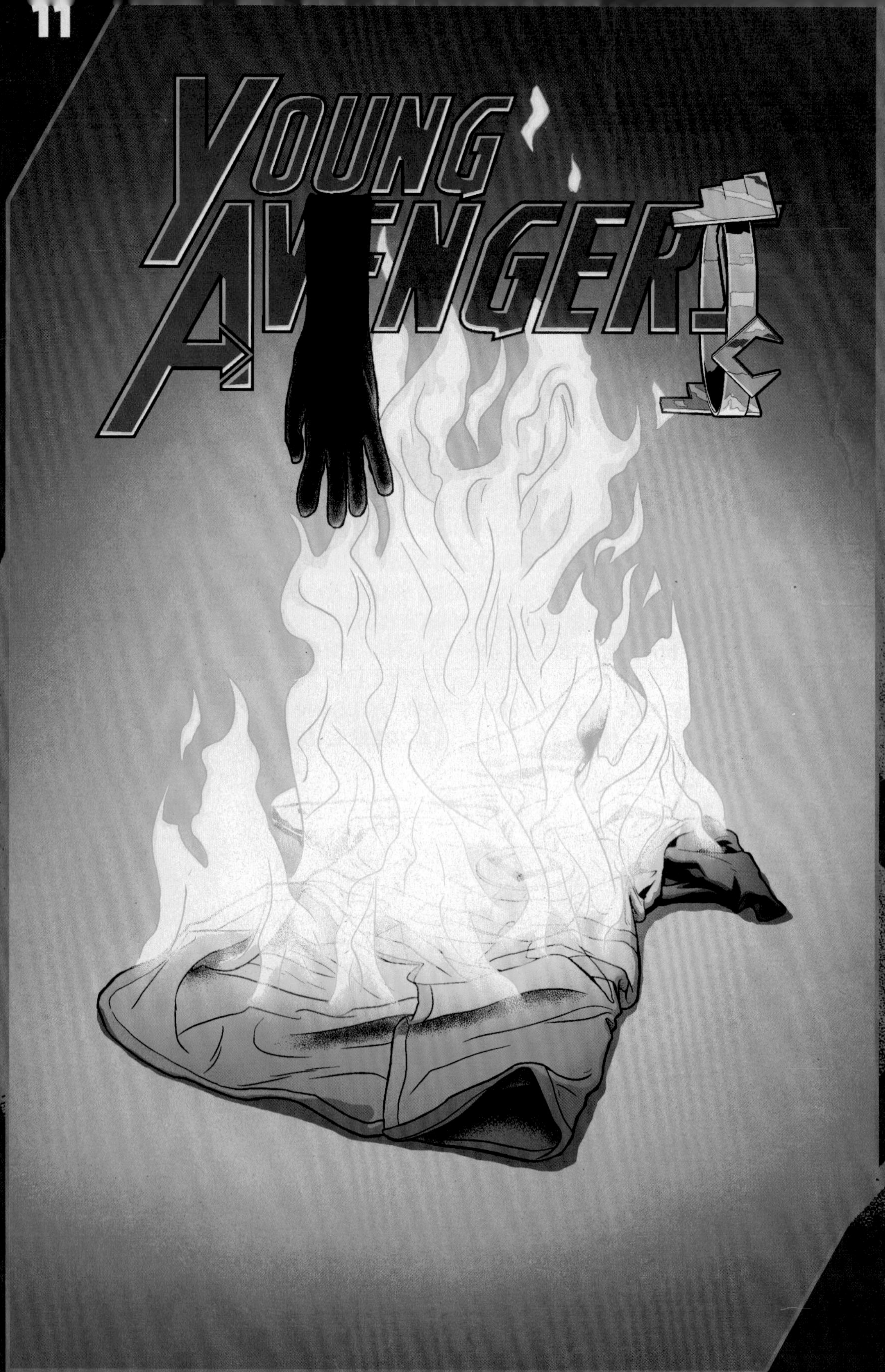
YOUNG

STAGE NERVOUS BREAKDOWN

yamblr.

search yamblr

- living on a snack
- special thanks
- to
- Idette
- Winecoor
- <3

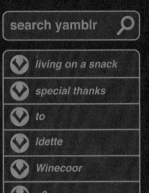

Hawkeye
not the hawkguy

Hulkling
shape-shifting alien hybrid guy

Loki
god of mischief

Marvel Boy
banished kree music lover

Miss America
interdimensional kicker of butt

Prodigy
knows pretty much everything

Wiccan
angsty chaos-magic user

ShumaGoRAD!

Back in Mother's super creepy dimension, Mother hungrily waits for Wiccan and his tasty, tasty powers to return so she can make a snack out of them. All she really needs is the right bait…

#dimension of the creeps #tasty powers are tasty #living on a snack

IceQueen

Loki, using a magic hologram-a-phone, pays a visit to Mother where it's revealed that he totally set up Wiccan in an attempt to double-cross Mother and take all the magic! What a jerky jerk jerk.

#trust loki #whisper sweet nothings #do not trust loki

AppleADay

After a rather tense game of Questions (Is there a mobile version of that game?), Loki leaves triumphant and Patri-not shows up, still acting all mysterious and whatnot. What's really up with that guy…?

#still creepy #did he just turn into smoke #oh snap he did

SnacksOnSnacks OnSnacks

Leah also joins in on the fun and pays a visit to Mother. She reveals that she intends to get her revenge on Loki for kinda sorta stranding her in the crazy distant past with no way home.

#revenge is a dish #hel hath no fury #other cliches

UltimateBillyIdol

With Teddy in tow, Leah takes him to a meeting of the angry exes of the Young Avengers. Thankfully, Teddy determines that they're all cray-cray and tries to leave. Wrong answer, buster. Teddy gets captured by Mother. Crap.

#worst support group ever #at least the coffee is good #dammit someone drank the last of it

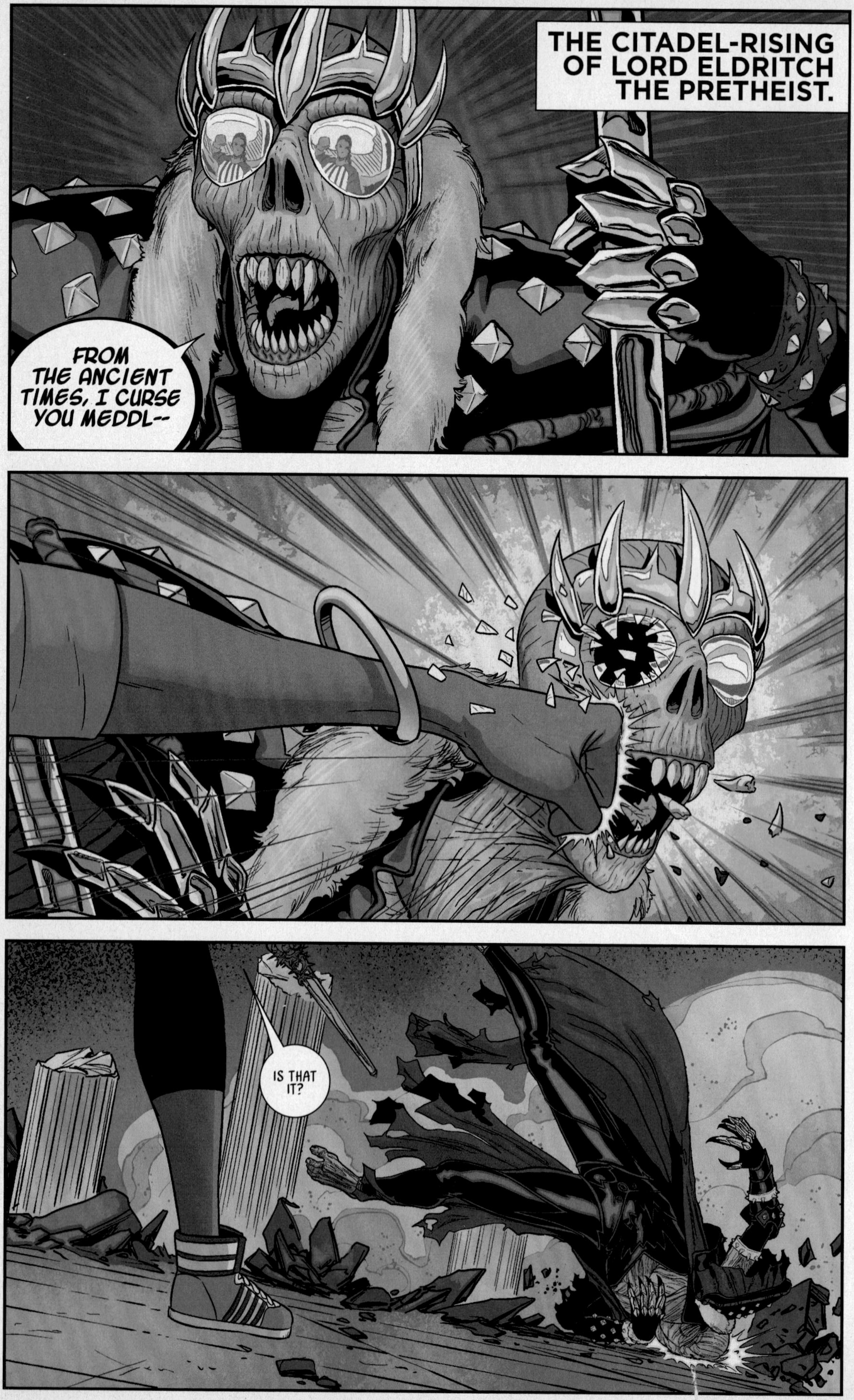
THE CITADEL-RISING OF LORD ELDRITCH THE PRETHEIST.
FROM THE ANCIENT TIMES, I CURSE YOU MEDDL--
IS THAT IT?

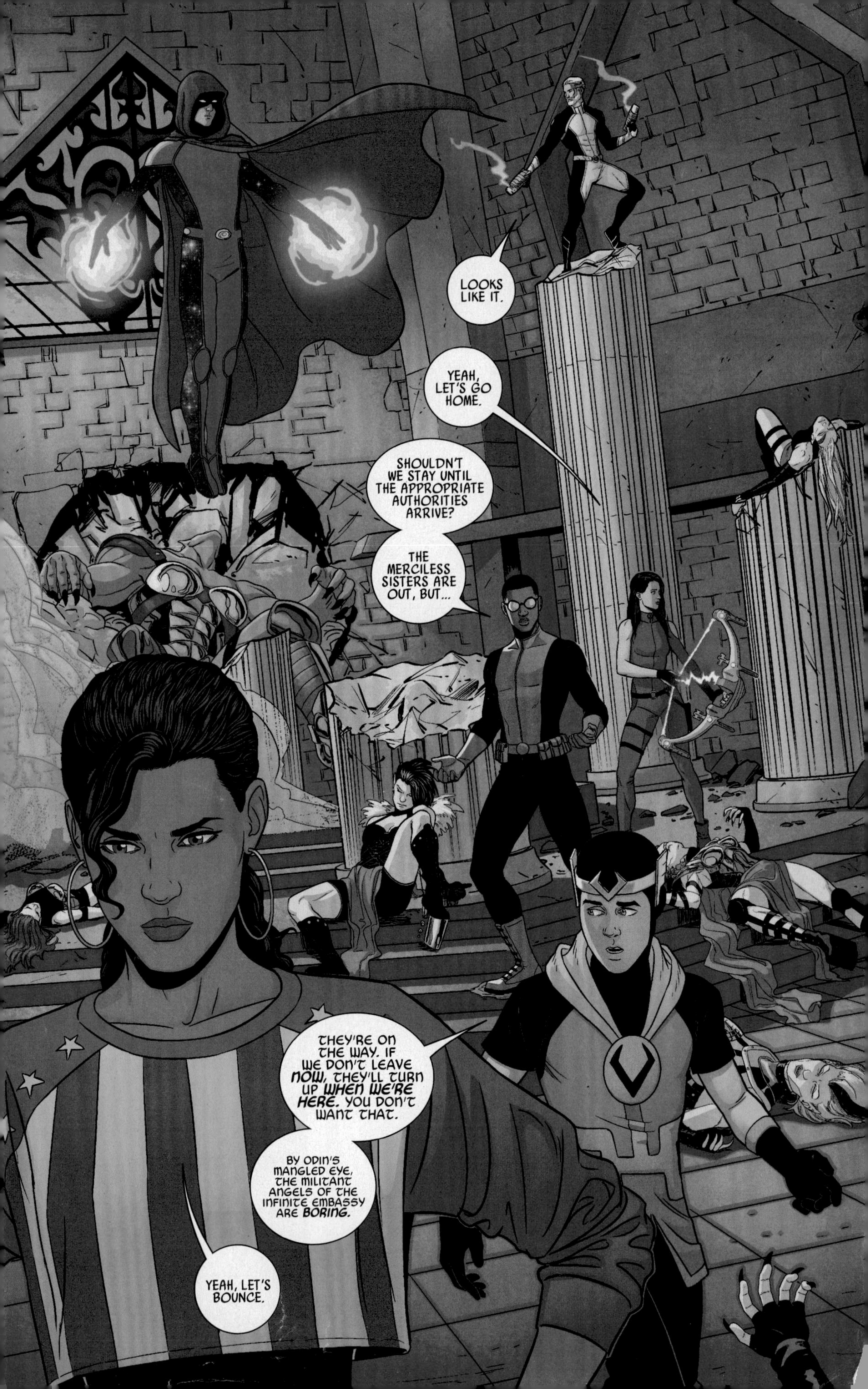

LOOKS LIKE IT.
YEAH, LET'S GO HOME.
SHOULDN'T WE STAY UNTIL THE APPROPRIATE AUTHORITIES ARRIVE?
THE MERCILESS SISTERS ARE OUT, BUT...
THEY'RE ON THE WAY. IF WE DON'T LEAVE NOW, THEY'LL TURN UP WHEN WE'RE HERE. YOU DON'T WANT THAT.
BY ODIN'S MANGLED EYE, THE MILITANT ANGELS OF THE INFINITE EMBASSY ARE BORING.
YEAH, LET'S BOUNCE.

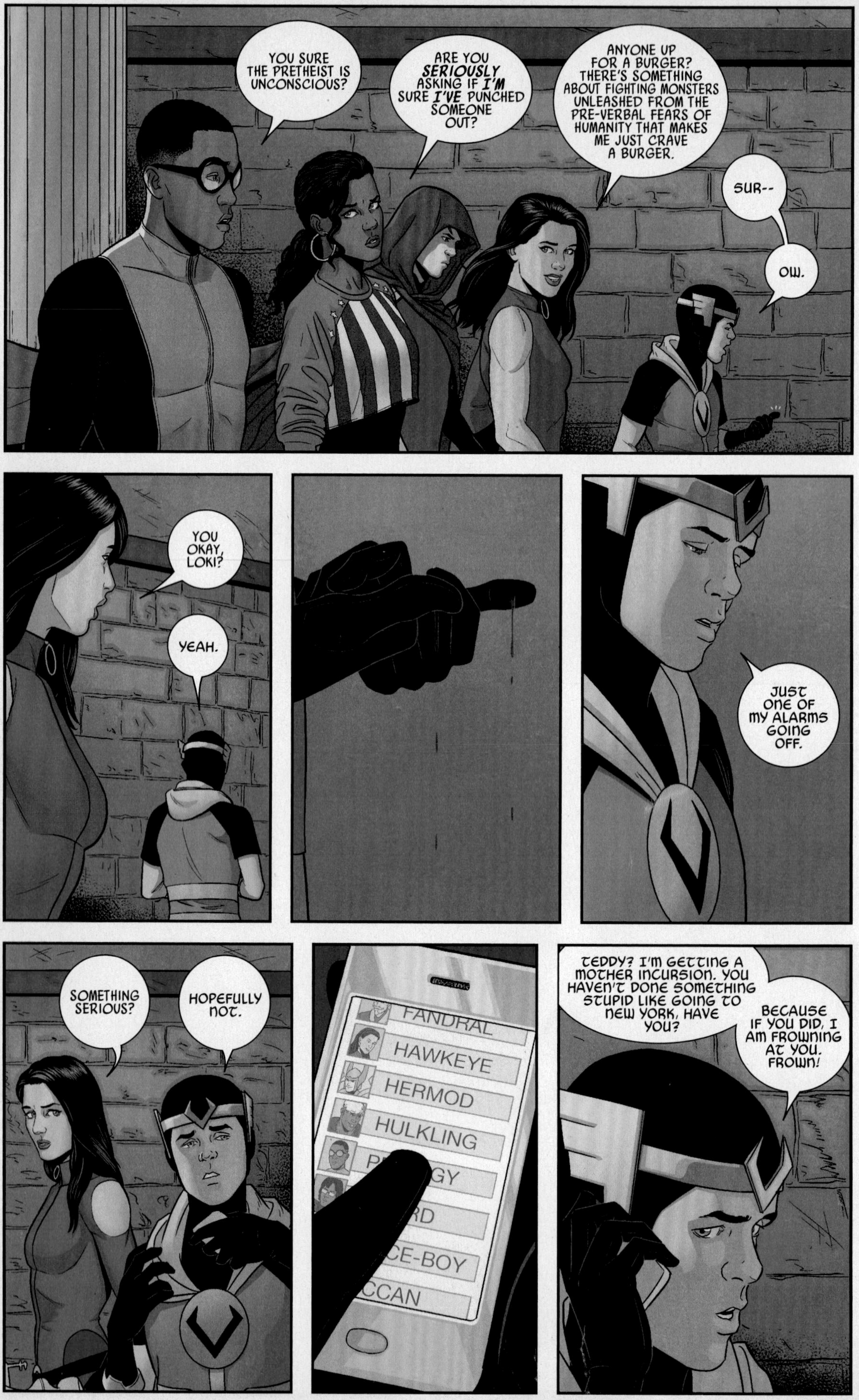
YOU SURE THE PRETHEIST IS UNCONSCIOUS?
ARE YOU SERIOUSLY ASKING IF I'M SURE I'VE PUNCHED SOMEONE OUT?
ANYONE UP FOR A BURGER? THERE'S SOMETHING ABOUT FIGHTING MONSTERS UNLEASHED FROM THE PRE-VERBAL FEARS OF HUMANITY THAT MAKES ME JUST CRAVE A BURGER.
SUR--
OW.
YOU OKAY, LOKI?
YEAH.
JUST ONE OF MY ALARMS GOING OFF.
SOMETHING SERIOUS?
HOPEFULLY NOT.
FANDRAL
HAWKEYE
HERMOD
HULKLING
TEDDY? I'M GETTING A MOTHER INCURSION. YOU HAVEN'T DONE SOMETHING STUPID LIKE GOING TO NEW YORK, HAVE YOU?
BECAUSE IF YOU DID, I AM FROWNING AT YOU. FROWN!

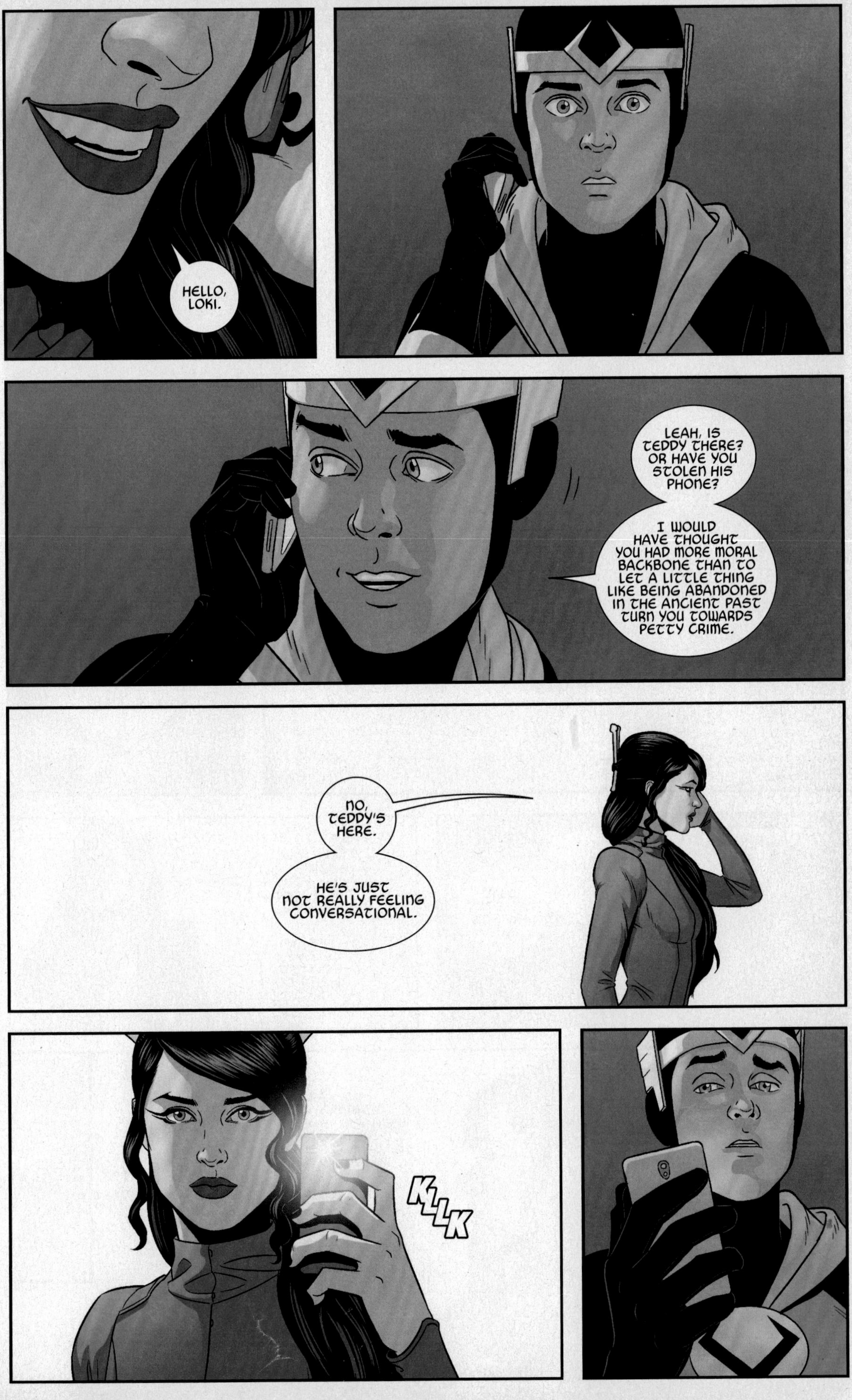
HELLO, LOKI.
LEAH, IS TEDDY THERE? OR HAVE YOU STOLEN HIS PHONE?
I WOULD HAVE THOUGHT YOU HAD MORE MORAL BACKBONE THAN TO LET A LITTLE THING LIKE BEING ABANDONED IN THE ANCIENT PAST TURN YOU TOWARDS PETTY CRIME.
NO, TEDDY'S HERE.
HE'S JUST NOT REALLY FEELING CONVERSATIONAL.
KLLK

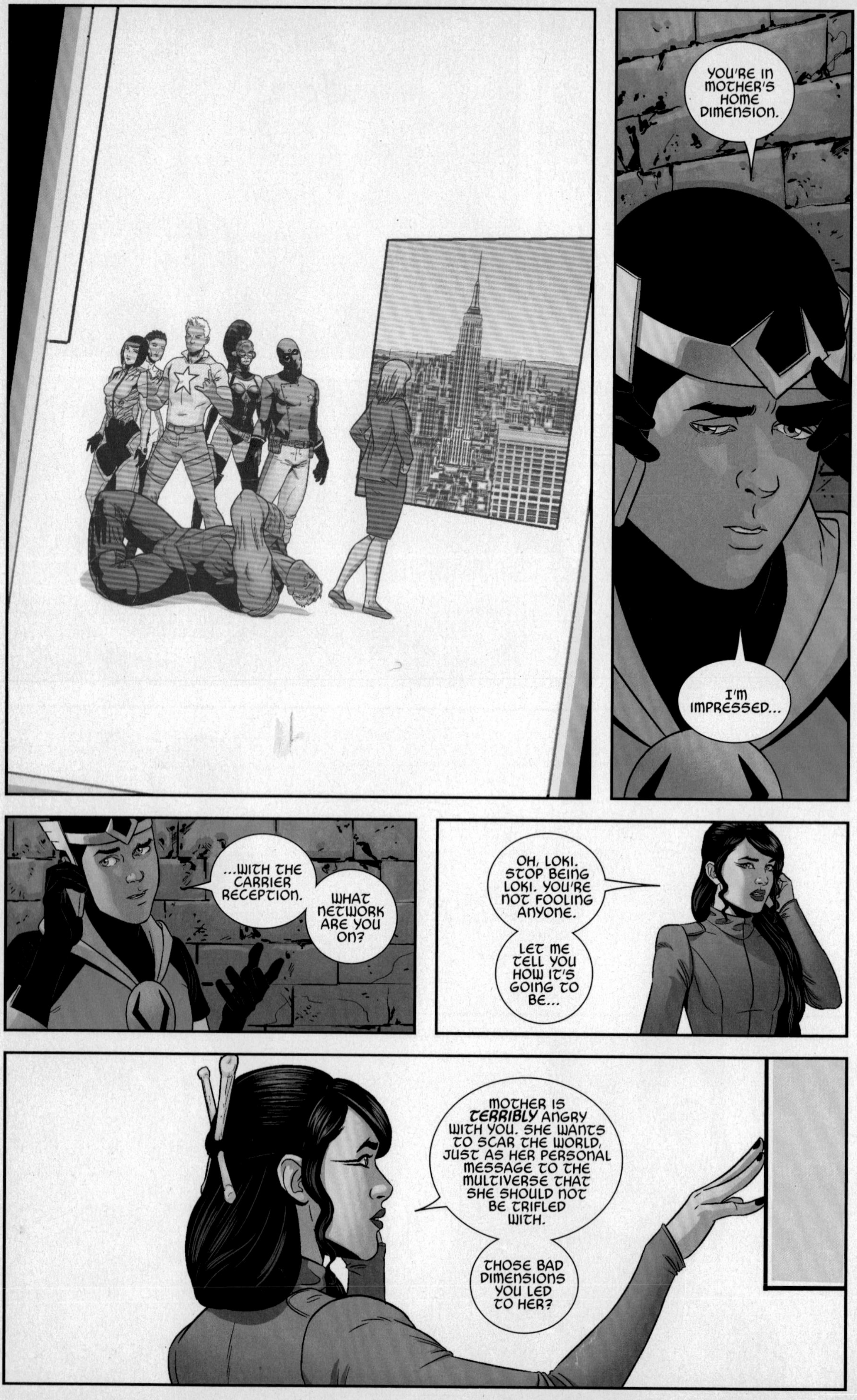
YOU'RE IN MOTHER'S HOME DIMENSION.
I'M IMPRESSED...
...WITH THE CARRIER RECEPTION.
WHAT NETWORK ARE YOU ON?
OH, LOKI. STOP BEING LOKI. YOU'RE NOT FOOLING ANYONE.
LET ME TELL YOU HOW IT'S GOING TO BE...
MOTHER IS *TERRIBLY* ANGRY WITH YOU. SHE WANTS TO SCAR THE WORLD, JUST AS HER PERSONAL MESSAGE TO THE MULTIVERSE THAT SHE SHOULD NOT BE TRIFLED WITH.
THOSE BAD DIMENSIONS YOU LED TO HER?

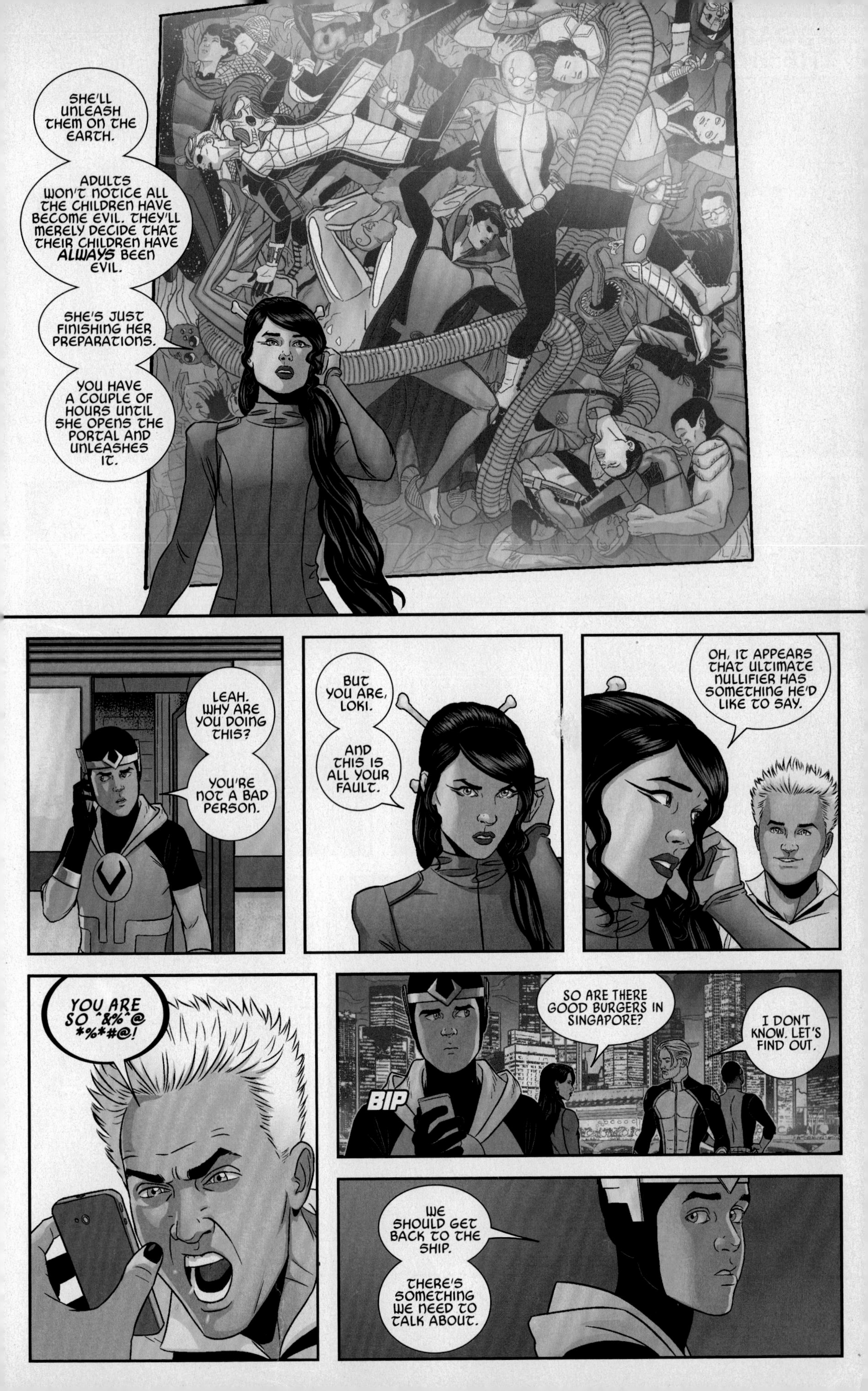
SHE'LL UNLEASH THEM ON THE EARTH.
ADULTS WON'T NOTICE ALL THE CHILDREN HAVE BECOME EVIL. THEY'LL MERELY DECIDE THAT THEIR CHILDREN HAVE *ALWAYS* BEEN EVIL.
SHE'S JUST FINISHING HER PREPARATIONS.
YOU HAVE A COUPLE OF HOURS UNTIL SHE OPENS THE PORTAL AND UNLEASHES IT.
LEAH. WHY ARE YOU DOING THIS?
YOU'RE NOT A BAD PERSON.
BUT YOU ARE, LOKI.
AND THIS IS ALL YOUR FAULT.
OH, IT APPEARS THAT ULTIMATE NULLIFIER HAS SOMETHING HE'D LIKE TO SAY.
YOU ARE SO ^&%^@ *%*#@!
BIP
SO ARE THERE GOOD BURGERS IN SINGAPORE?
I DON'T KNOW. LET'S FIND OUT.
WE SHOULD GET BACK TO THE SHIP.
THERE'S SOMETHING WE NEED TO TALK ABOUT.

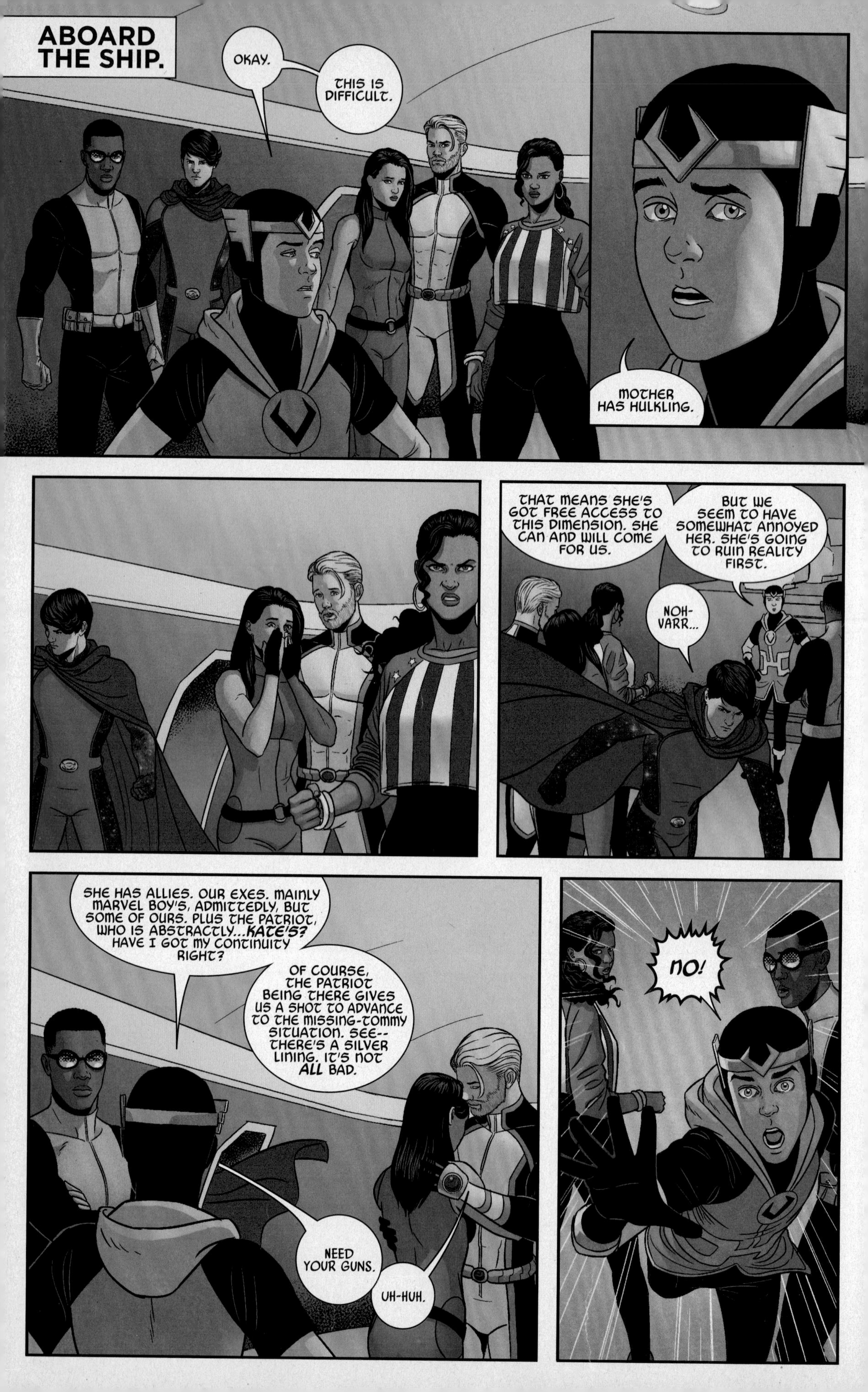
ABOARD THE SHIP.
OKAY.
THIS IS DIFFICULT.
MOTHER HAS HULKLING.
THAT MEANS SHE'S GOT FREE ACCESS TO THIS DIMENSION. SHE CAN AND WILL COME FOR US.
BUT WE SEEM TO HAVE SOMEWHAT ANNOYED HER. SHE'S GOING TO RUIN REALITY FIRST.
NOH-VARR...
SHE HAS ALLIES. OUR EXES. MAINLY MARVEL BOY'S, ADMITTEDLY, BUT SOME OF OURS. PLUS THE PATRIOT, WHO IS ABSTRACTLY...KATE'S? HAVE I GOT MY CONTINUITY RIGHT?
OF COURSE, THE PATRIOT BEING THERE GIVES US A SHOT TO ADVANCE TO THE MISSING-TOMMY SITUATION. SEE--THERE'S A SILVER LINING. IT'S NOT ALL BAD.
NEED YOUR GUNS.
UH-HUH.
NO!

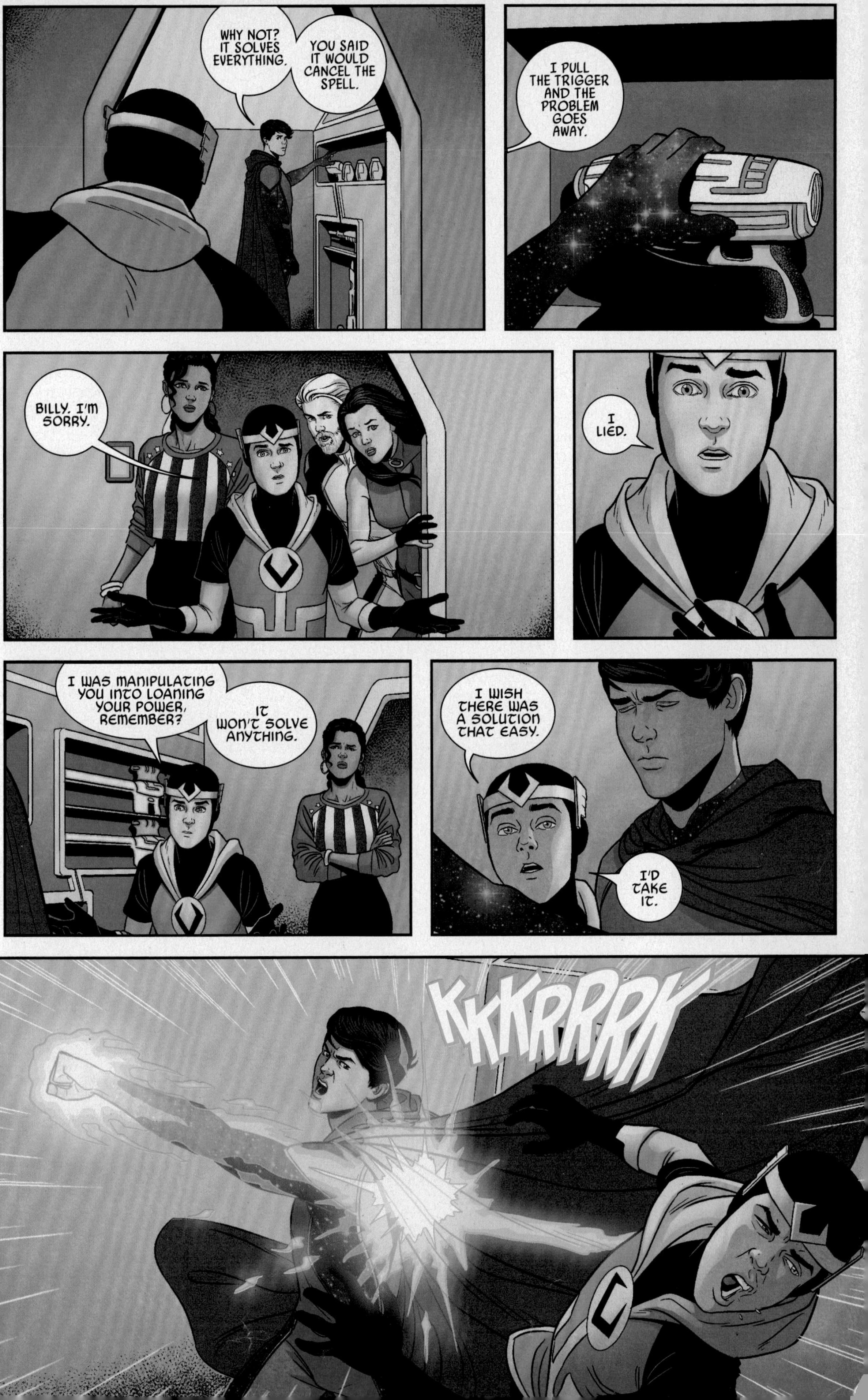
WHY NOT? IT SOLVES EVERYTHING.
YOU SAID IT WOULD CANCEL THE SPELL.
I PULL THE TRIGGER AND THE PROBLEM GOES AWAY.
BILLY. I'M SORRY.
I LIED.
I WAS MANIPULATING YOU INTO LOANING YOUR POWER, REMEMBER?
IT WON'T SOLVE ANYTHING.
I WISH THERE WAS A SOLUTION THAT EASY.
I'D TAKE IT.
KKKRRRK

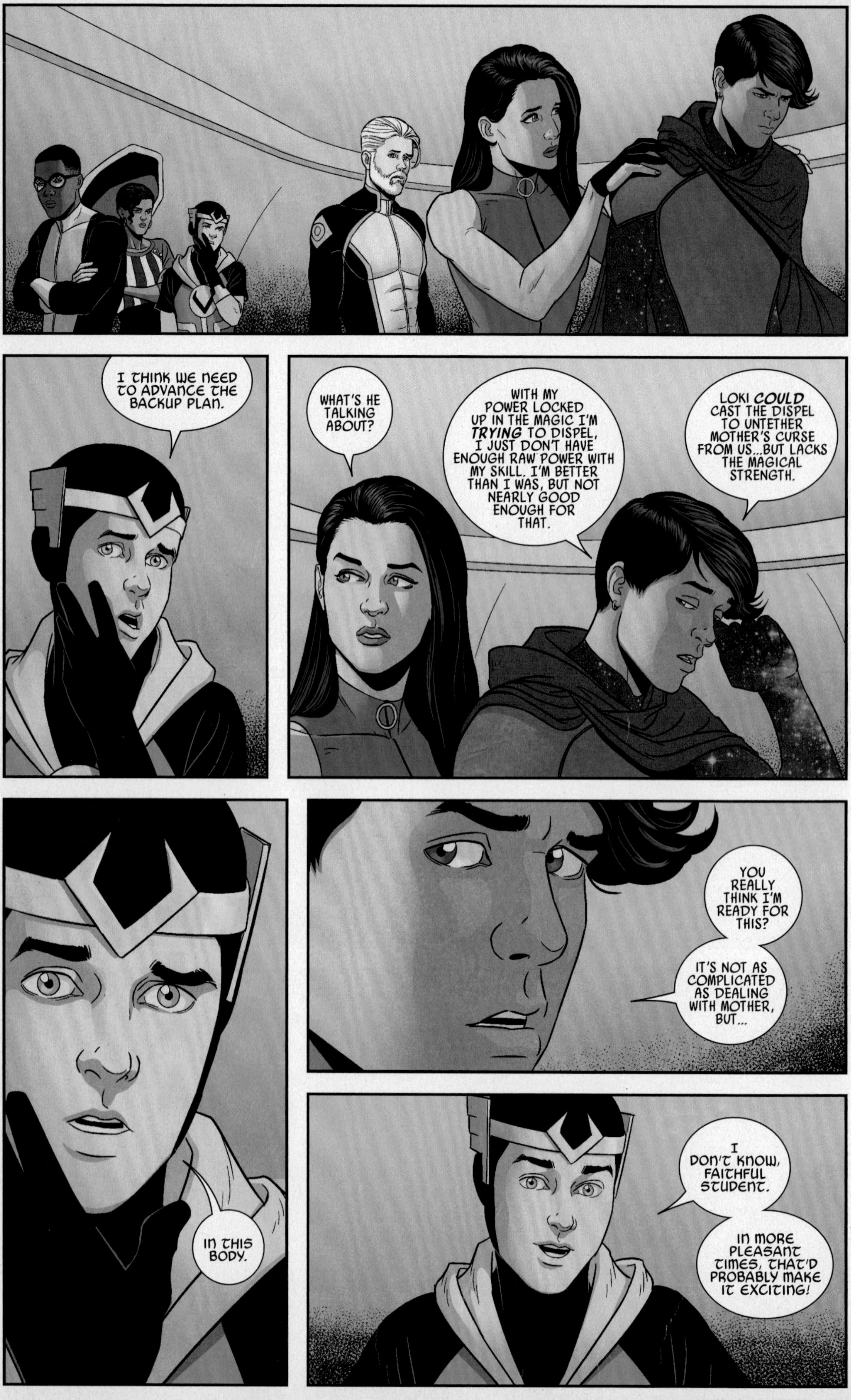
I THINK WE NEED TO ADVANCE THE BACKUP PLAN.
WHAT'S HE TALKING ABOUT?
WITH MY POWER LOCKED UP IN THE MAGIC I'M TRYING TO DISPEL, I JUST DON'T HAVE ENOUGH RAW POWER WITH MY SKILL. I'M BETTER THAN I WAS, BUT NOT NEARLY GOOD ENOUGH FOR THAT.
LOKI COULD CAST THE DISPEL TO UNTETHER MOTHER'S CURSE FROM US...BUT LACKS THE MAGICAL STRENGTH.
IN THIS BODY.
YOU REALLY THINK I'M READY FOR THIS?
IT'S NOT AS COMPLICATED AS DEALING WITH MOTHER, BUT...
I DON'T KNOW, FAITHFUL STUDENT.
IN MORE PLEASANT TIMES, THAT'D PROBABLY MAKE IT EXCITING!

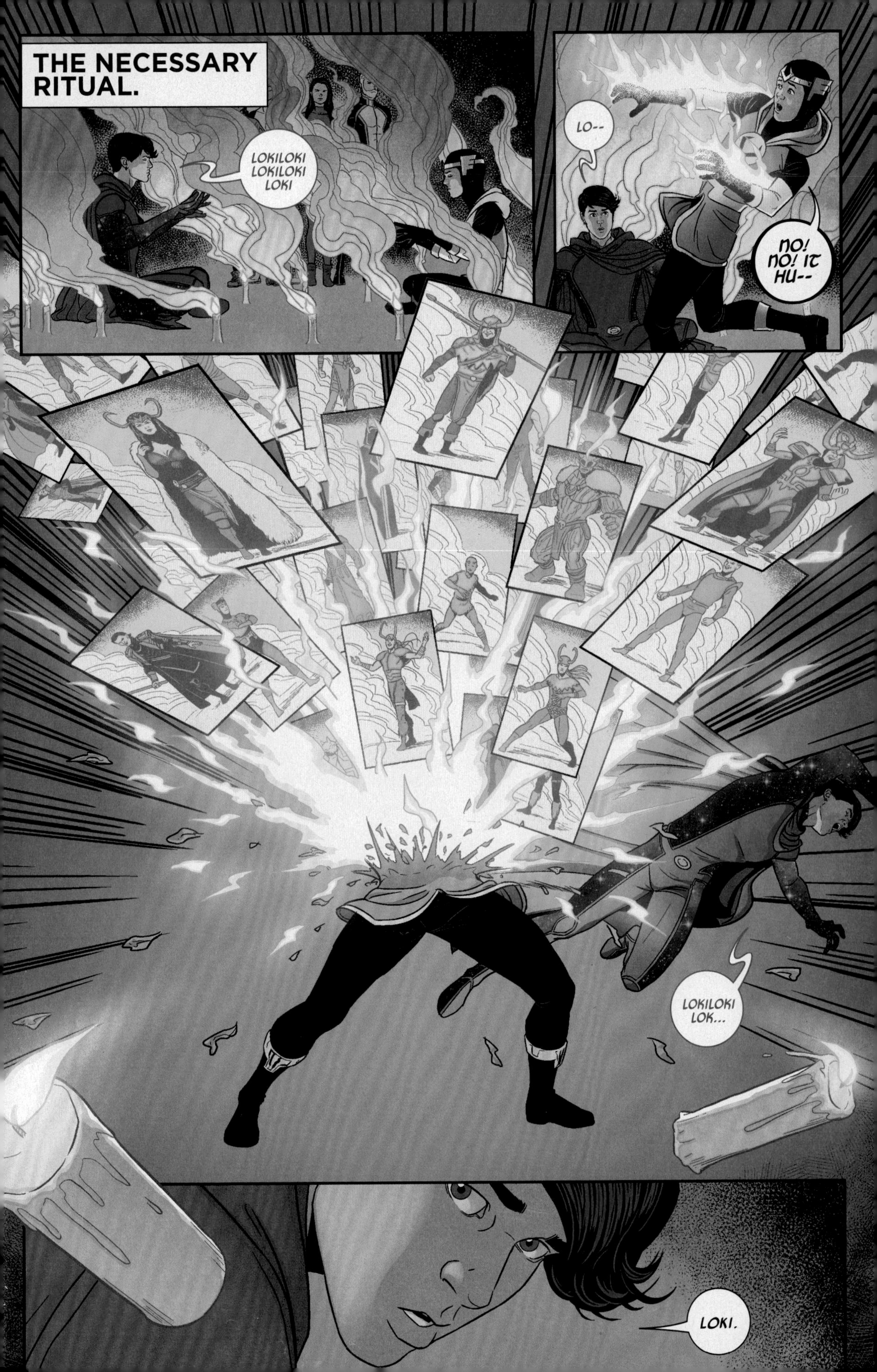
THE NECESSARY RITUAL.
LOKILOKI LOKILOKI LOKI
LO--
NO! NO! IT HU--
LOKILOKI LOK...
LOKI.

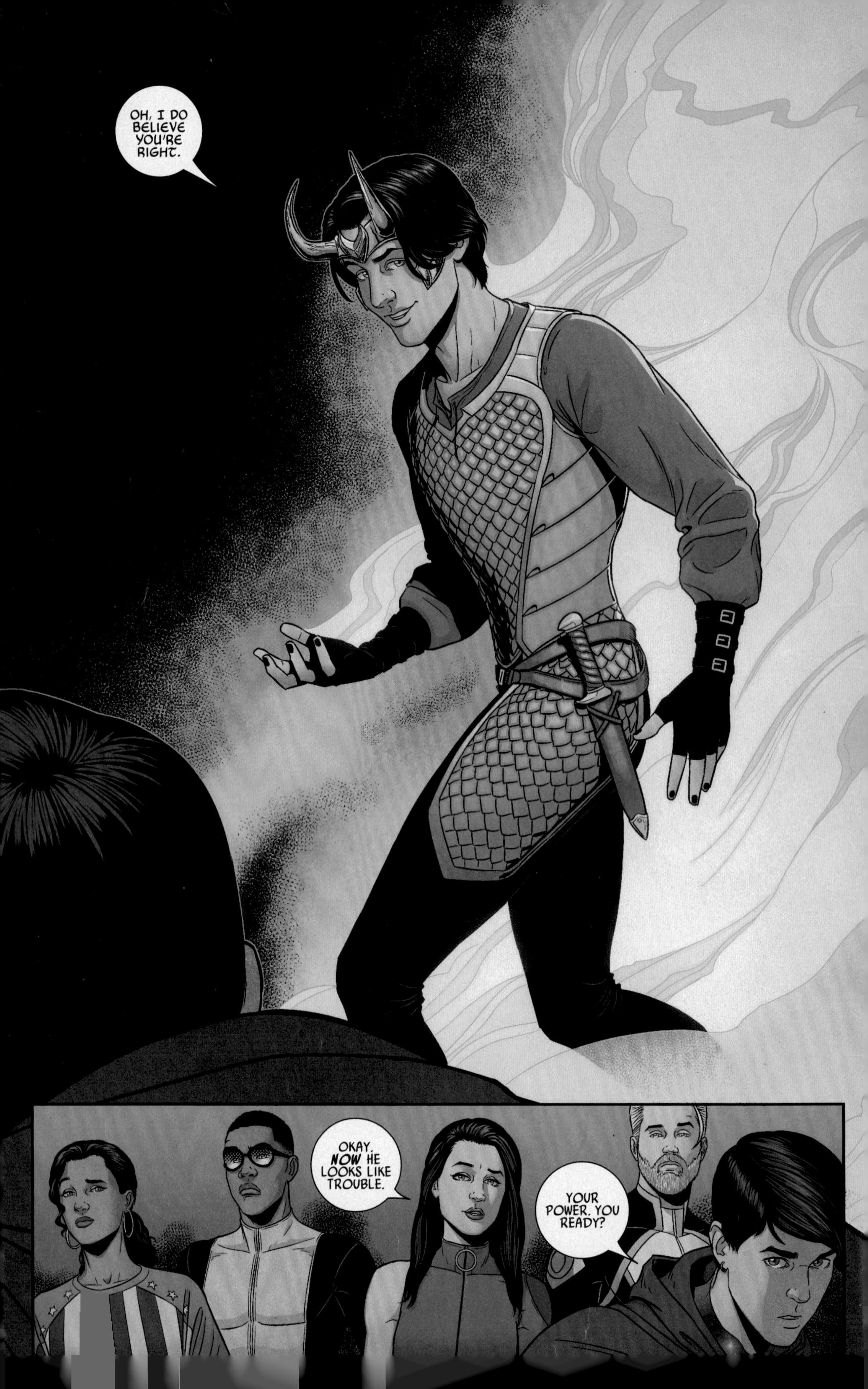
OH, I DO BELIEVE YOU'RE RIGHT.
OKAY. NOW HE LOOKS LIKE TROUBLE.
YOUR POWER. YOU READY?

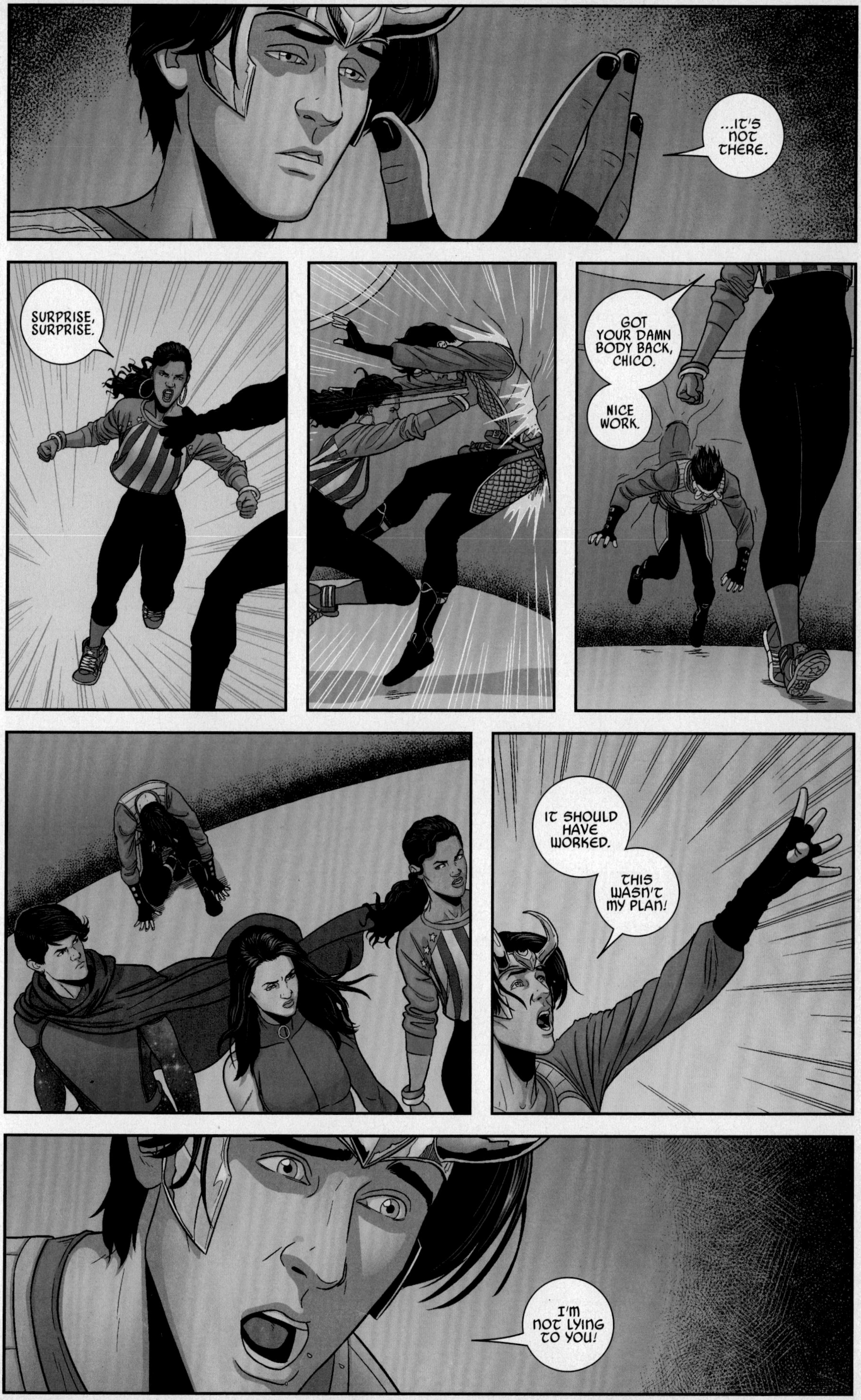
...IT'S NOT THERE.
SURPRISE, SURPRISE.
GOT YOUR DAMN BODY BACK, CHICO.
NICE WORK.
IT SHOULD HAVE WORKED.
THIS WASN'T MY PLAN!
I'M NOT LYING TO YOU!

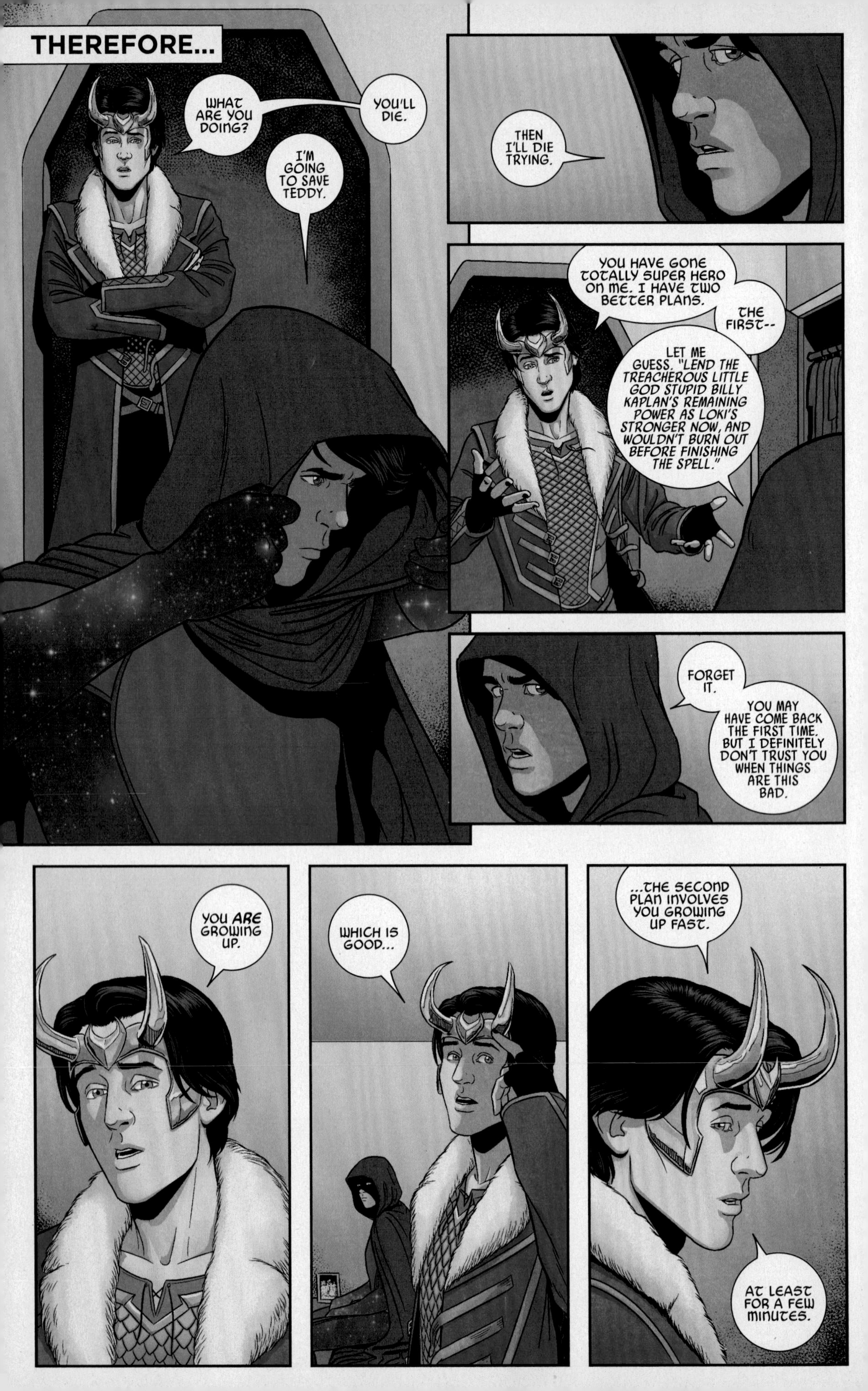

THEREFORE...
WHAT ARE YOU DOING?
I'M GOING TO SAVE TEDDY.
YOU'LL DIE.
THEN I'LL DIE TRYING.
YOU HAVE GONE TOTALLY SUPER HERO ON ME. I HAVE TWO BETTER PLANS.
THE FIRST--
LET ME GUESS. "LEND THE TREACHEROUS LITTLE GOD STUPID BILLY KAPLAN'S REMAINING POWER AS LOKI'S STRONGER NOW, AND WOULDN'T BURN OUT BEFORE FINISHING THE SPELL."
FORGET IT.
YOU MAY HAVE COME BACK THE FIRST TIME. BUT I DEFINITELY DON'T TRUST YOU WHEN THINGS ARE THIS BAD.
YOU ARE GROWING UP.
WHICH IS GOOD...
...THE SECOND PLAN INVOLVES YOU GROWING UP FAST.
AT LEAST FOR A FEW MINUTES.

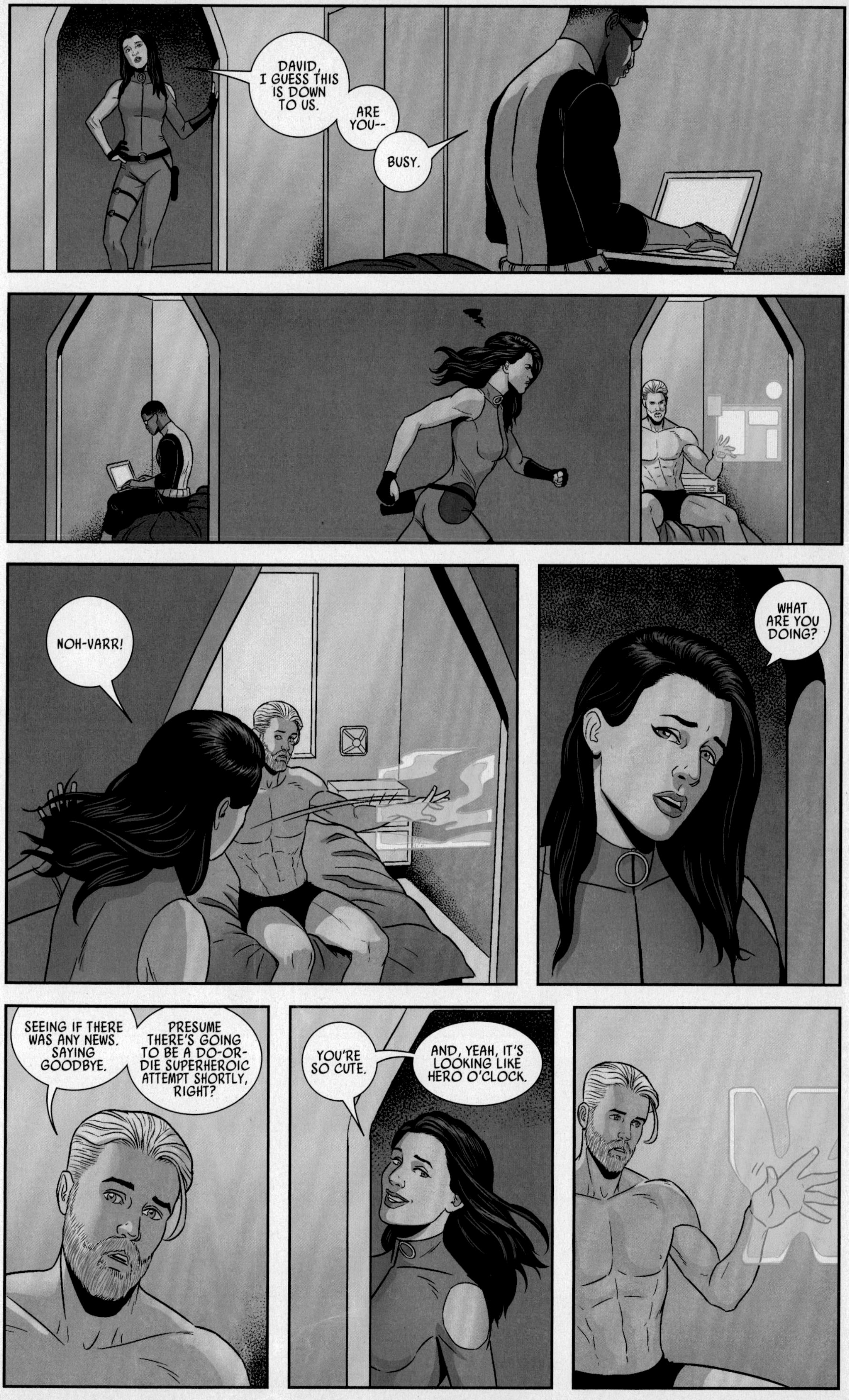
DAVID, I GUESS THIS IS DOWN TO US.
ARE YOU--
BUSY.
NOH-VARR!
WHAT ARE YOU DOING?
SEEING IF THERE WAS ANY NEWS. SAYING GOODBYE.
PRESUME THERE'S GOING TO BE A DO-OR-DIE SUPERHEROIC ATTEMPT SHORTLY, RIGHT?
YOU'RE SO CUTE.
AND, YEAH, IT'S LOOKING LIKE HERO O'CLOCK.

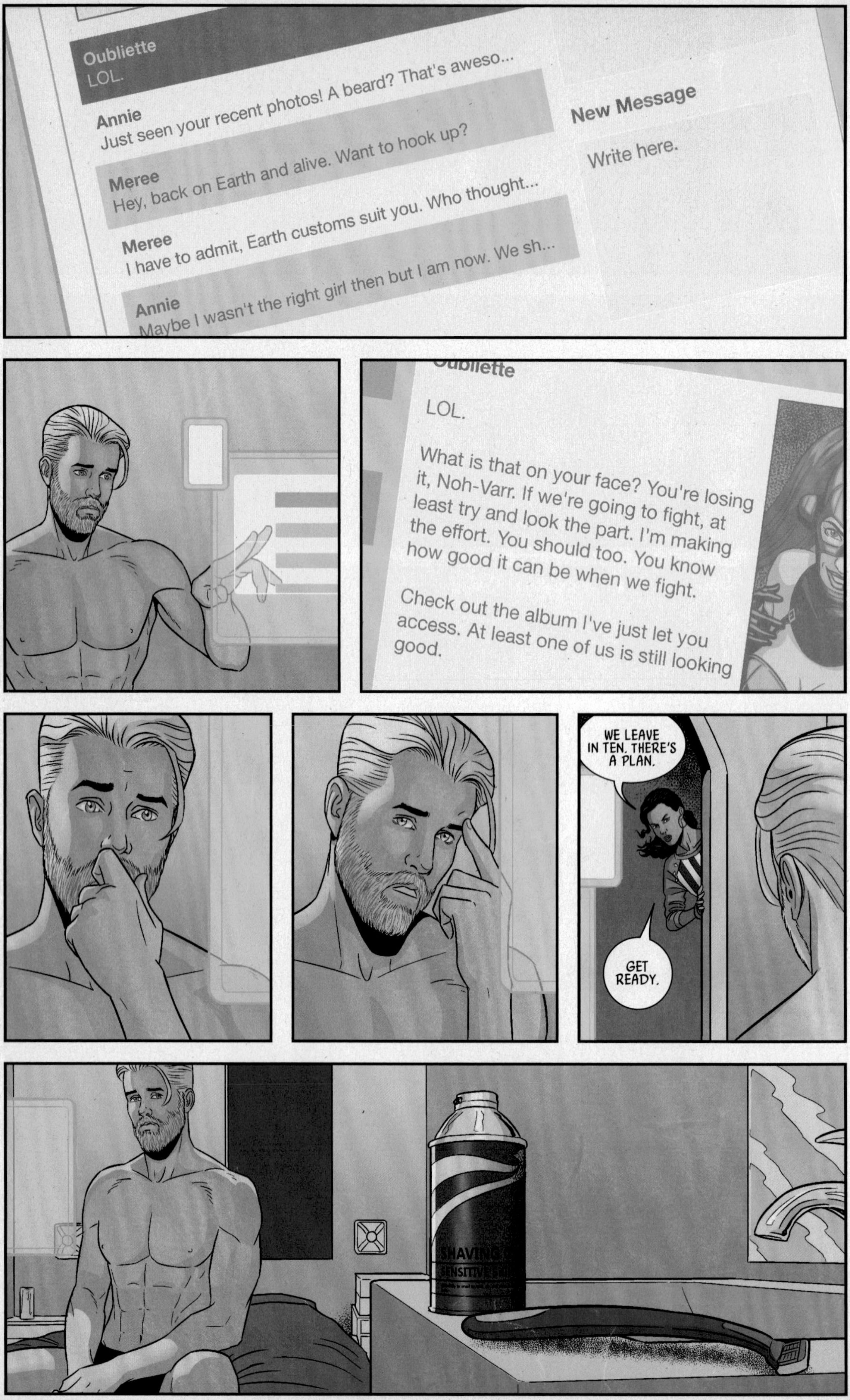
Oubliette
LOL.
Annie
Just seen your recent photos! A beard? That's aweso...
Meree
Hey, back on Earth and alive. Want to hook up?
Meree
I have to admit, Earth customs suit you. Who thought...
Annie
Maybe I wasn't the right girl then but I am now. We sh...
New Message
Write here.
LOL.
What is that on your face? You're losing it, Noh-Varr. If we're going to fight, at least try and look the part. I'm making the effort. You should too. You know how good it can be when we fight.
Check out the album I've just let you access. At least one of us is still looking good.
WE LEAVE IN TEN. THERE'S A PLAN.
GET READY.

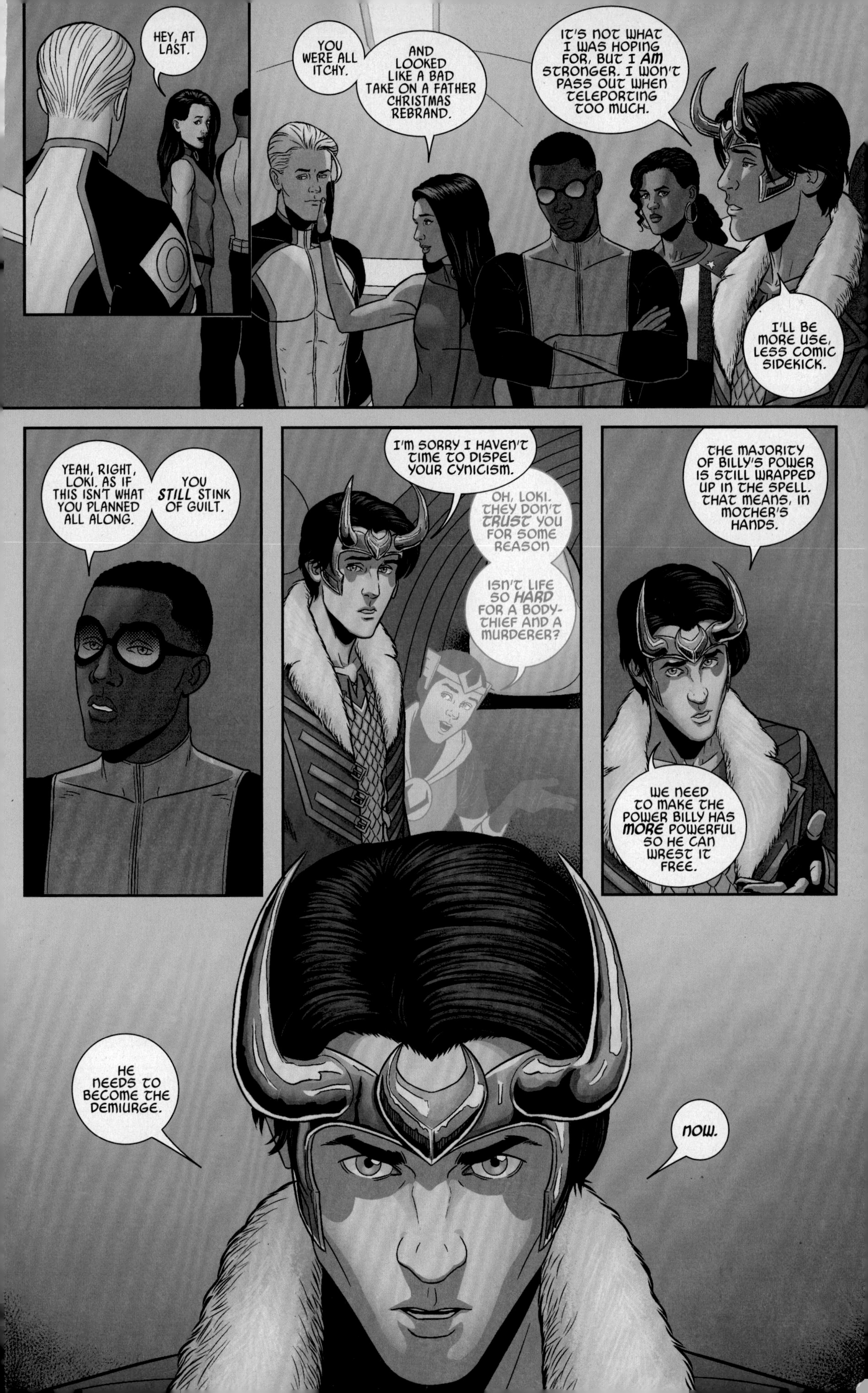
HEY, AT LAST.
YOU WERE ALL ITCHY.
AND LOOKED LIKE A BAD TAKE ON A FATHER CHRISTMAS REBRAND.
IT'S NOT WHAT I WAS HOPING FOR, BUT I AM STRONGER. I WON'T PASS OUT WHEN TELEPORTING TOO MUCH.
I'LL BE MORE USE, LESS COMIC SIDEKICK.
YEAH, RIGHT, LOKI. AS IF THIS ISN'T WHAT YOU PLANNED ALL ALONG.
YOU STILL STINK OF GUILT.
I'M SORRY I HAVEN'T TIME TO DISPEL YOUR CYNICISM.
OH, LOKI. THEY DON'T TRUST YOU FOR SOME REASON
ISN'T LIFE SO HARD FOR A BODY-THIEF AND A MURDERER?
THE MAJORITY OF BILLY'S POWER IS STILL WRAPPED UP IN THE SPELL. THAT MEANS, IN MOTHER'S HANDS.
WE NEED TO MAKE THE POWER BILLY HAS MORE POWERFUL SO HE CAN WREST IT FREE.
HE NEEDS TO BECOME THE DEMIURGE.
NOW.

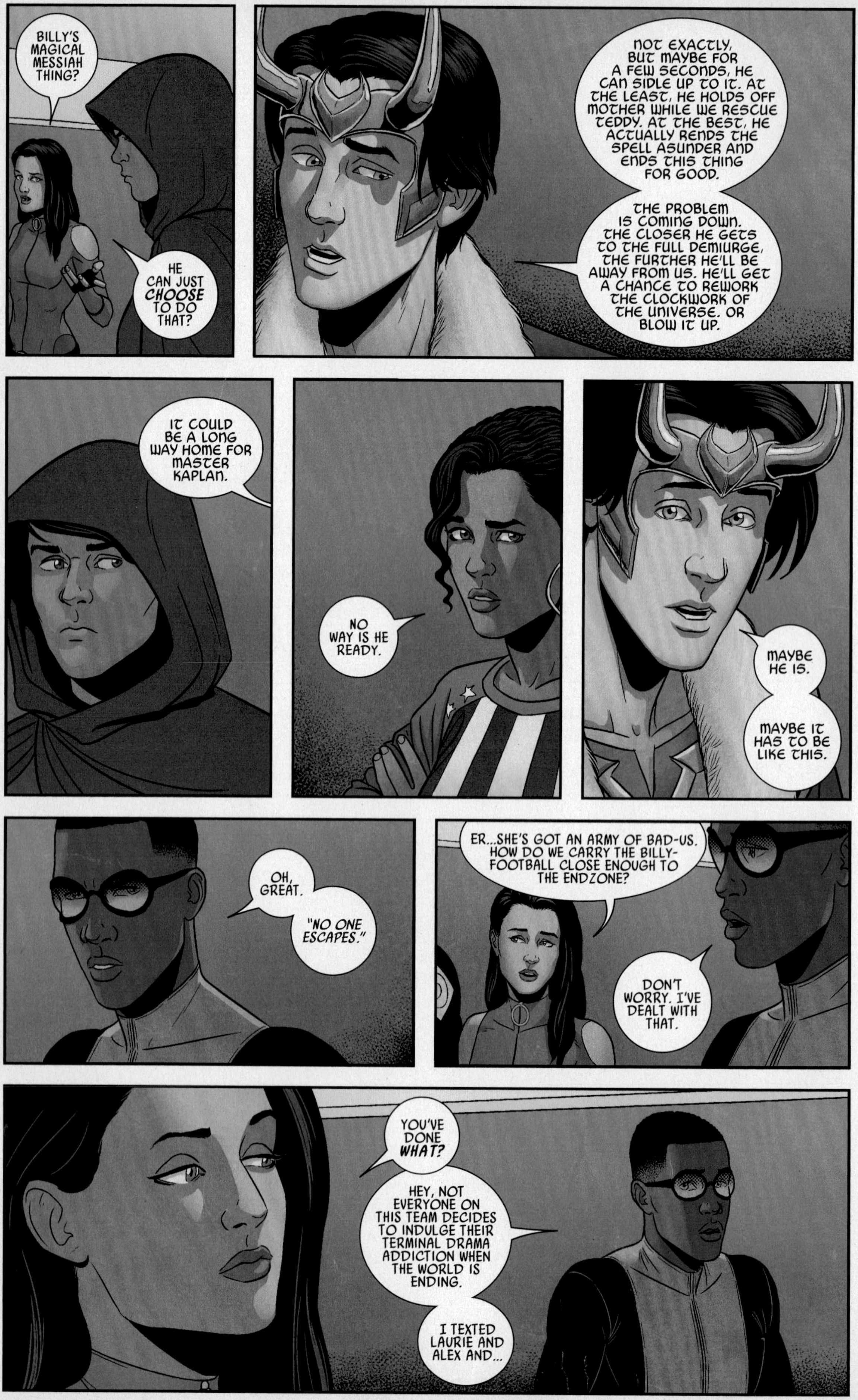
BILLY'S MAGICAL MESSIAH THING?
HE CAN JUST *CHOOSE* TO DO THAT?
NOT EXACTLY, BUT MAYBE FOR A FEW SECONDS, HE CAN SIDLE UP TO IT. AT THE LEAST, HE HOLDS OFF MOTHER WHILE WE RESCUE TEDDY. AT THE BEST, HE ACTUALLY RENDS THE SPELL ASUNDER AND ENDS THIS THING FOR GOOD.
THE PROBLEM IS COMING DOWN. THE CLOSER HE GETS TO THE FULL DEMIURGE, THE FURTHER HE'LL BE AWAY FROM US. HE'LL GET A CHANCE TO REWORK THE CLOCKWORK OF THE UNIVERSE. OR BLOW IT UP.
IT COULD BE A LONG WAY HOME FOR MASTER KAPLAN.
NO WAY IS HE READY.
MAYBE HE IS.
MAYBE IT HAS TO BE LIKE THIS.
OH, GREAT.
"NO ONE ESCAPES."
ER...SHE'S GOT AN ARMY OF BAD-US. HOW DO WE CARRY THE BILLY-FOOTBALL CLOSE ENOUGH TO THE ENDZONE?
DON'T WORRY. I'VE DEALT WITH THAT.
YOU'VE DONE *WHAT?*
HEY, NOT EVERYONE ON THIS TEAM DECIDES TO INDULGE THEIR TERMINAL DRAMA ADDICTION WHEN THE WORLD IS ENDING.
I TEXTED LAURIE AND ALEX AND...

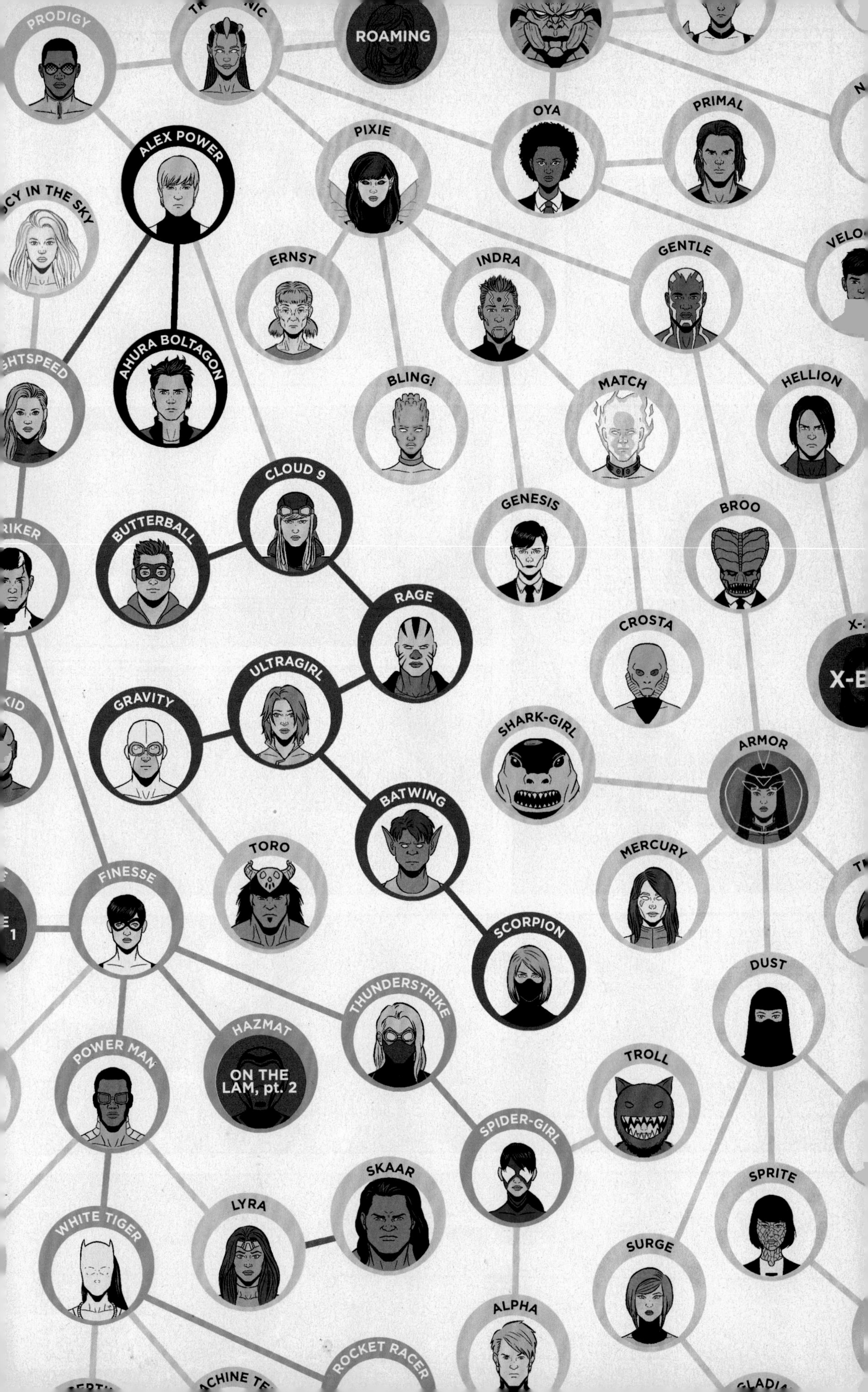
PRODIGY
ROAMING
ALEX POWER
AHURA BOLTAGON
PIXIE
OYA
PRIMAL
ERNST
INDRA
GENTLE
BLING!
MATCH
HELLION
CLOUD 9
BUTTERBALL
GENESIS
BROO
RAGE
CROSTA
ULTRAGIRL
GRAVITY
SHARK-GIRL
ARMOR
BATWING
TORO
FINESSE
MERCURY
SCORPION
DUST
THUNDERSTRIKE
HAZMAT
ON THE LAM, pt. 2
POWER MAN
TROLL
SPIDER-GIRL
SKAAR
SPRITE
LYRA
WHITE TIGER
SURGE
ALPHA
ROCKET RACER

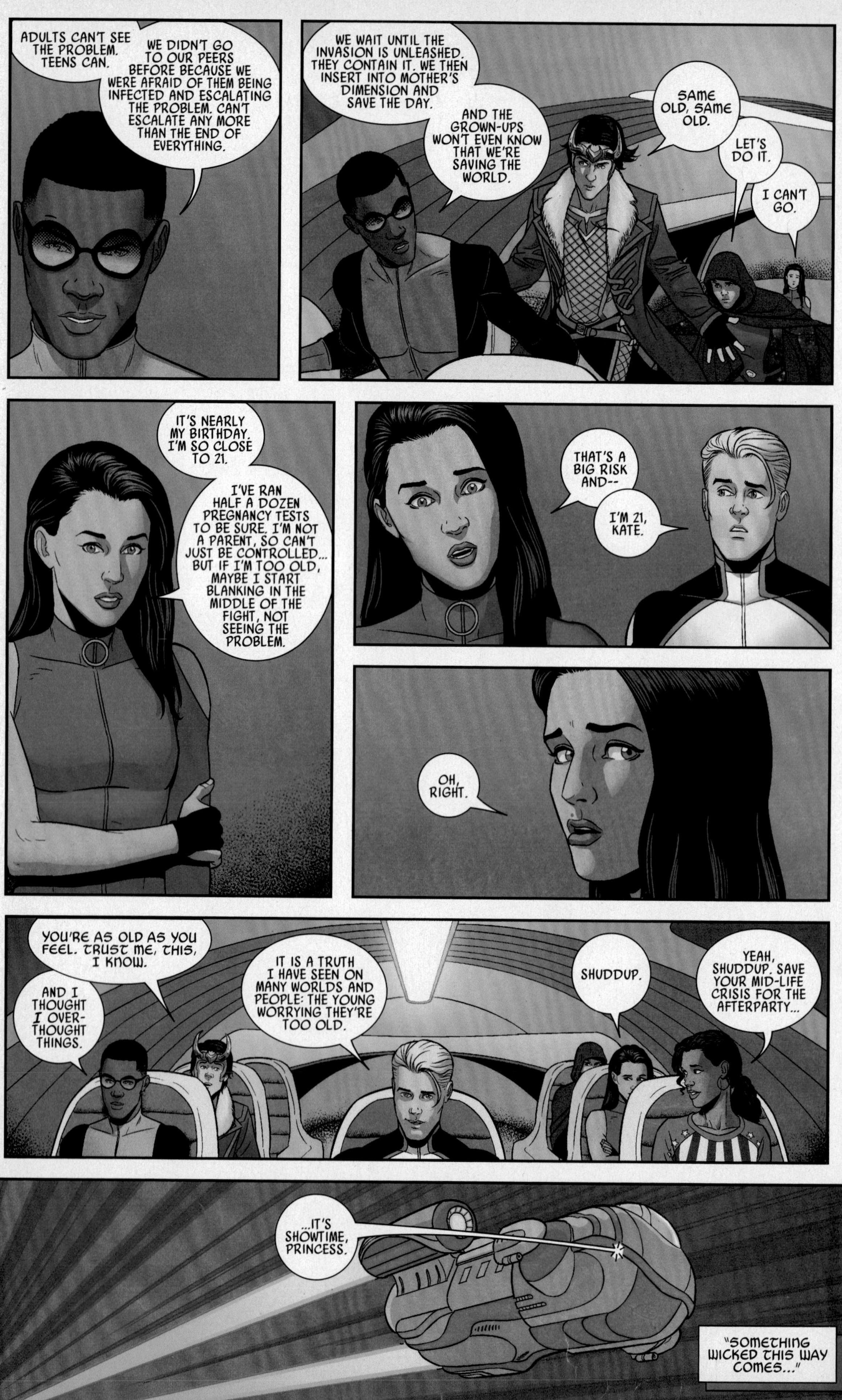
ADULTS CAN'T SEE THE PROBLEM. TEENS CAN.
WE DIDN'T GO TO OUR PEERS BEFORE BECAUSE WE WERE AFRAID OF THEM BEING INFECTED AND ESCALATING THE PROBLEM. CAN'T ESCALATE ANY MORE THAN THE END OF EVERYTHING.
WE WAIT UNTIL THE INVASION IS UNLEASHED. THEY CONTAIN IT. WE THEN INSERT INTO MOTHER'S DIMENSION AND SAVE THE DAY.
AND THE GROWN-UPS WON'T EVEN KNOW THAT WE'RE SAVING THE WORLD.
SAME OLD, SAME OLD.
LET'S DO IT.
I CAN'T GO.
IT'S NEARLY MY BIRTHDAY. I'M SO CLOSE TO 21.
I'VE RAN HALF A DOZEN PREGNANCY TESTS TO BE SURE. I'M NOT A PARENT, SO CAN'T JUST BE CONTROLLED... BUT IF I'M TOO OLD, MAYBE I START BLANKING IN THE MIDDLE OF THE FIGHT, NOT SEEING THE PROBLEM.
THAT'S A BIG RISK AND--
I'M 21, KATE.
OH, RIGHT.
YOU'RE AS OLD AS YOU FEEL. TRUST ME, THIS, I KNOW.
AND I THOUGHT I OVER-THOUGHT THINGS.
IT IS A TRUTH I HAVE SEEN ON MANY WORLDS AND PEOPLE: THE YOUNG WORRYING THEY'RE TOO OLD.
SHUDDUP.
YEAH, SHUDDUP. SAVE YOUR MID-LIFE CRISIS FOR THE AFTERPARTY...
...IT'S SHOWTIME, PRINCESS.
"SOMETHING WICKED THIS WAY COMES..."

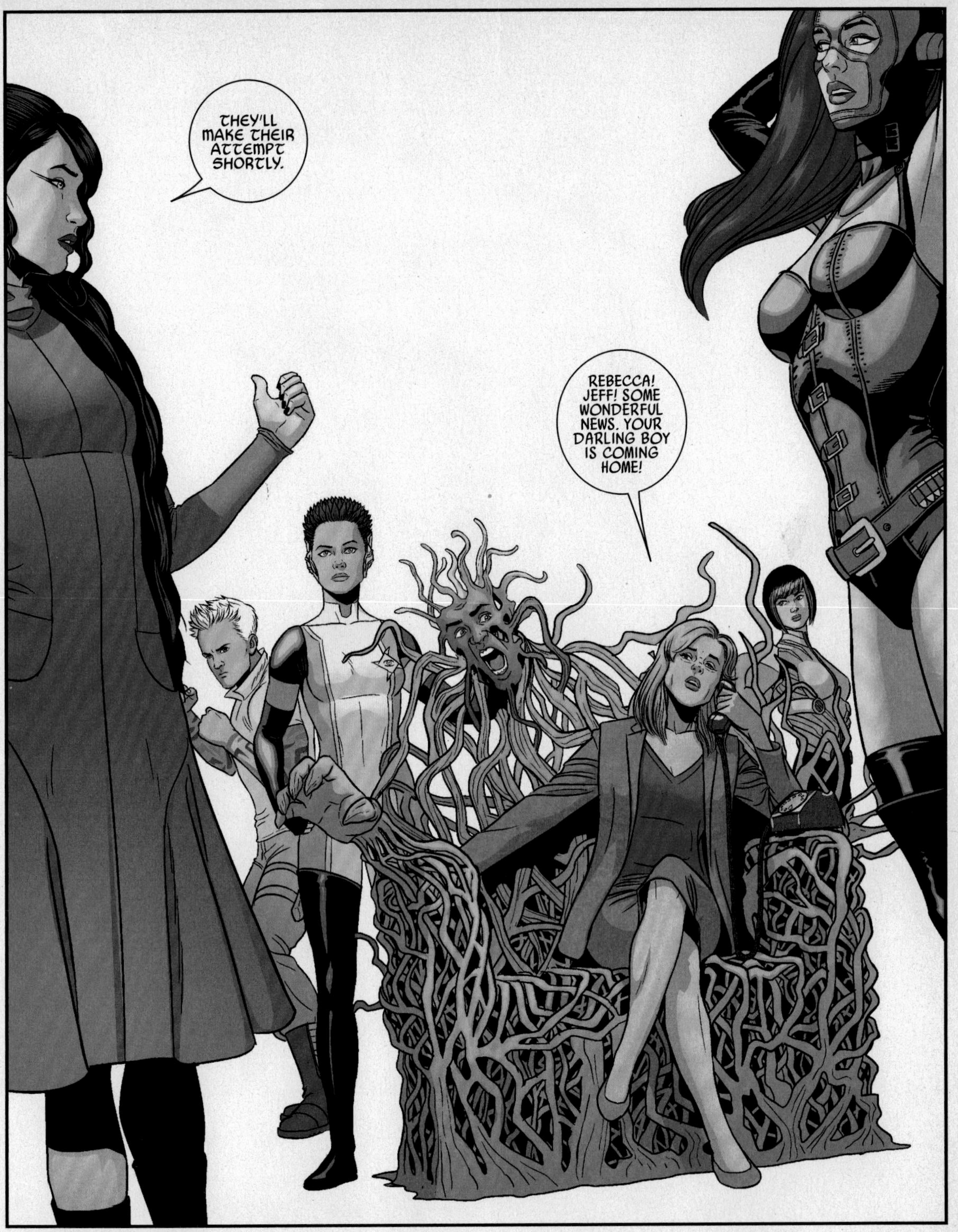
THEY'LL MAKE THEIR ATTEMPT SHORTLY.
REBECCA! JEFF! SOME WONDERFUL NEWS. YOUR DARLING BOY IS COMING HOME!

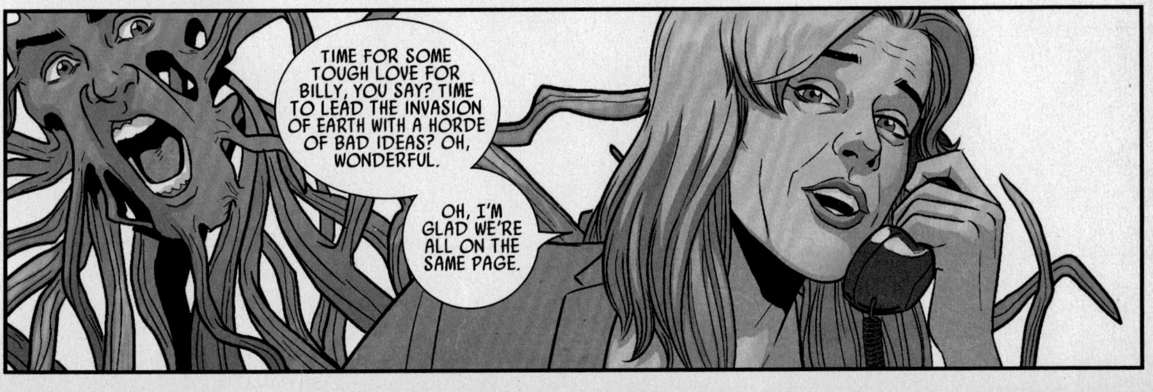
TIME FOR SOME TOUGH LOVE FOR BILLY, YOU SAY? TIME TO LEAD THE INVASION OF EARTH WITH A HORDE OF BAD IDEAS? OH, WONDERFUL.
OH, I'M GLAD WE'RE ALL ON THE SAME PAGE.

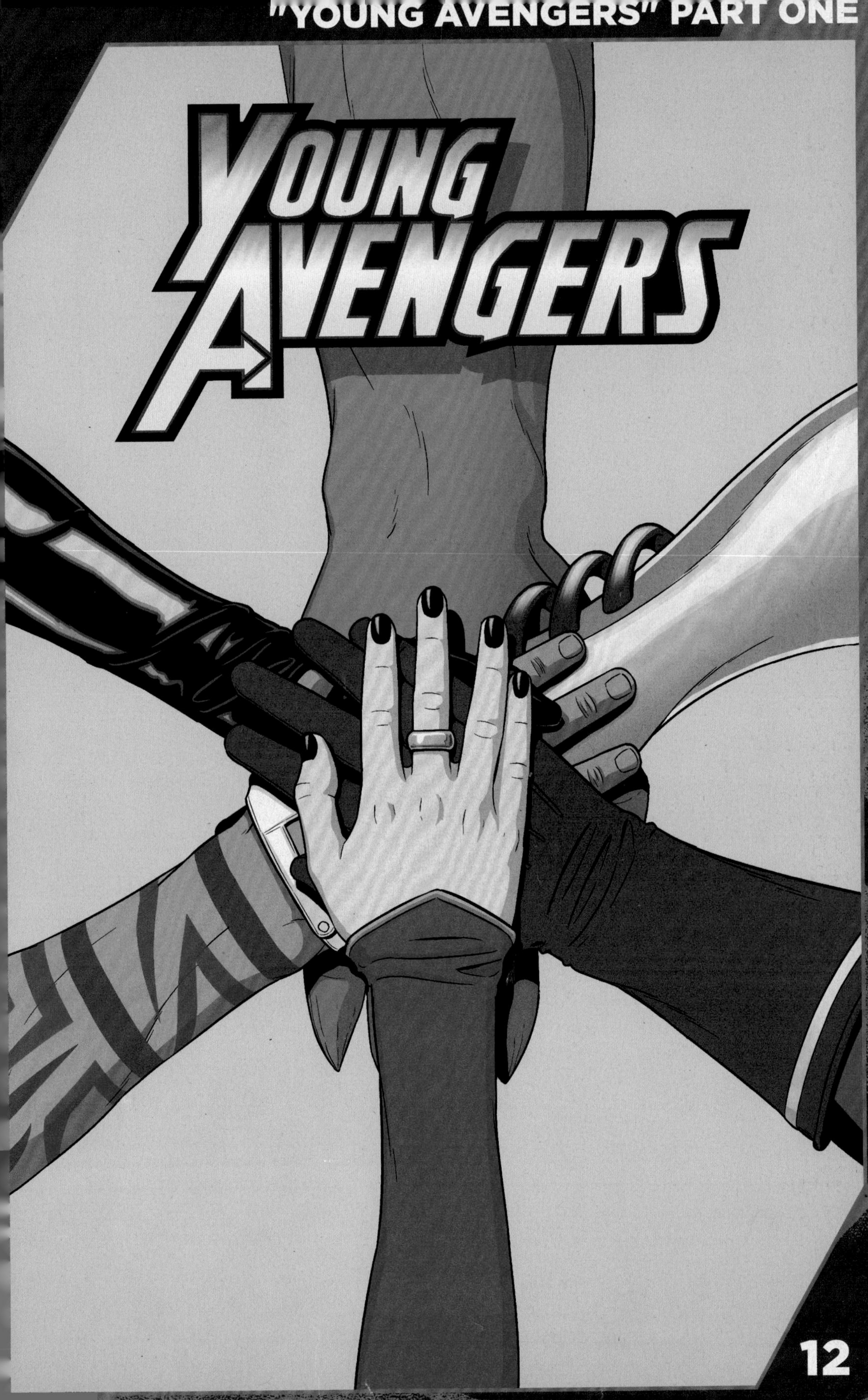
"YOUNG AVENGERS" PART ONE
YOUNG AVENGERS
12

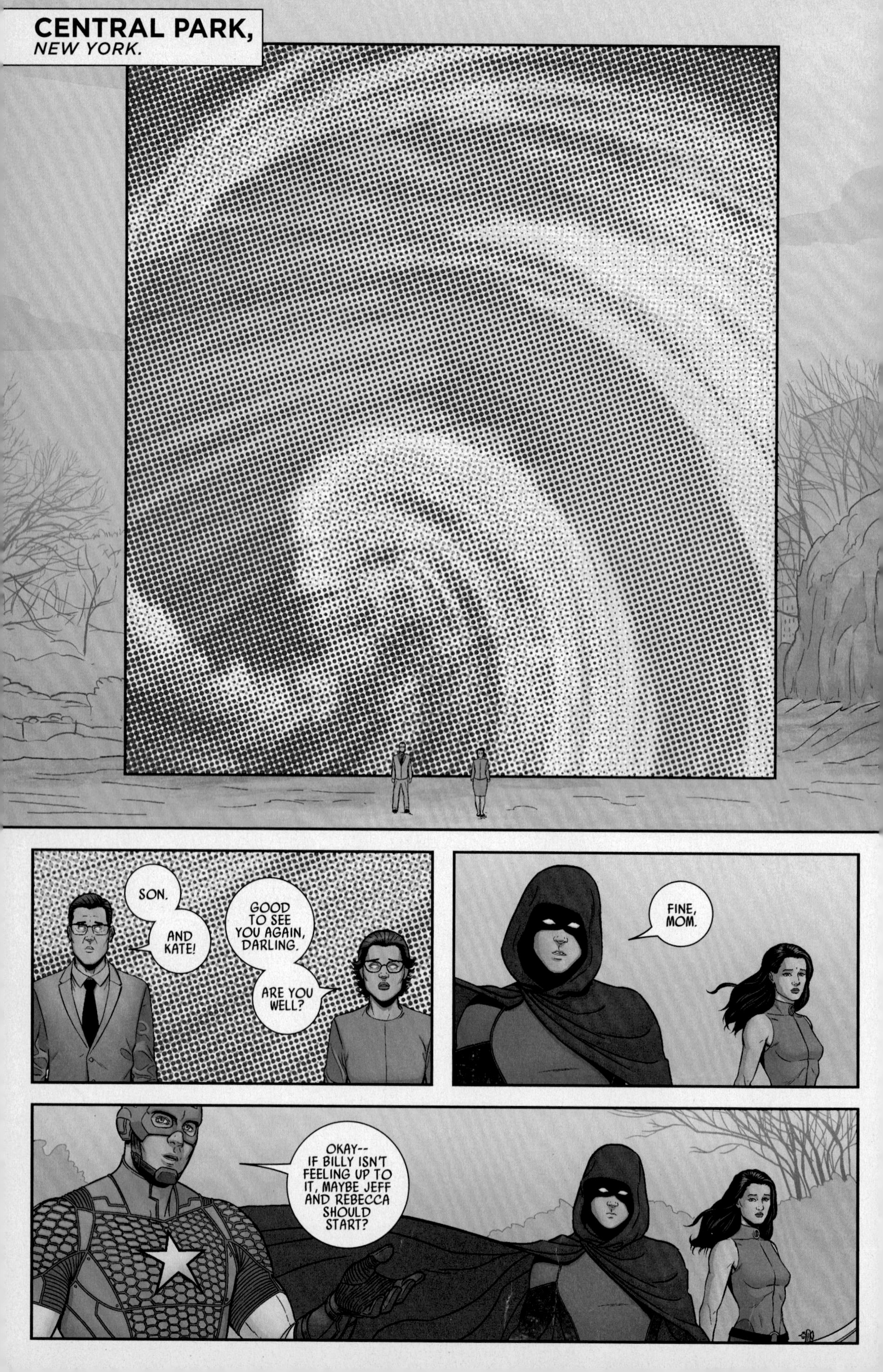
CENTRAL PARK,
NEW YORK.
SON.
AND KATE!
GOOD TO SEE YOU AGAIN, DARLING.
ARE YOU WELL?
FINE, MOM.
OKAY-- IF BILLY ISN'T FEELING UP TO IT, MAYBE JEFF AND REBECCA SHOULD START?

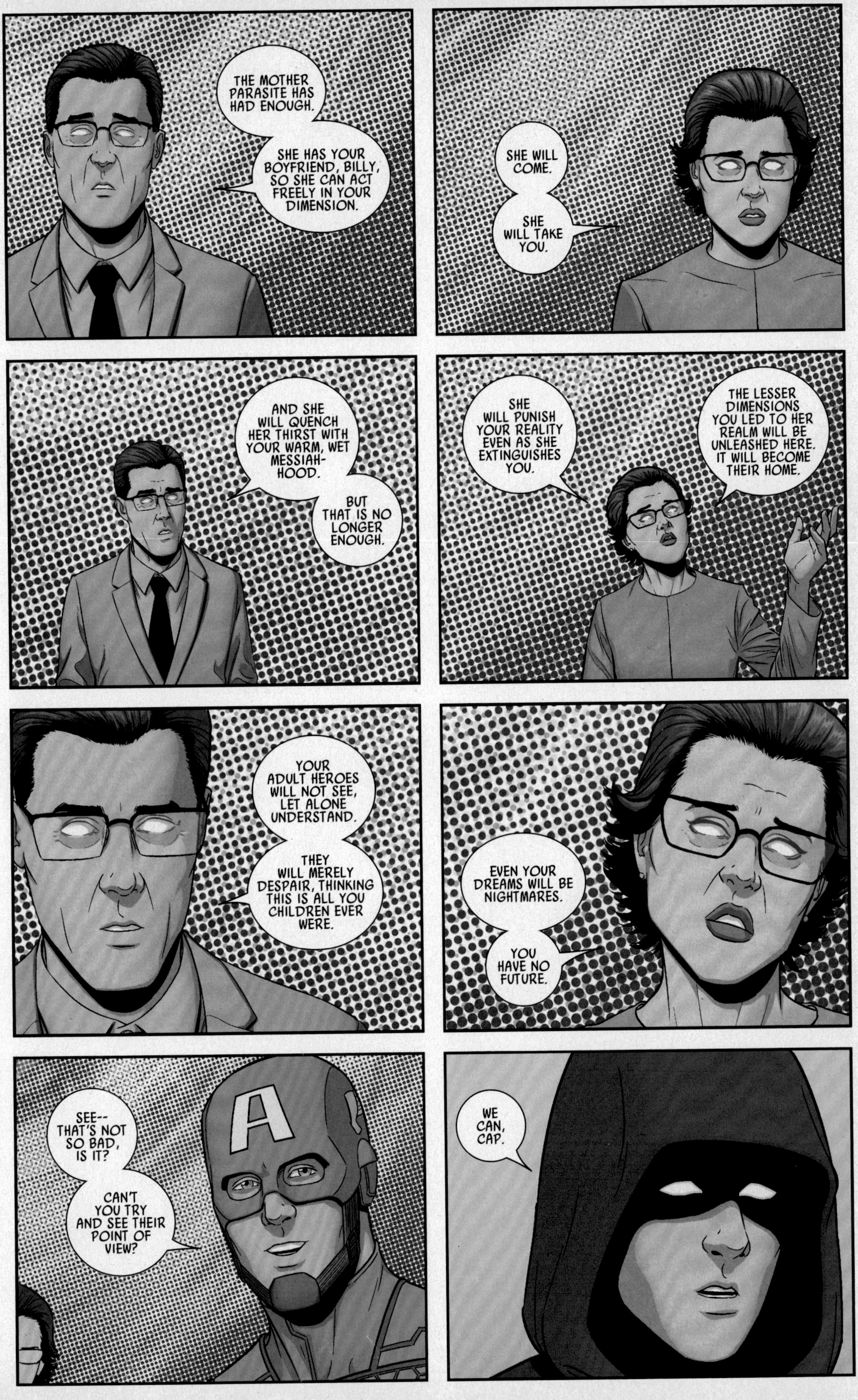
THE MOTHER PARASITE HAS HAD ENOUGH.
SHE HAS YOUR BOYFRIEND, BILLY, SO SHE CAN ACT FREELY IN YOUR DIMENSION.
SHE WILL COME.
SHE WILL TAKE YOU.
AND SHE WILL QUENCH HER THIRST WITH YOUR WARM, WET MESSIAH-HOOD.
BUT THAT IS NO LONGER ENOUGH.
SHE WILL PUNISH YOUR REALITY EVEN AS SHE EXTINGUISHES YOU.
THE LESSER DIMENSIONS YOU LED TO HER REALM WILL BE UNLEASHED HERE. IT WILL BECOME THEIR HOME.
YOUR ADULT HEROES WILL NOT SEE, LET ALONE UNDERSTAND.
THEY WILL MERELY DESPAIR, THINKING THIS IS ALL YOU CHILDREN EVER WERE.
EVEN YOUR DREAMS WILL BE NIGHTMARES.
YOU HAVE NO FUTURE.
SEE-- THAT'S NOT SO BAD, IS IT?
CAN'T YOU TRY AND SEE THEIR POINT OF VIEW?
WE CAN, CAP.

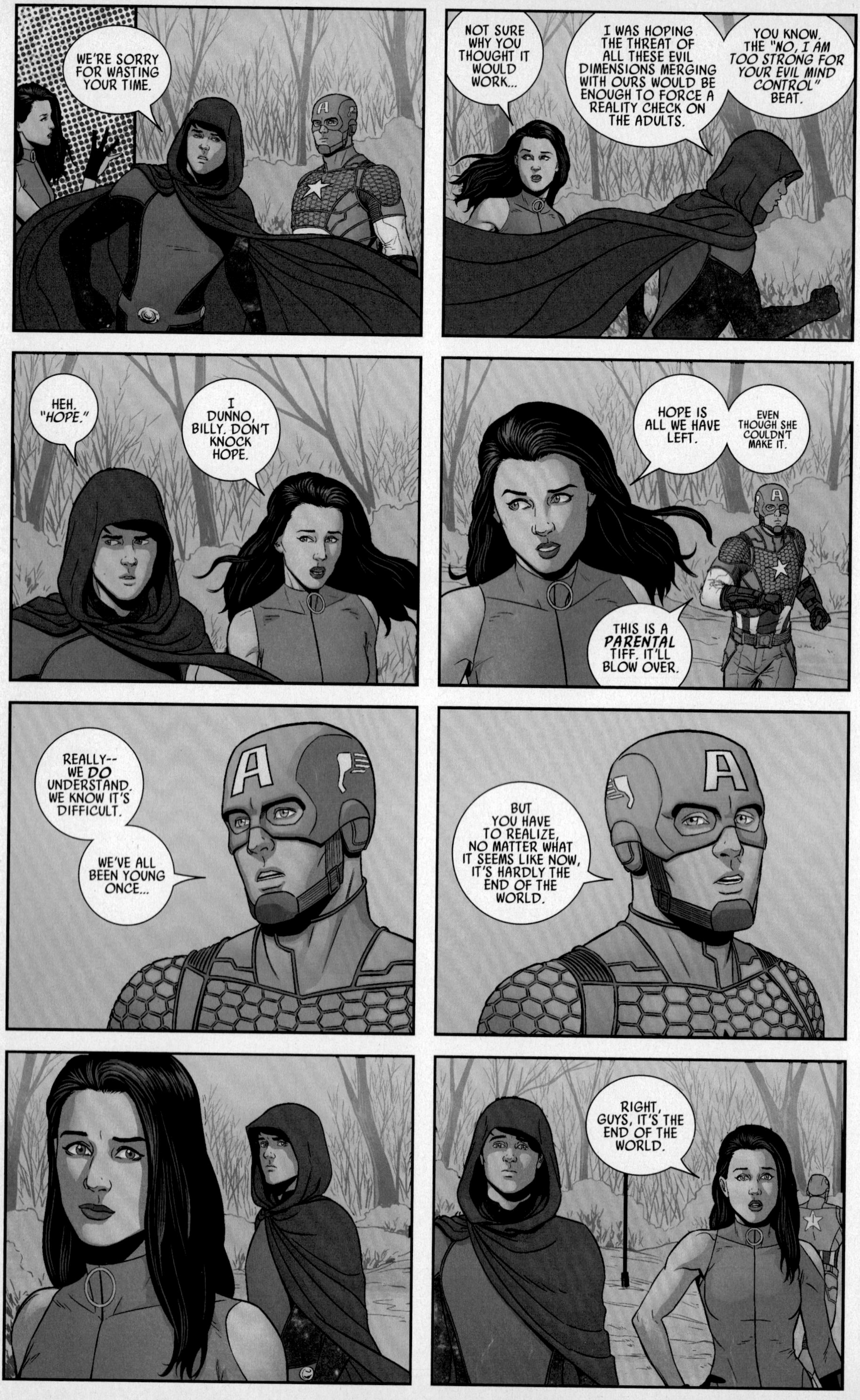
WE'RE SORRY FOR WASTING YOUR TIME.
NOT SURE WHY YOU THOUGHT IT WOULD WORK...
I WAS HOPING THE THREAT OF ALL THESE EVIL DIMENSIONS MERGING WITH OURS WOULD BE ENOUGH TO FORCE A REALITY CHECK ON THE ADULTS.
YOU KNOW. THE "NO, I AM TOO STRONG FOR YOUR EVIL MIND CONTROL" BEAT.
HEH. "HOPE."
I DUNNO, BILLY. DON'T KNOCK HOPE.
HOPE IS ALL WE HAVE LEFT.
EVEN THOUGH SHE COULDN'T MAKE IT.
THIS IS A PARENTAL TIFF. IT'LL BLOW OVER.
REALLY-- WE DO UNDERSTAND. WE KNOW IT'S DIFFICULT.
WE'VE ALL BEEN YOUNG ONCE...
BUT YOU HAVE TO REALIZE, NO MATTER WHAT IT SEEMS LIKE NOW, IT'S HARDLY THE END OF THE WORLD.
RIGHT, GUYS, IT'S THE END OF THE WORLD.

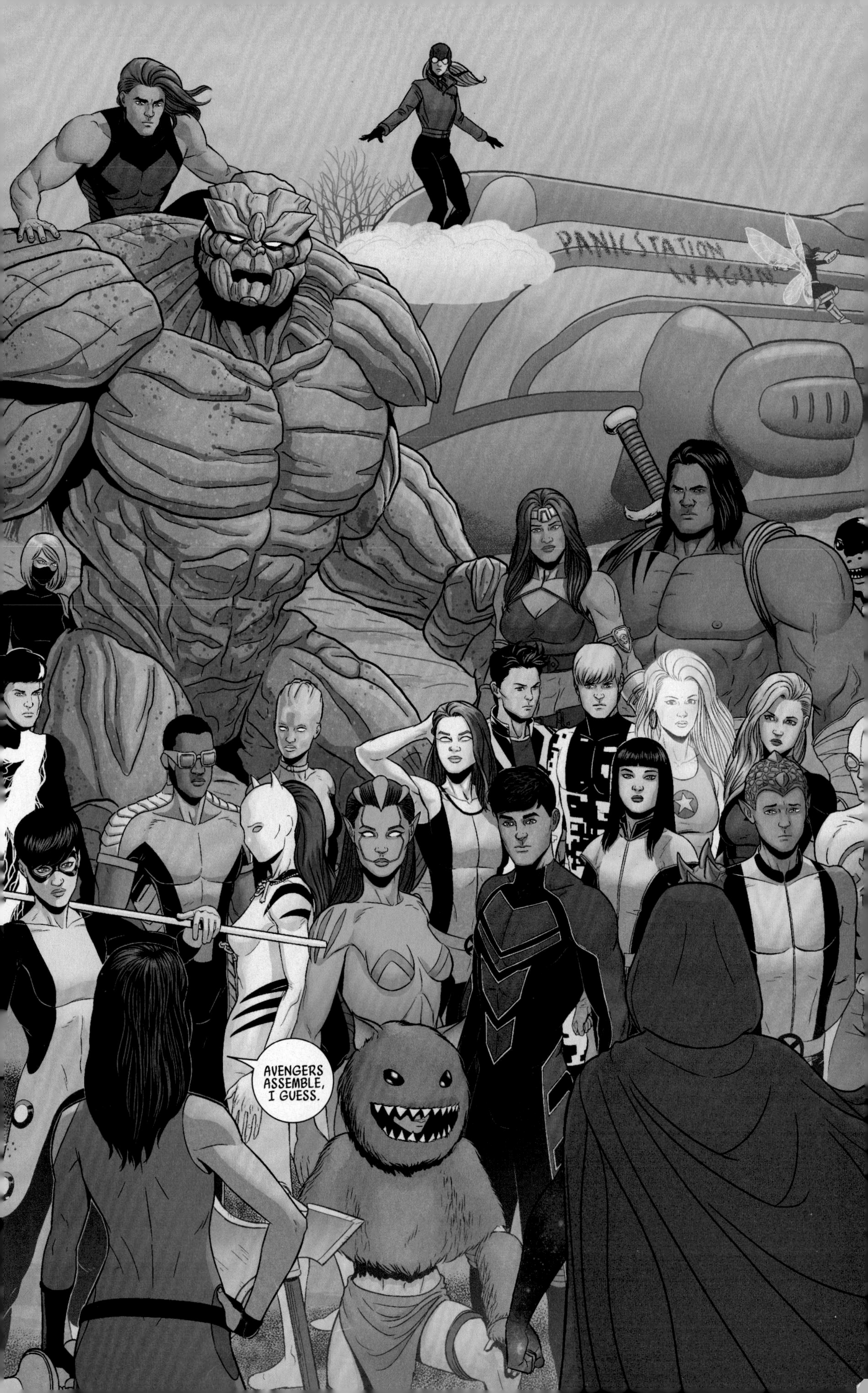
PANIC STATION WAGON
AVENGERS ASSEMBLE, I GUESS.

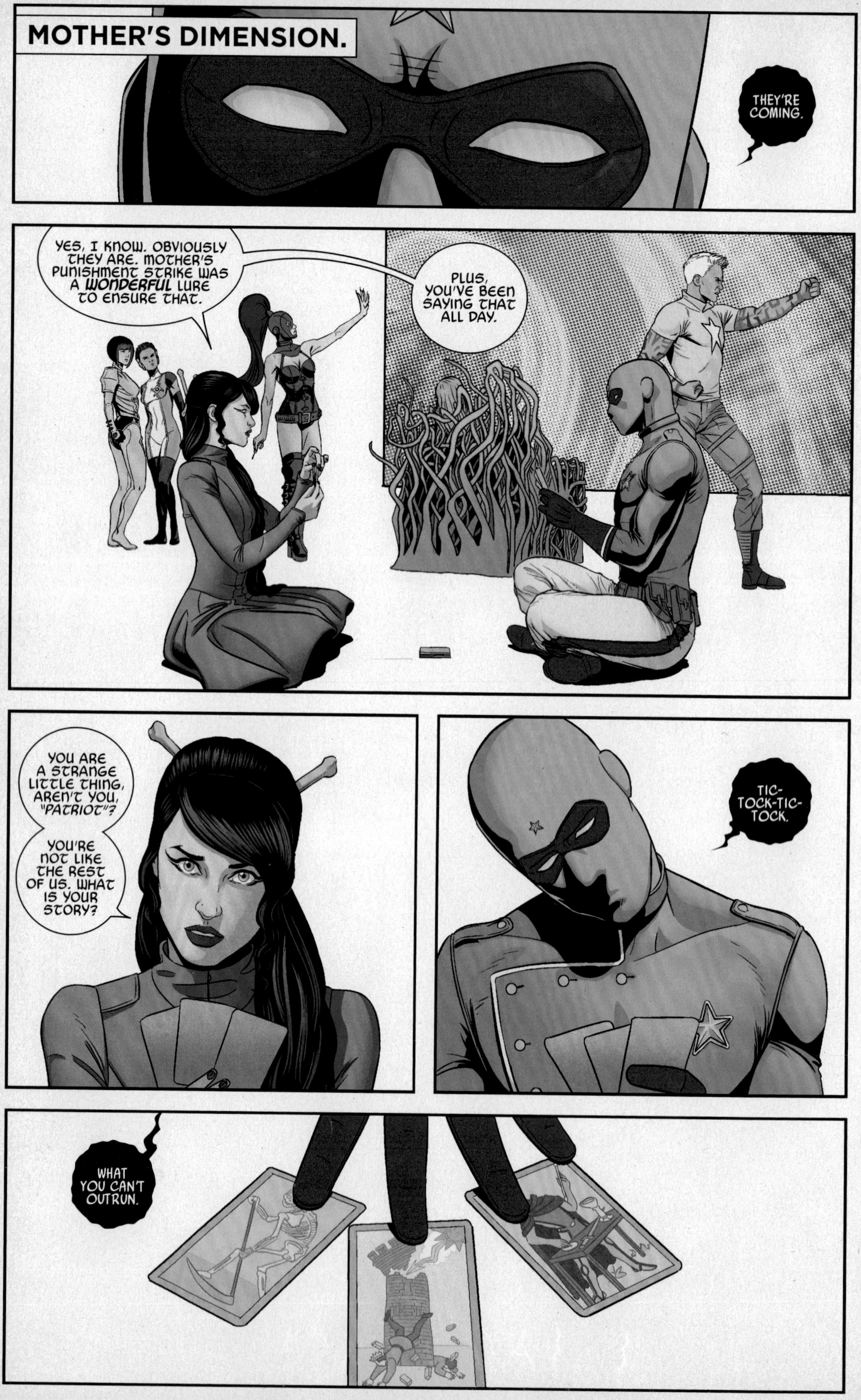
MOTHER'S DIMENSION.
THEY'RE COMING.
YES, I KNOW. OBVIOUSLY THEY ARE. MOTHER'S PUNISHMENT STRIKE WAS A WONDERFUL LURE TO ENSURE THAT.
PLUS, YOU'VE BEEN SAYING THAT ALL DAY.
YOU ARE A STRANGE LITTLE THING, AREN'T YOU, "PATRIOT"?
YOU'RE NOT LIKE THE REST OF US. WHAT IS YOUR STORY?
TIC-TOCK-TIC-TOCK.
WHAT YOU CAN'T OUTRUN.

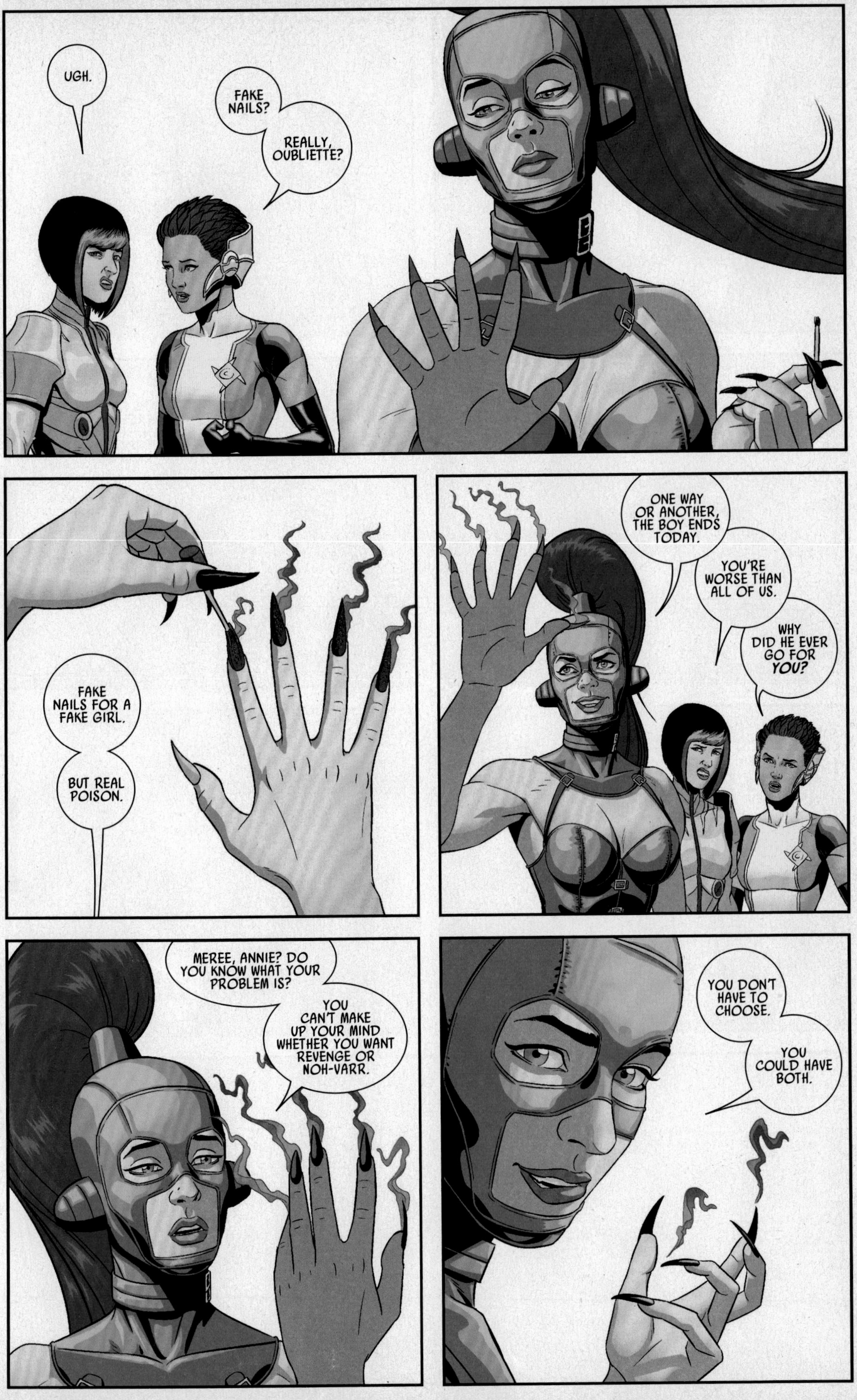
UGH.
FAKE NAILS?
REALLY, OUBLIETTE?
FAKE NAILS FOR A FAKE GIRL.
BUT REAL POISON.
ONE WAY OR ANOTHER, THE BOY ENDS TODAY.
YOU'RE WORSE THAN ALL OF US.
WHY DID HE EVER GO FOR YOU?
MEREE, ANNIE? DO YOU KNOW WHAT YOUR PROBLEM IS?
YOU CAN'T MAKE UP YOUR MIND WHETHER YOU WANT REVENGE OR NOH-VARR.
YOU DON'T HAVE TO CHOOSE.
YOU COULD HAVE BOTH.

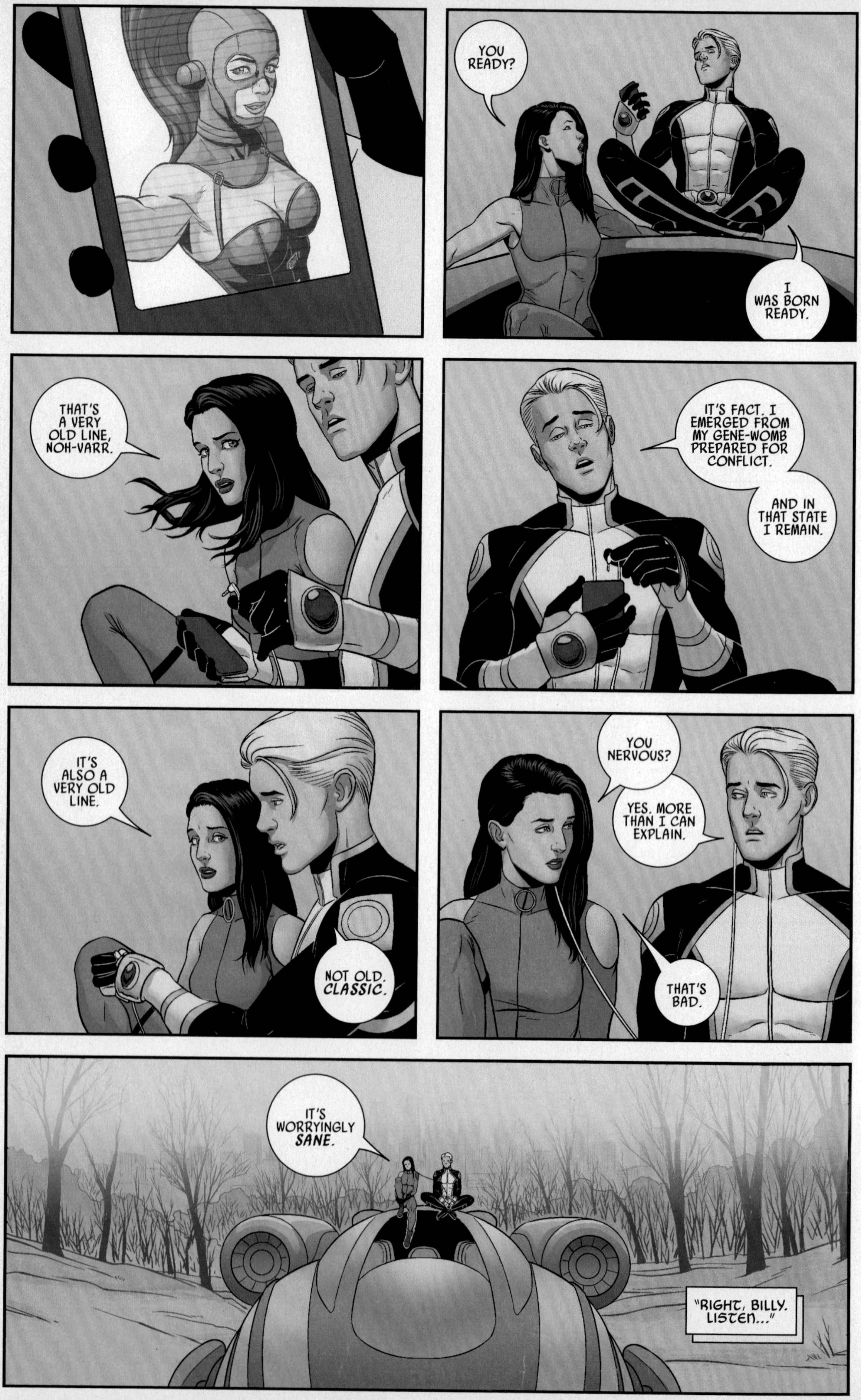
YOU READY?
I WAS BORN READY.
THAT'S A VERY OLD LINE, NOH-VARR.
IT'S FACT. I EMERGED FROM MY GENE-WOMB PREPARED FOR CONFLICT.
AND IN THAT STATE I REMAIN.
IT'S ALSO A VERY OLD LINE.
NOT OLD. CLASSIC.
YOU NERVOUS?
YES. MORE THAN I CAN EXPLAIN.
THAT'S BAD.
IT'S WORRYINGLY SANE.
"RIGHT, BILLY. LISTEN..."

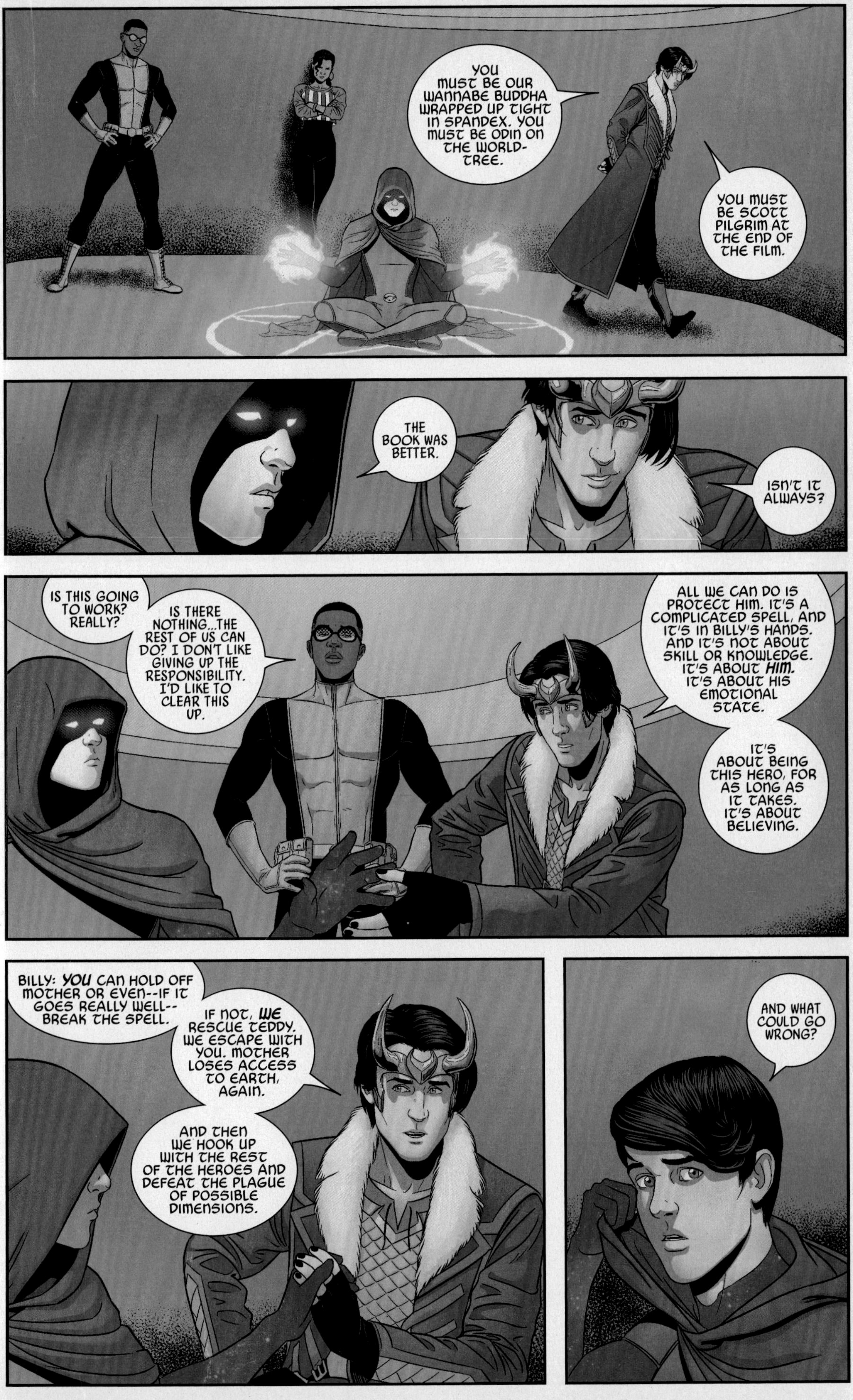
YOU MUST BE OUR WANNABE BUDDHA WRAPPED UP TIGHT IN SPANDEX. YOU MUST BE ODIN ON THE WORLD-TREE.
YOU MUST BE SCOTT PILGRIM AT THE END OF THE FILM.
THE BOOK WAS BETTER.
ISN'T IT ALWAYS?
IS THIS GOING TO WORK? REALLY?
IS THERE NOTHING...THE REST OF US CAN DO? I DON'T LIKE GIVING UP THE RESPONSIBILITY. I'D LIKE TO CLEAR THIS UP.
ALL WE CAN DO IS PROTECT HIM. IT'S A COMPLICATED SPELL, AND IT'S IN BILLY'S HANDS. AND IT'S NOT ABOUT SKILL OR KNOWLEDGE. IT'S ABOUT HIM. IT'S ABOUT HIS EMOTIONAL STATE.
IT'S ABOUT BEING THIS HERO, FOR AS LONG AS IT TAKES. IT'S ABOUT BELIEVING.
BILLY: YOU CAN HOLD OFF MOTHER OR EVEN--IF IT GOES REALLY WELL--BREAK THE SPELL.
IF NOT, WE RESCUE TEDDY. WE ESCAPE WITH YOU. MOTHER LOSES ACCESS TO EARTH, AGAIN.
AND THEN WE HOOK UP WITH THE REST OF THE HEROES AND DEFEAT THE PLAGUE OF POSSIBLE DIMENSIONS.
AND WHAT COULD GO WRONG?

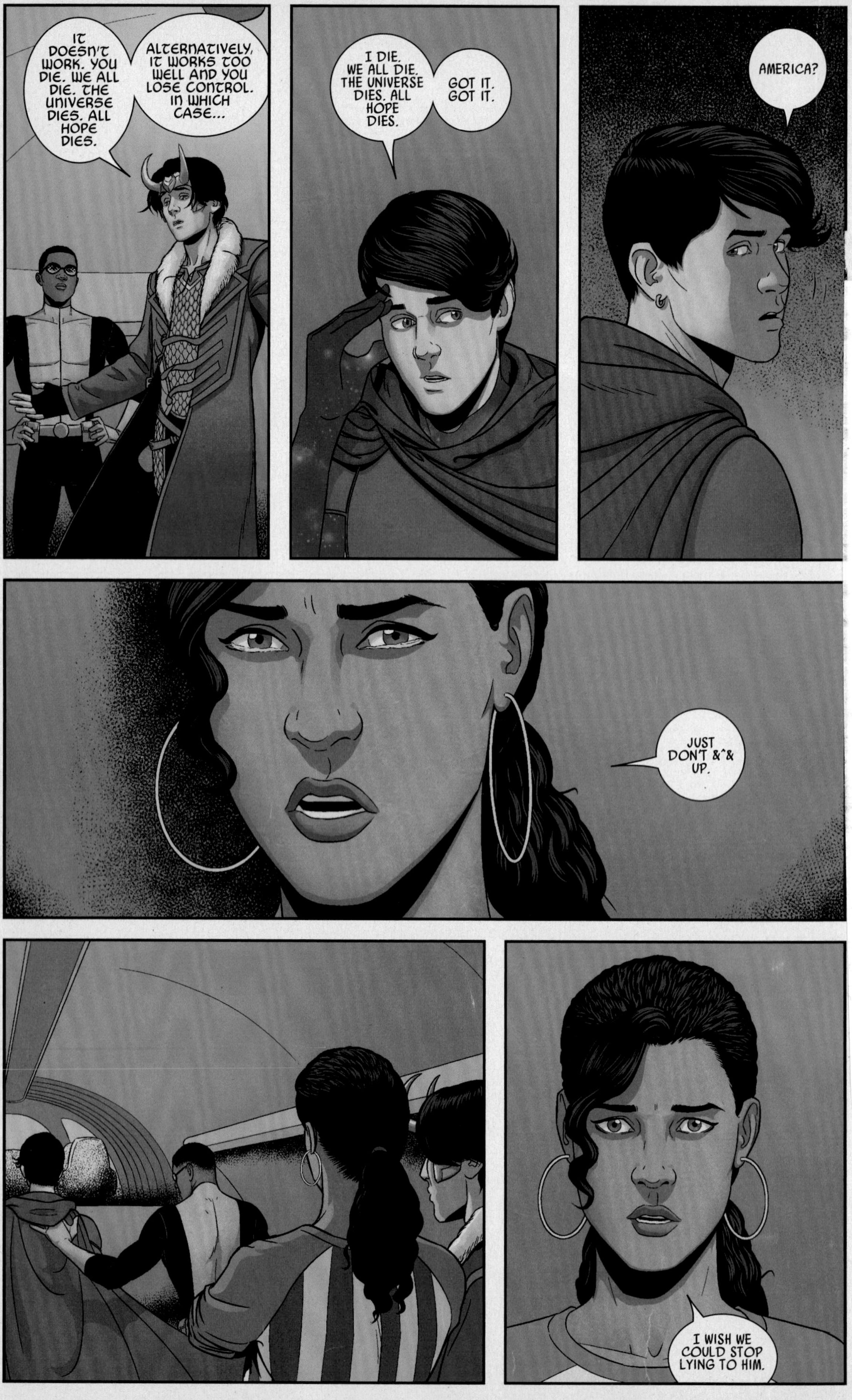
IT DOESN'T WORK. YOU DIE. WE ALL DIE. THE UNIVERSE DIES. ALL HOPE DIES.
ALTERNATIVELY, IT WORKS TOO WELL AND YOU LOSE CONTROL. IN WHICH CASE...
I DIE. WE ALL DIE. THE UNIVERSE DIES. ALL HOPE DIES.
GOT IT. GOT IT.
AMERICA?
JUST DON'T &^& UP.
I WISH WE COULD STOP LYING TO HIM.

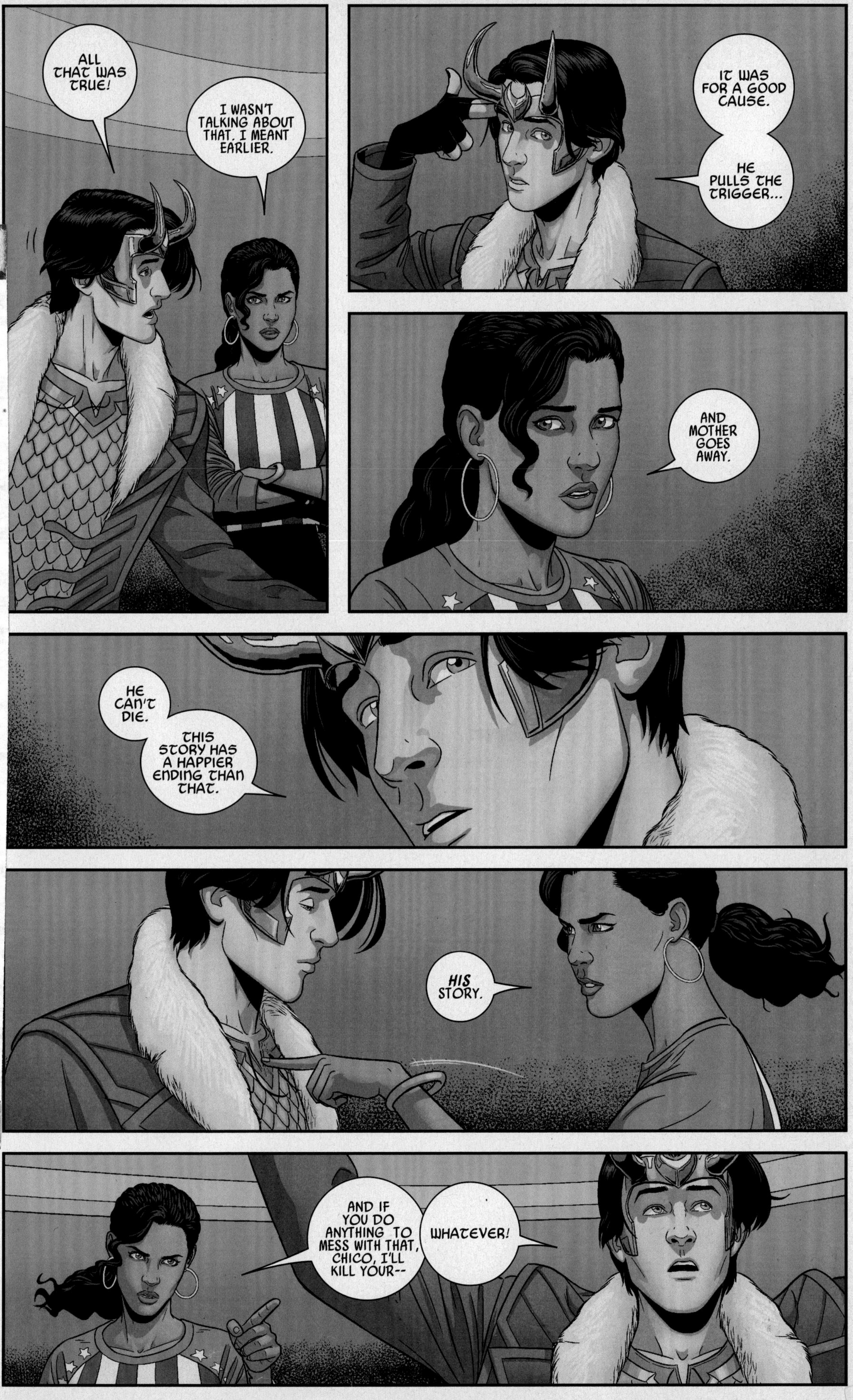
ALL THAT WAS TRUE!
I WASN'T TALKING ABOUT THAT. I MEANT EARLIER.
IT WAS FOR A GOOD CAUSE.
HE PULLS THE TRIGGER...
AND MOTHER GOES AWAY.
HE CAN'T DIE.
THIS STORY HAS A HAPPIER ENDING THAN THAT.
HIS STORY.
AND IF YOU DO ANYTHING TO MESS WITH THAT, CHICO, I'LL KILL YOUR--
WHATEVER!

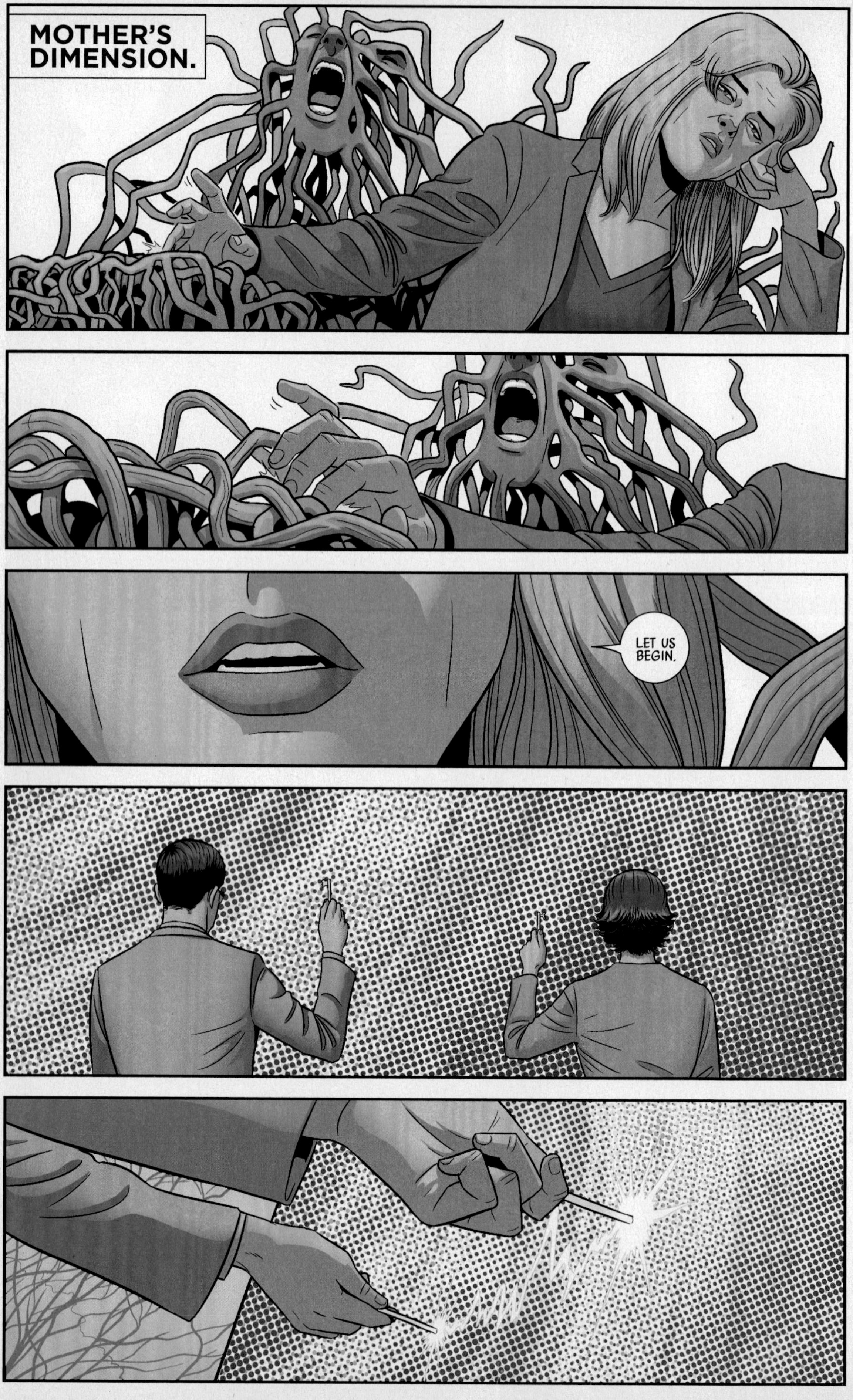
MOTHER'S DIMENSION.
LET US BEGIN.

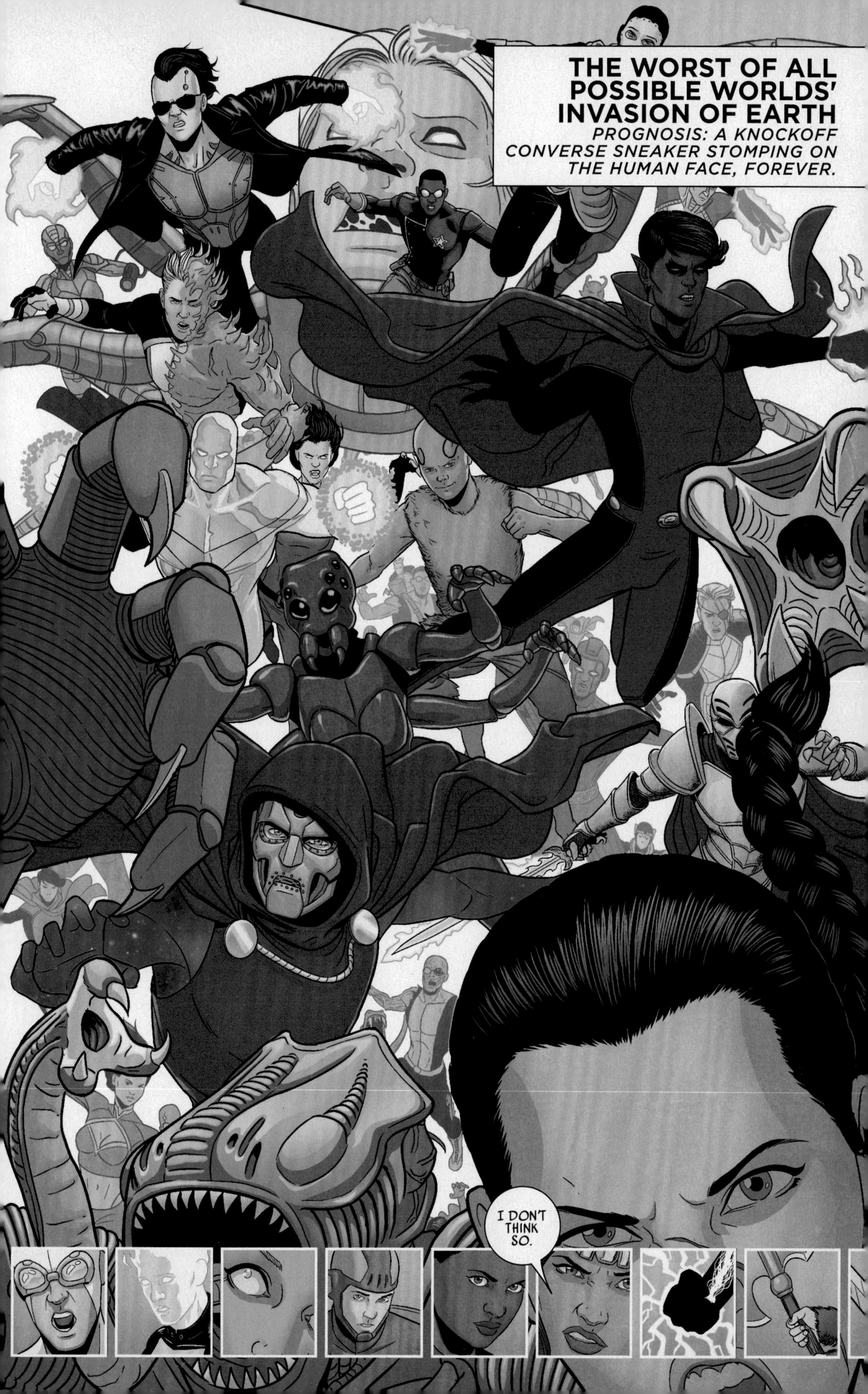
THE WORST OF ALL POSSIBLE WORLDS' INVASION OF EARTH
PROGNOSIS: A KNOCKOFF CONVERSE SNEAKER STOMPING ON THE HUMAN FACE, FOREVER.
I DON'T THINK SO.

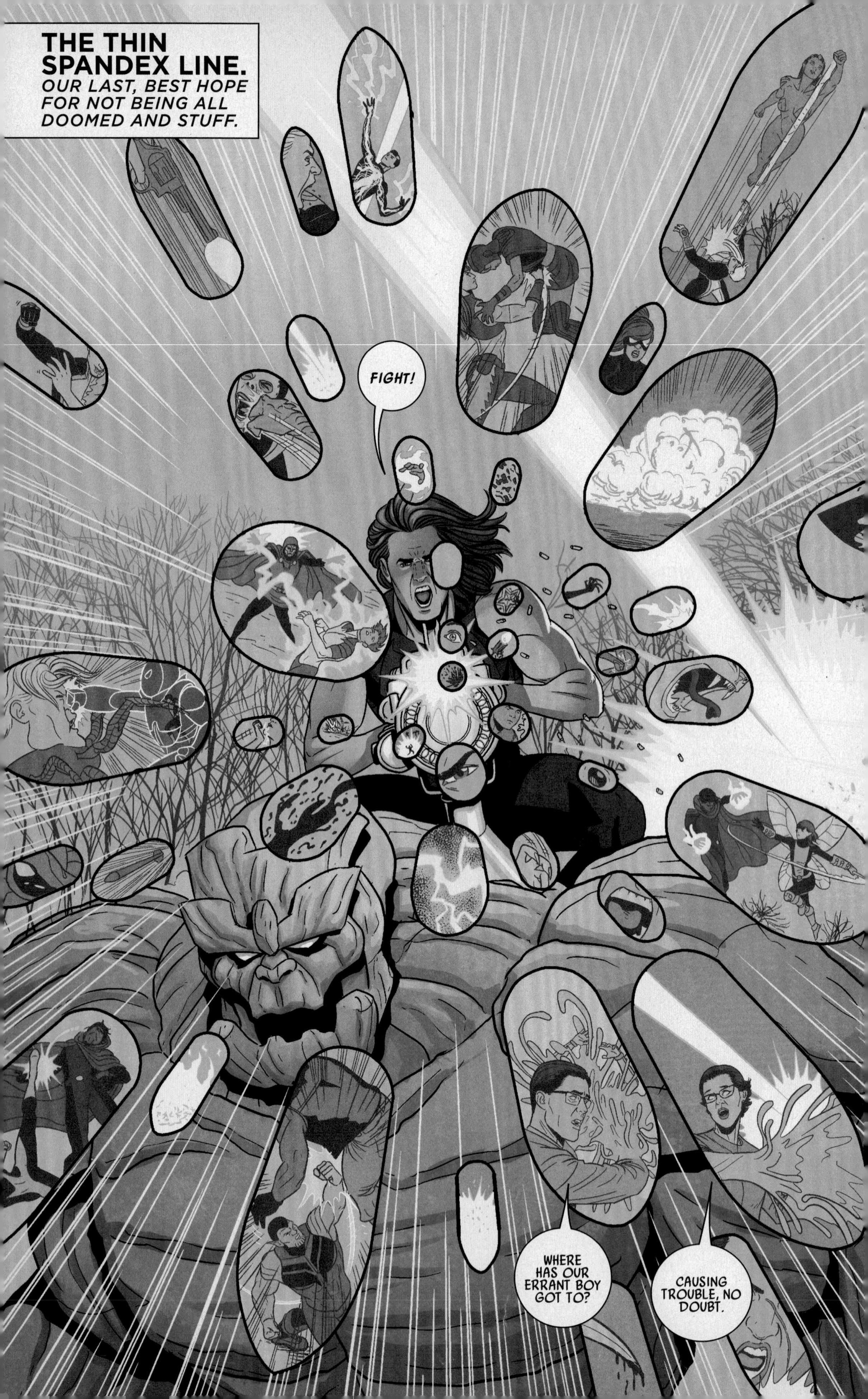
THE THIN SPANDEX LINE.
OUR LAST, BEST HOPE FOR NOT BEING ALL DOOMED AND STUFF.
FIGHT!
WHERE HAS OUR ERRANT BOY GOT TO?
CAUSING TROUBLE, NO DOUBT.

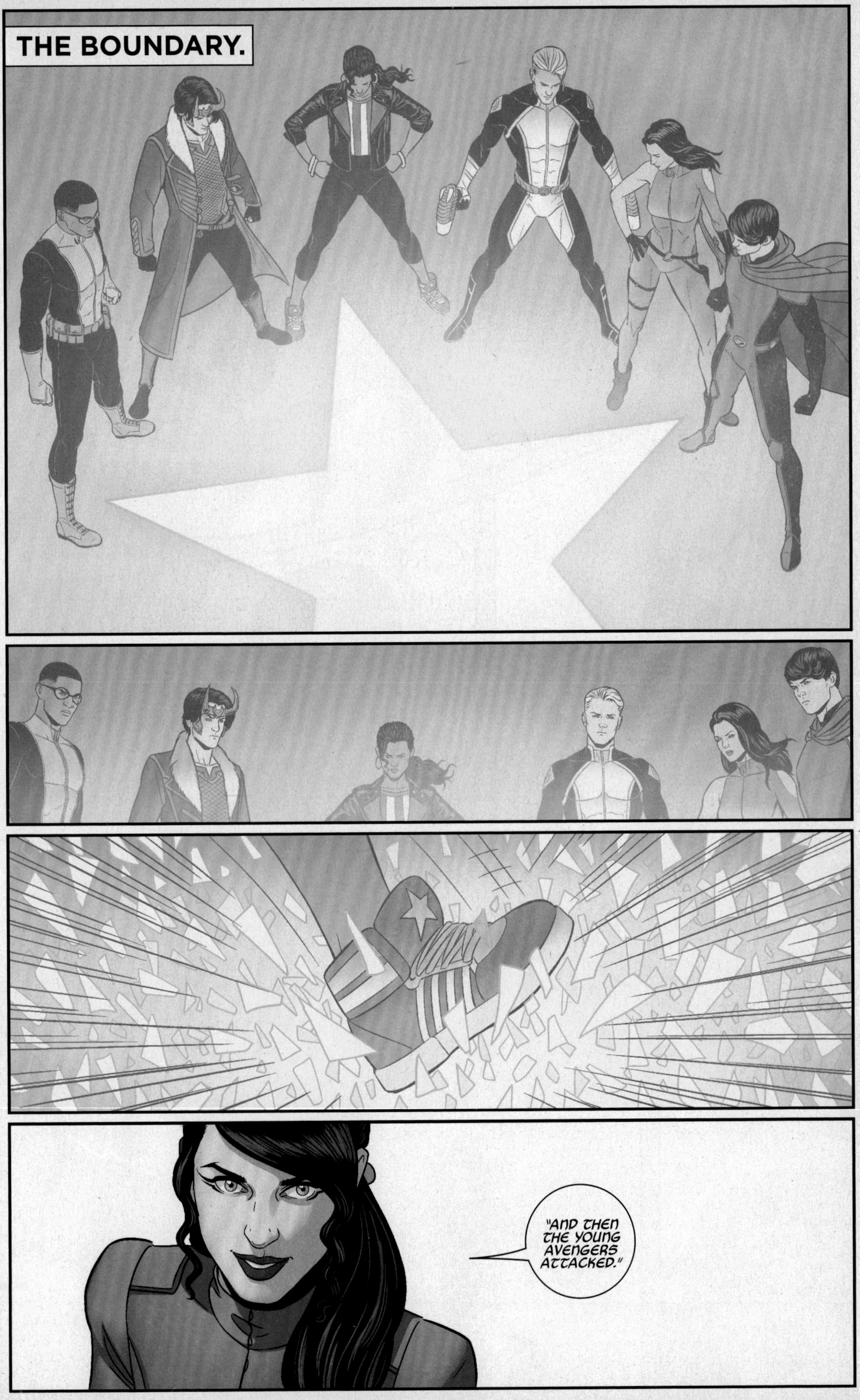
THE BOUNDARY.
"AND THEN THE YOUNG AVENGERS ATTACKED."

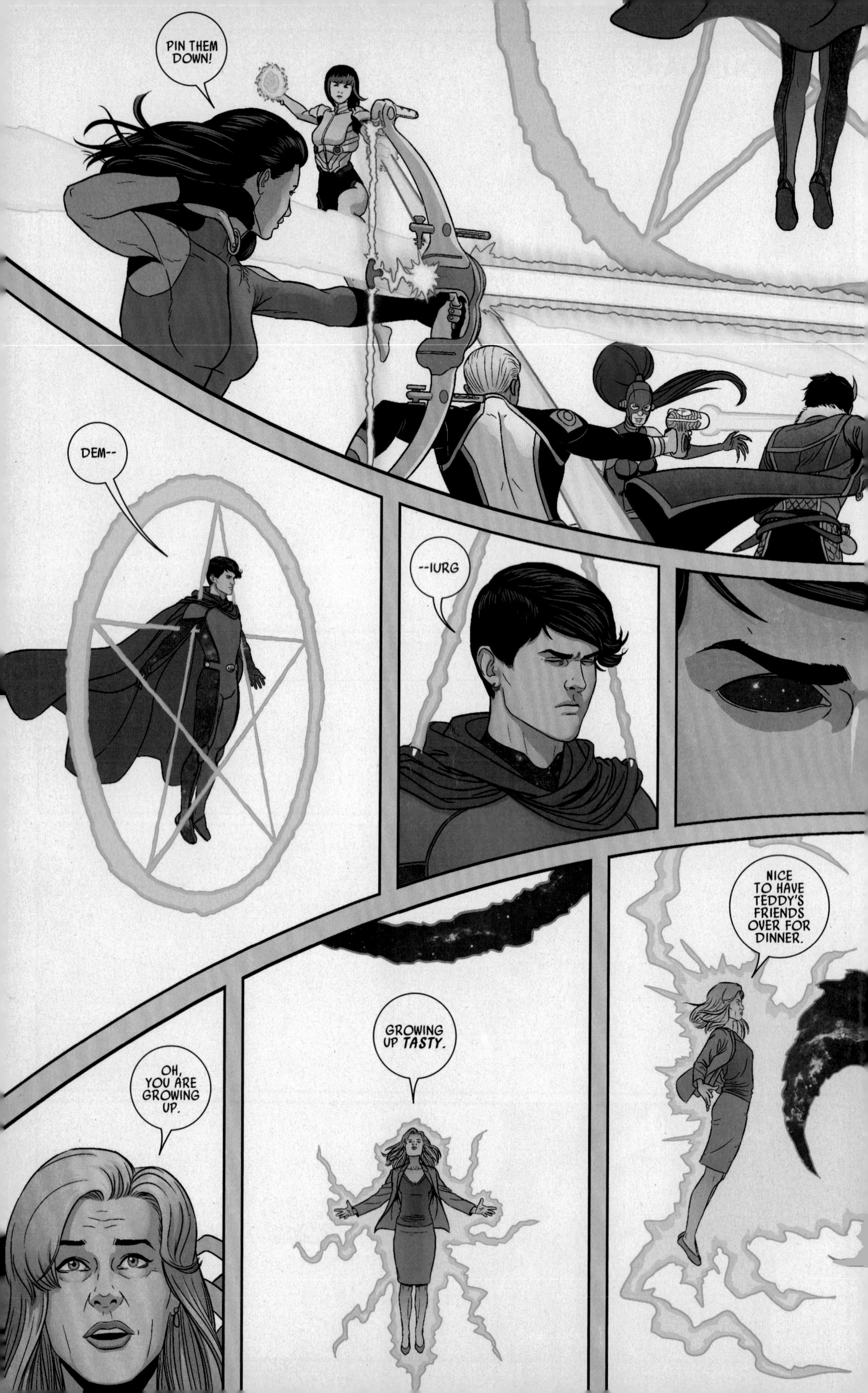
PIN THEM DOWN!
DEM--
--IURG
NICE TO HAVE TEDDY'S FRIENDS OVER FOR DINNER.
GROWING UP *TASTY*.
OH, YOU ARE GROWING UP.

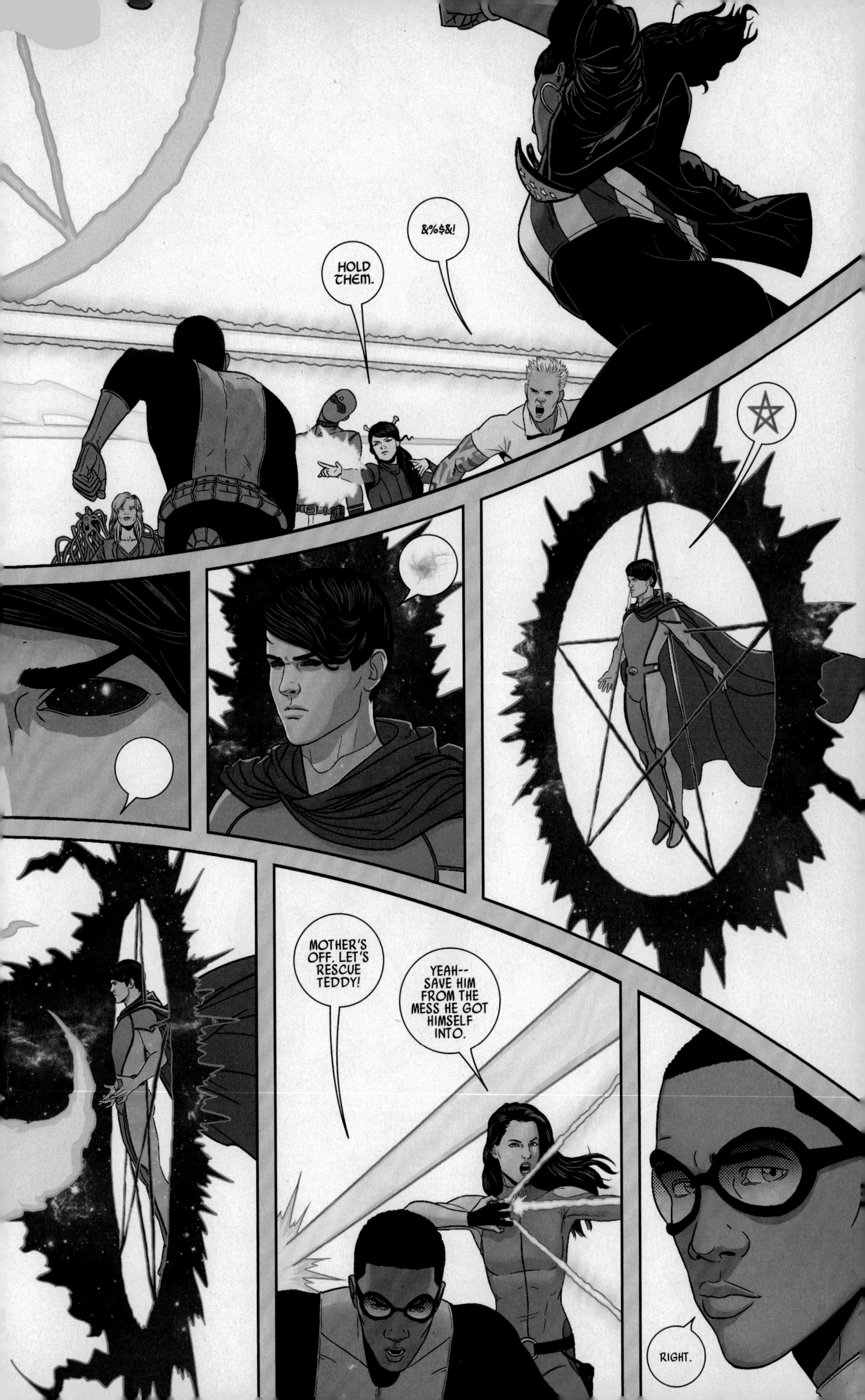
HOLD THEM.
&%$&!
MOTHER'S OFF. LET'S RESCUE TEDDY!
YEAH-- SAVE HIM FROM THE MESS HE GOT HIMSELF INTO.
RIGHT.

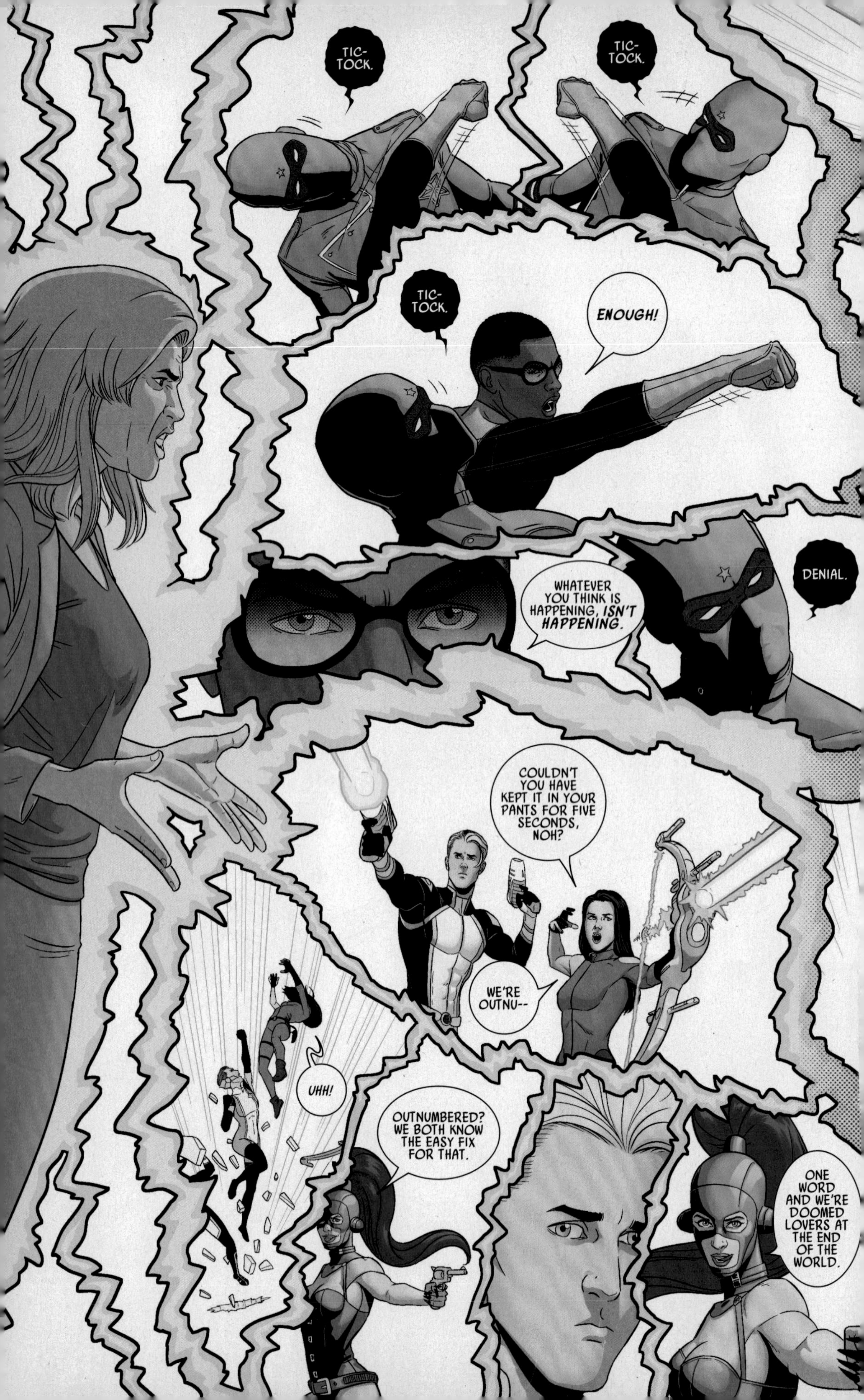

TIC-TOCK.
TIC-TOCK.
TIC-TOCK.
ENOUGH!
WHATEVER YOU THINK IS HAPPENING, ISN'T HAPPENING.
DENIAL.
COULDN'T YOU HAVE KEPT IT IN YOUR PANTS FOR FIVE SECONDS, NOH?
WE'RE OUTNU--
UHH!
OUTNUMBERED? WE BOTH KNOW THE EASY FIX FOR THAT.
ONE WORD AND WE'RE DOOMED LOVERS AT THE END OF THE WORLD.

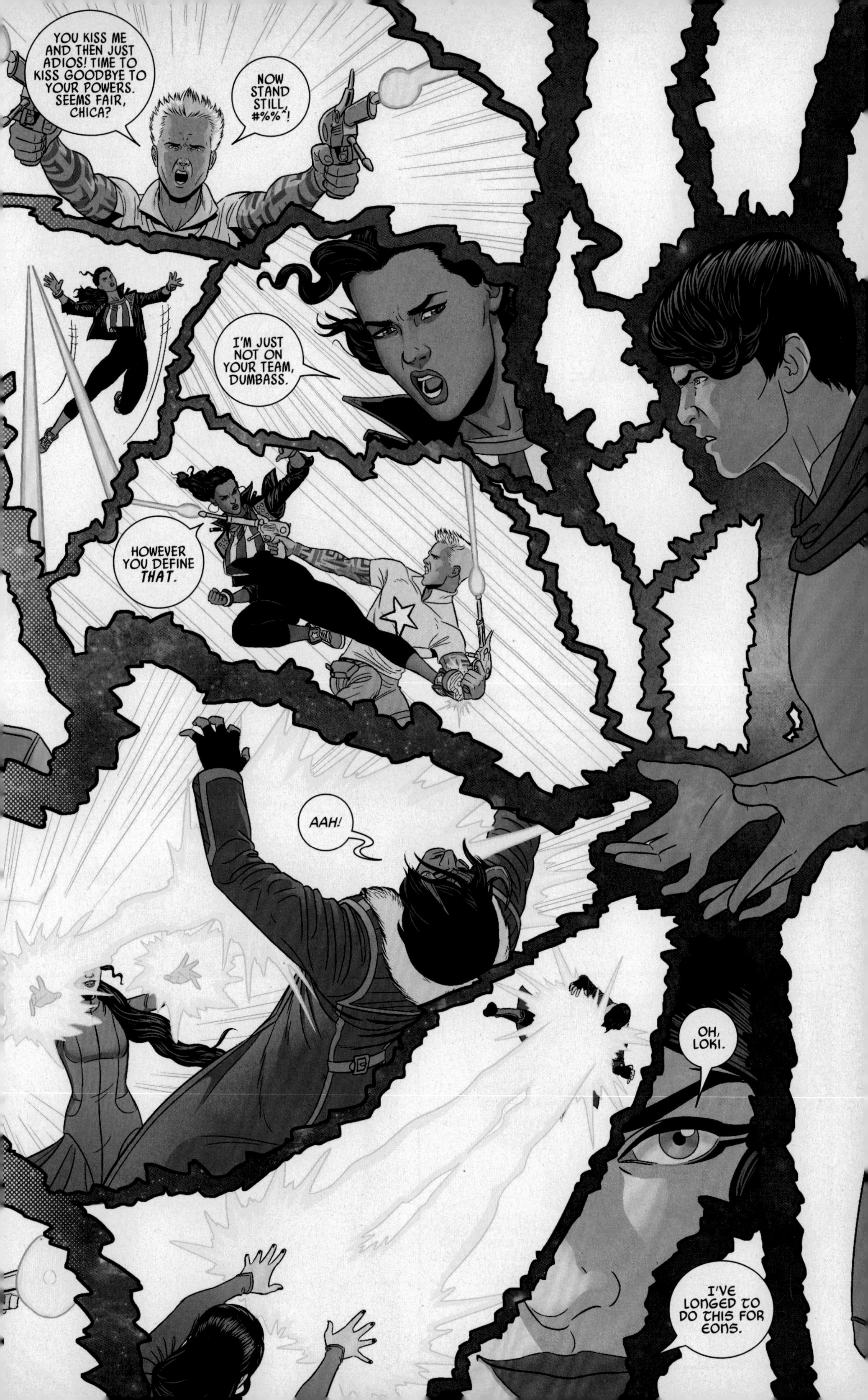
YOU KISS ME AND THEN JUST ADIOS! TIME TO KISS GOODBYE TO YOUR POWERS. SEEMS FAIR, CHICA?
NOW STAND STILL, #%%^!
I'M JUST NOT ON YOUR TEAM, DUMBASS.
HOWEVER YOU DEFINE THAT.
AAH!
OH, LOKI.
I'VE LONGED TO DO THIS FOR EONS.

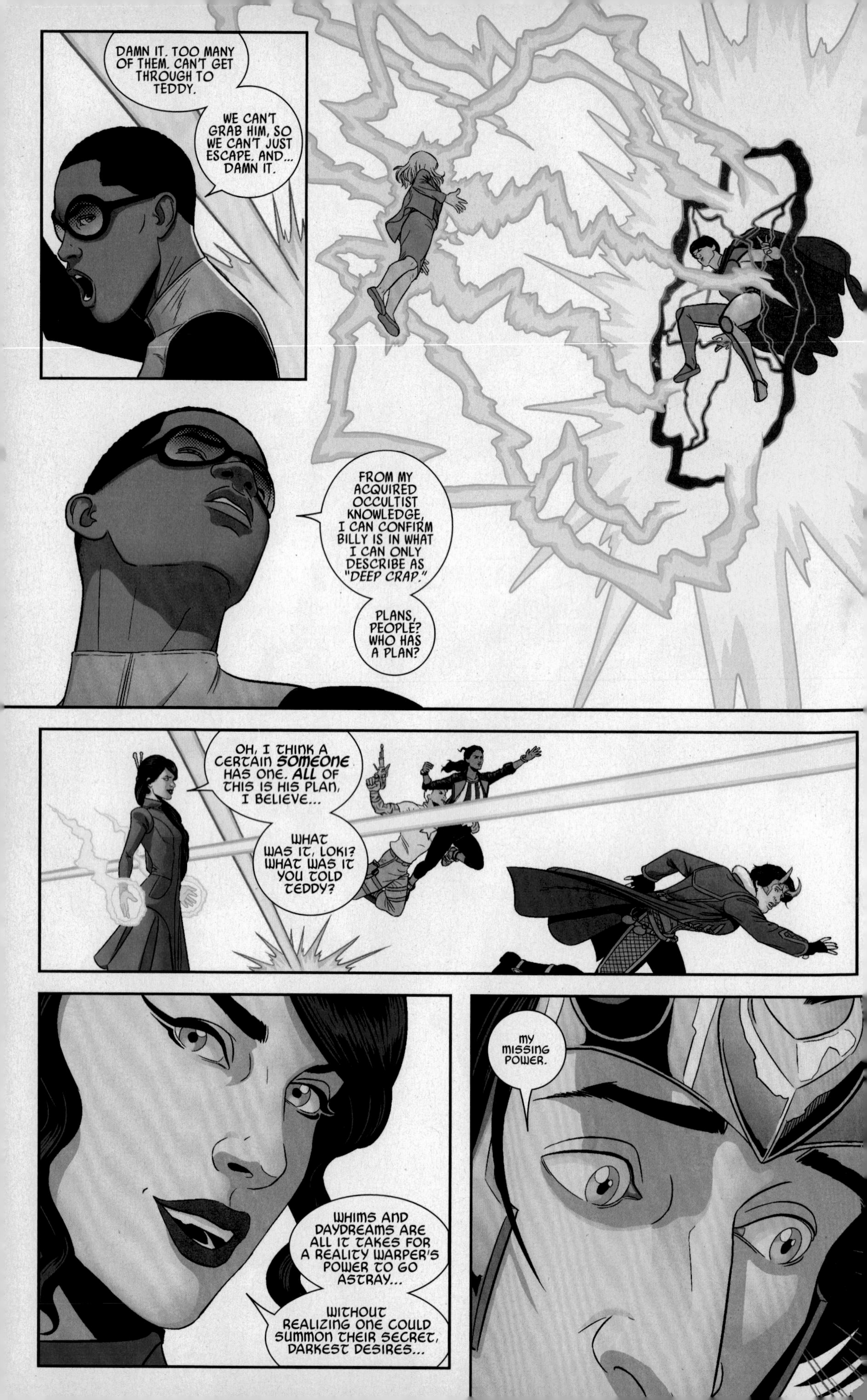
DAMN IT. TOO MANY OF THEM. CAN'T GET THROUGH TO TEDDY.
WE CAN'T GRAB HIM, SO WE CAN'T JUST ESCAPE. AND... DAMN IT.
FROM MY ACQUIRED OCCULTIST KNOWLEDGE, I CAN CONFIRM BILLY IS IN WHAT I CAN ONLY DESCRIBE AS "DEEP CRAP."
PLANS, PEOPLE? WHO HAS A PLAN?
OH, I THINK A CERTAIN SOMEONE HAS ONE. ALL OF THIS IS HIS PLAN, I BELIEVE...
WHAT WAS IT, LOKI? WHAT WAS IT YOU TOLD TEDDY?
WHIMS AND DAYDREAMS ARE ALL IT TAKES FOR A REALITY WARPER'S POWER TO GO ASTRAY...
WITHOUT REALIZING ONE COULD SUMMON THEIR SECRET, DARKEST DESIRES...
MY MISSING POWER.

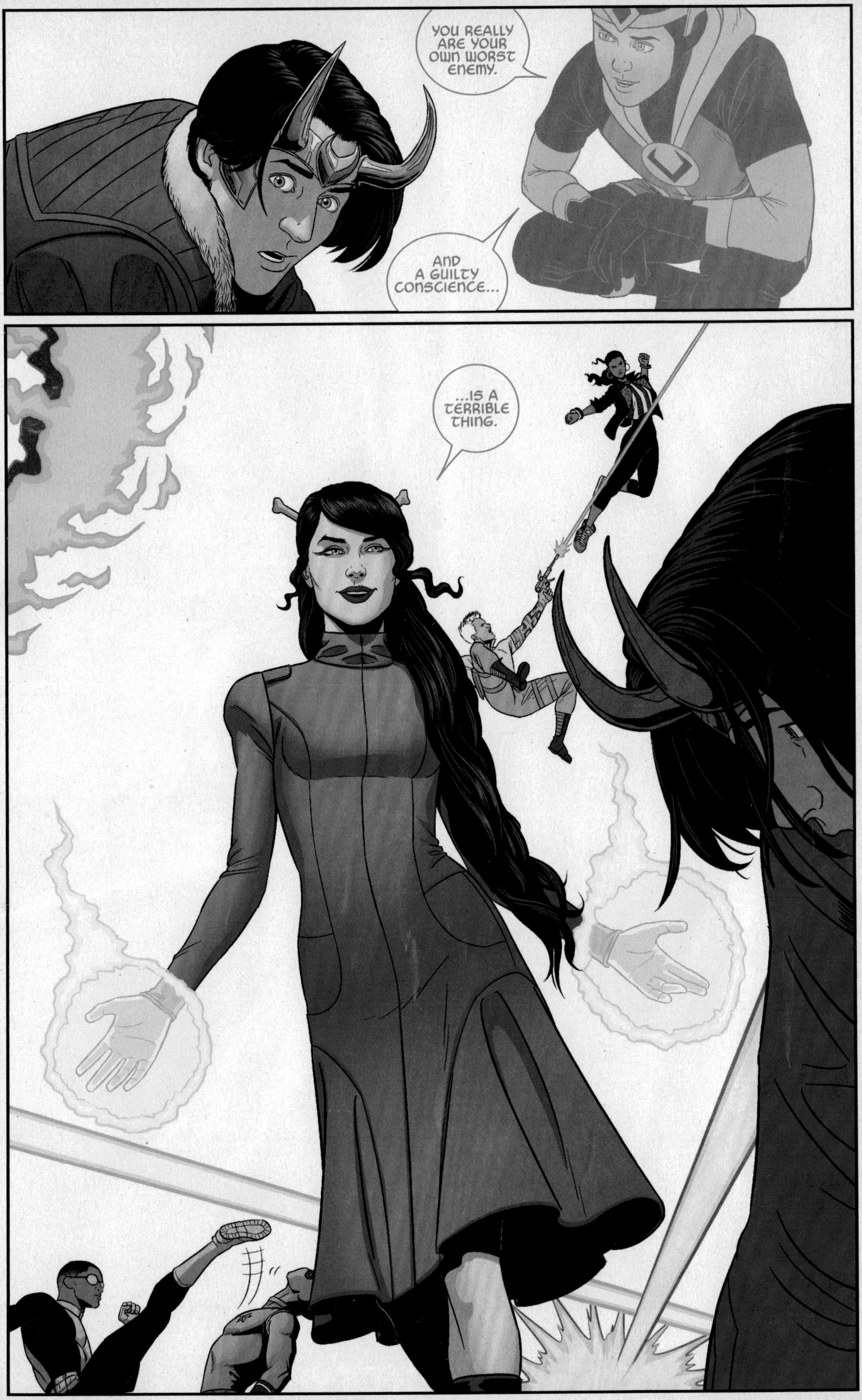
YOU REALLY ARE YOUR OWN WORST ENEMY.
AND A GUILTY CONSCIENCE...
...IS A TERRIBLE THING.

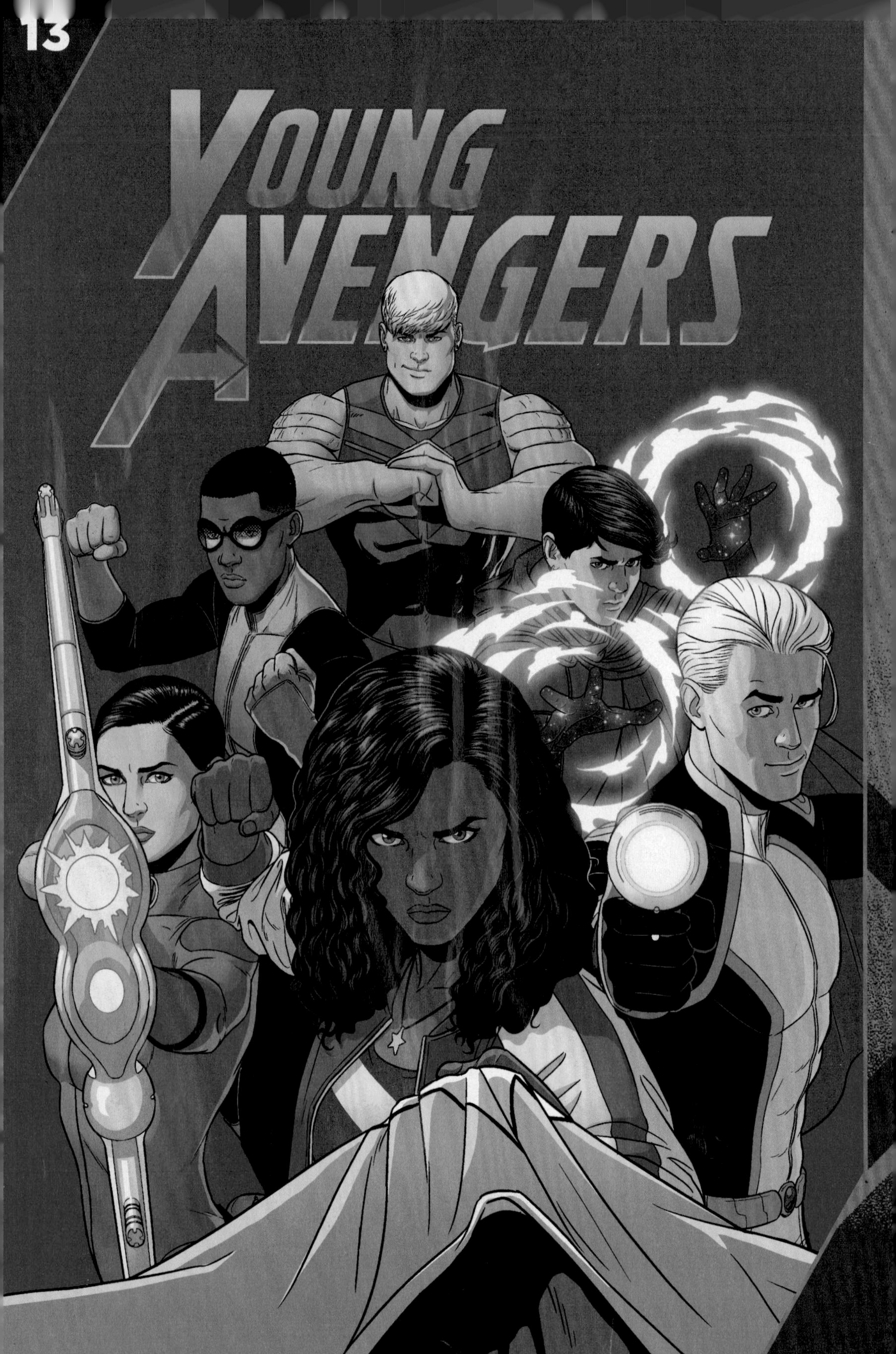
13
YOUNG AVENGERS

"YOUNG AVENGERS" PART TWO

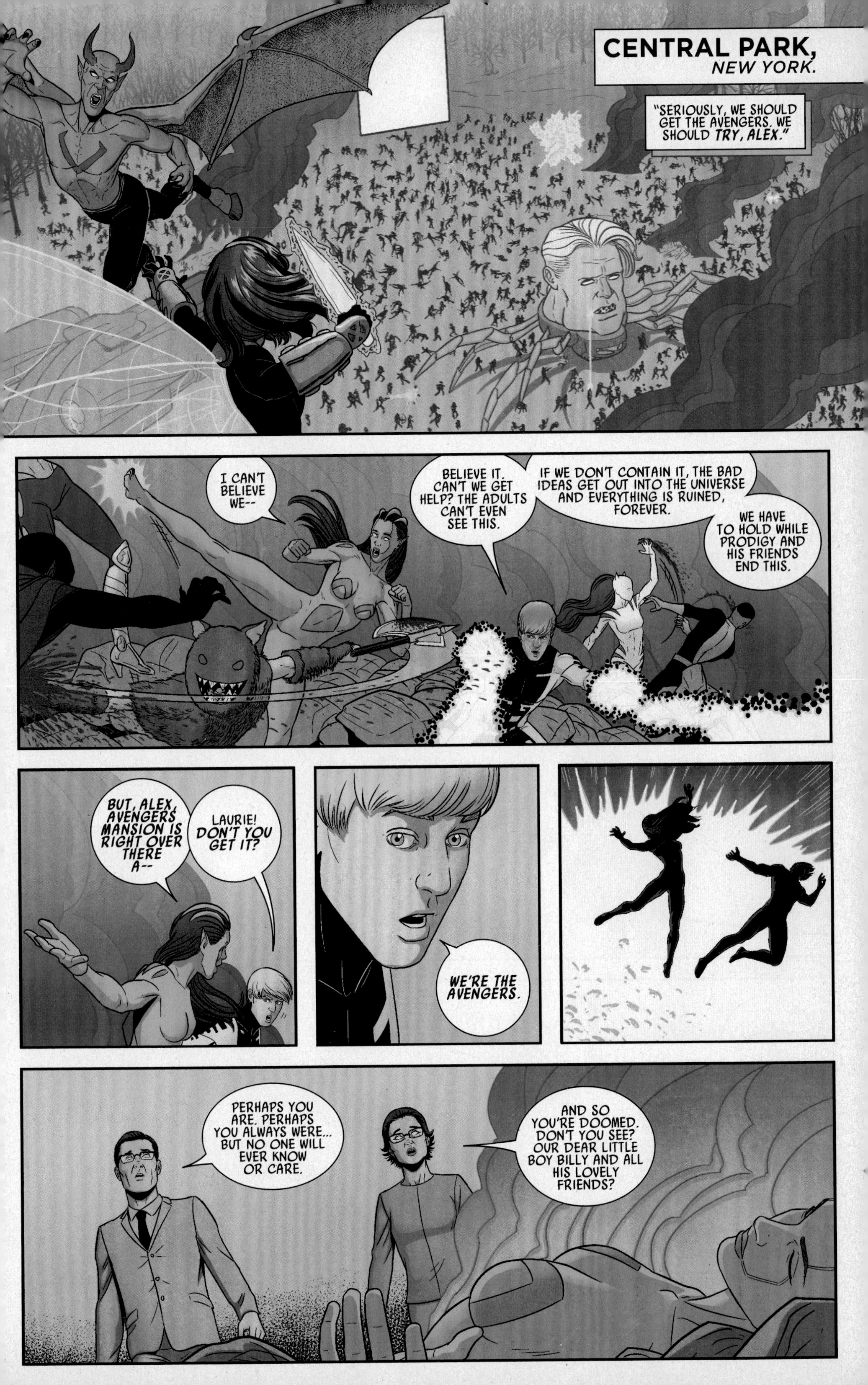
CENTRAL PARK, NEW YORK.
"SERIOUSLY, WE SHOULD GET THE AVENGERS. WE SHOULD TRY, ALEX."
I CAN'T BELIEVE WE--
BELIEVE IT. CAN'T WE GET HELP? THE ADULTS CAN'T EVEN SEE THIS.
IF WE DON'T CONTAIN IT, THE BAD IDEAS GET OUT INTO THE UNIVERSE AND EVERYTHING IS RUINED, FOREVER.
WE HAVE TO HOLD WHILE PRODIGY AND HIS FRIENDS END THIS.
BUT, ALEX, AVENGERS MANSION IS RIGHT OVER THERE A--
LAURIE! DON'T YOU GET IT?
WE'RE THE AVENGERS.
PERHAPS YOU ARE. PERHAPS YOU ALWAYS WERE... BUT NO ONE WILL EVER KNOW OR CARE.
AND SO YOU'RE DOOMED. DON'T YOU SEE? OUR DEAR LITTLE BOY BILLY AND ALL HIS LOVELY FRIENDS?

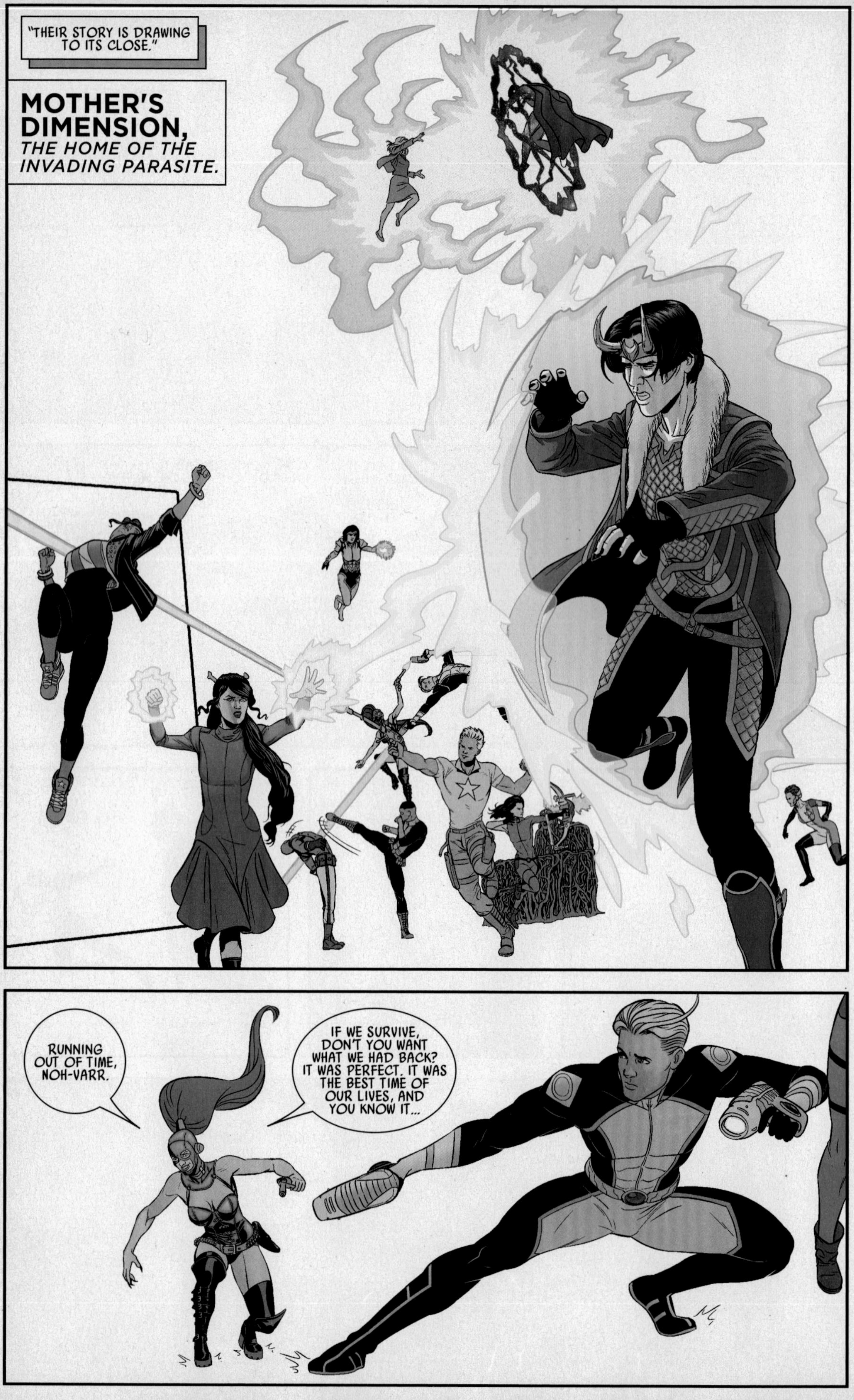
"THEIR STORY IS DRAWING TO ITS CLOSE."
MOTHER'S DIMENSION, THE HOME OF THE INVADING PARASITE.
RUNNING OUT OF TIME, NOH-VARR.
IF WE SURVIVE, DON'T YOU WANT WHAT WE HAD BACK? IT WAS PERFECT. IT WAS THE BEST TIME OF OUR LIVES, AND YOU KNOW IT...

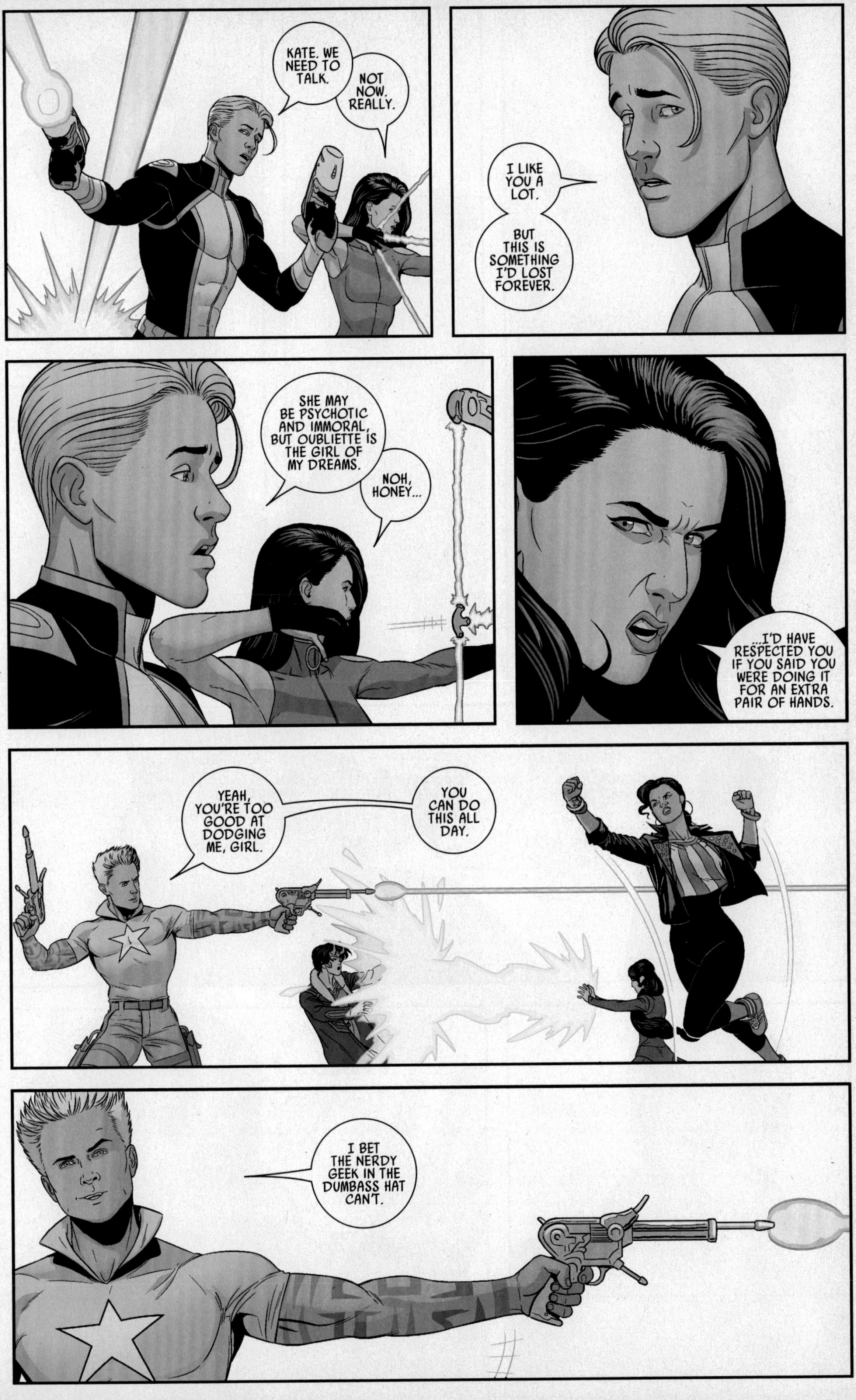
KATE, WE NEED TO TALK.
NOT NOW. REALLY.
I LIKE YOU A LOT.
BUT THIS IS SOMETHING I'D LOST FOREVER.
SHE MAY BE PSYCHOTIC AND IMMORAL, BUT OUBLIETTE IS THE GIRL OF MY DREAMS.
NOH, HONEY...
...I'D HAVE RESPECTED YOU IF YOU SAID YOU WERE DOING IT FOR AN EXTRA PAIR OF HANDS.
YEAH, YOU'RE TOO GOOD AT DODGING ME, GIRL.
YOU CAN DO THIS ALL DAY.
I BET THE NERDY GEEK IN THE DUMBASS HAT CAN'T.

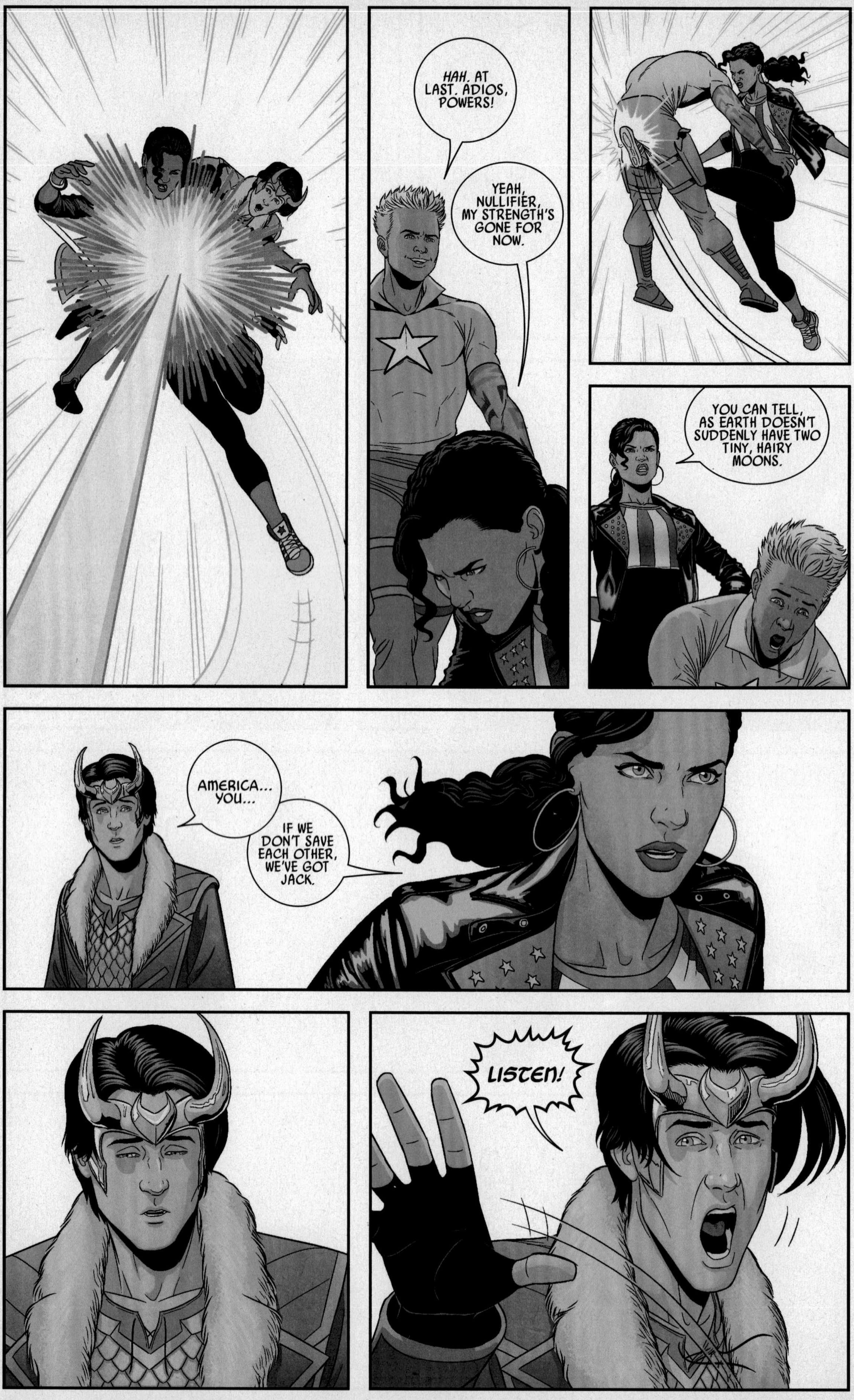

HAH. AT LAST. ADIOS, POWERS!
YEAH, NULLIFIER, MY STRENGTH'S GONE FOR NOW.
YOU CAN TELL, AS EARTH DOESN'T SUDDENLY HAVE TWO TINY, HAIRY MOONS.
AMERICA... YOU...
IF WE DON'T SAVE EACH OTHER, WE'VE GOT JACK.
LISTEN!

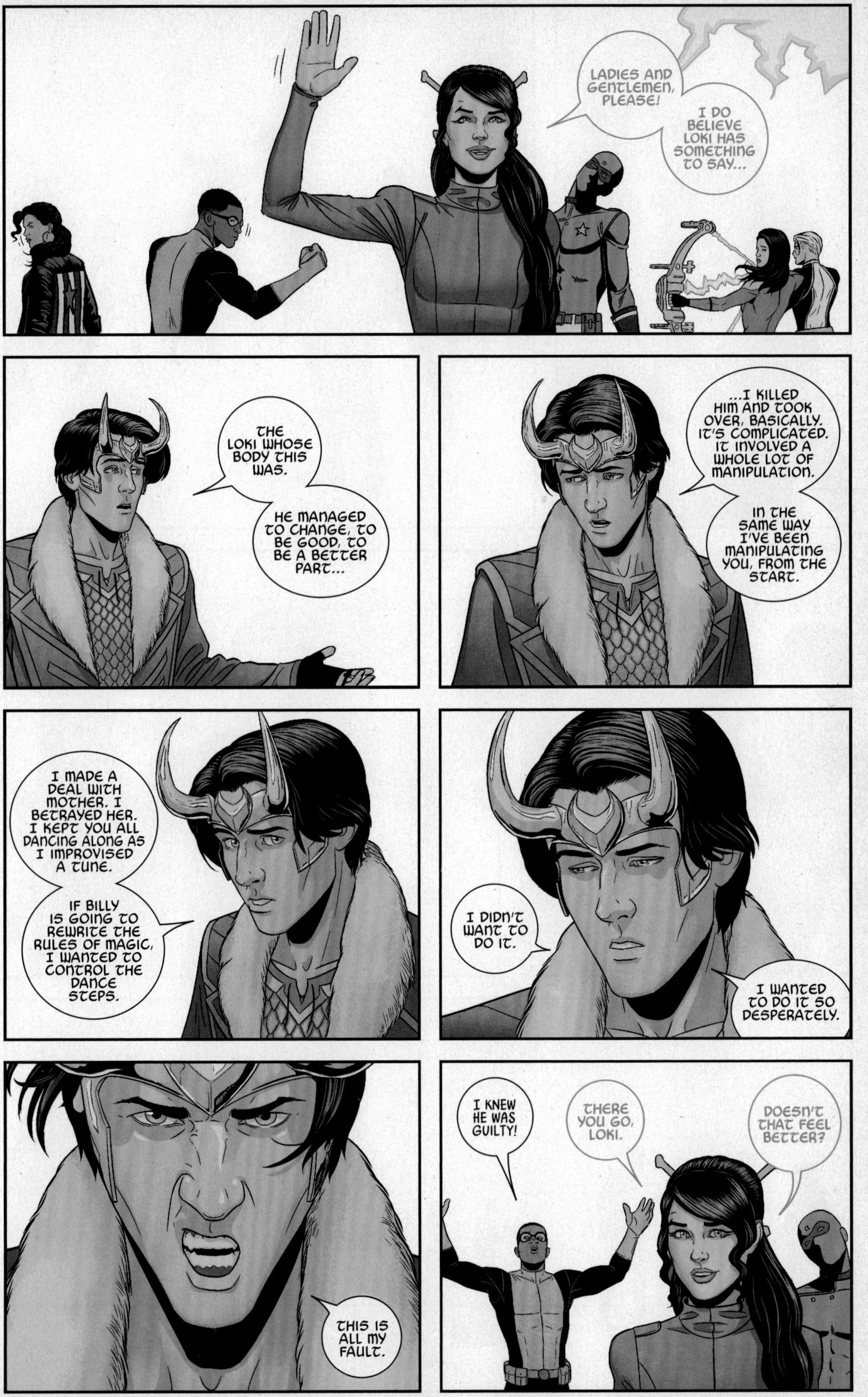
LADIES AND GENTLEMEN, PLEASE!
I DO BELIEVE LOKI HAS SOMETHING TO SAY...
THE LOKI WHOSE BODY THIS WAS.
HE MANAGED TO CHANGE, TO BE GOOD, TO BE A BETTER PART...
...I KILLED HIM AND TOOK OVER, BASICALLY. IT'S COMPLICATED. IT INVOLVED A WHOLE LOT OF MANIPULATION.
IN THE SAME WAY I'VE BEEN MANIPULATING YOU, FROM THE START.
I MADE A DEAL WITH MOTHER. I BETRAYED HER. I KEPT YOU ALL DANCING ALONG AS I IMPROVISED A TUNE.
IF BILLY IS GOING TO REWRITE THE RULES OF MAGIC, I WANTED TO CONTROL THE DANCE STEPS.
I DIDN'T WANT TO DO IT.
I WANTED TO DO IT SO DESPERATELY.
THIS IS ALL MY FAULT.
I KNEW HE WAS GUILTY!
THERE YOU GO, LOKI.
DOESN'T THAT FEEL BETTER?

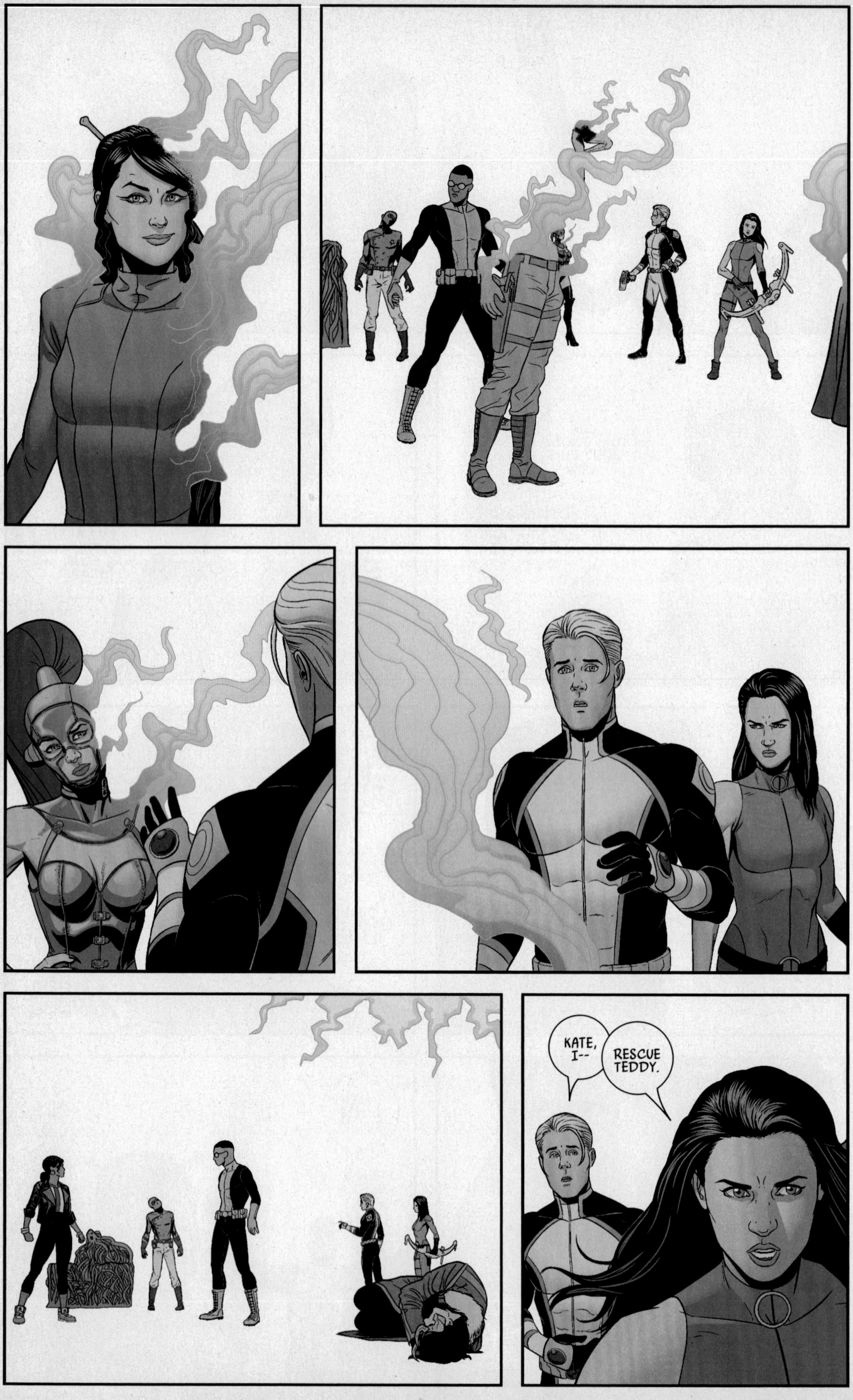
KATE, I--
RESCUE TEDDY.

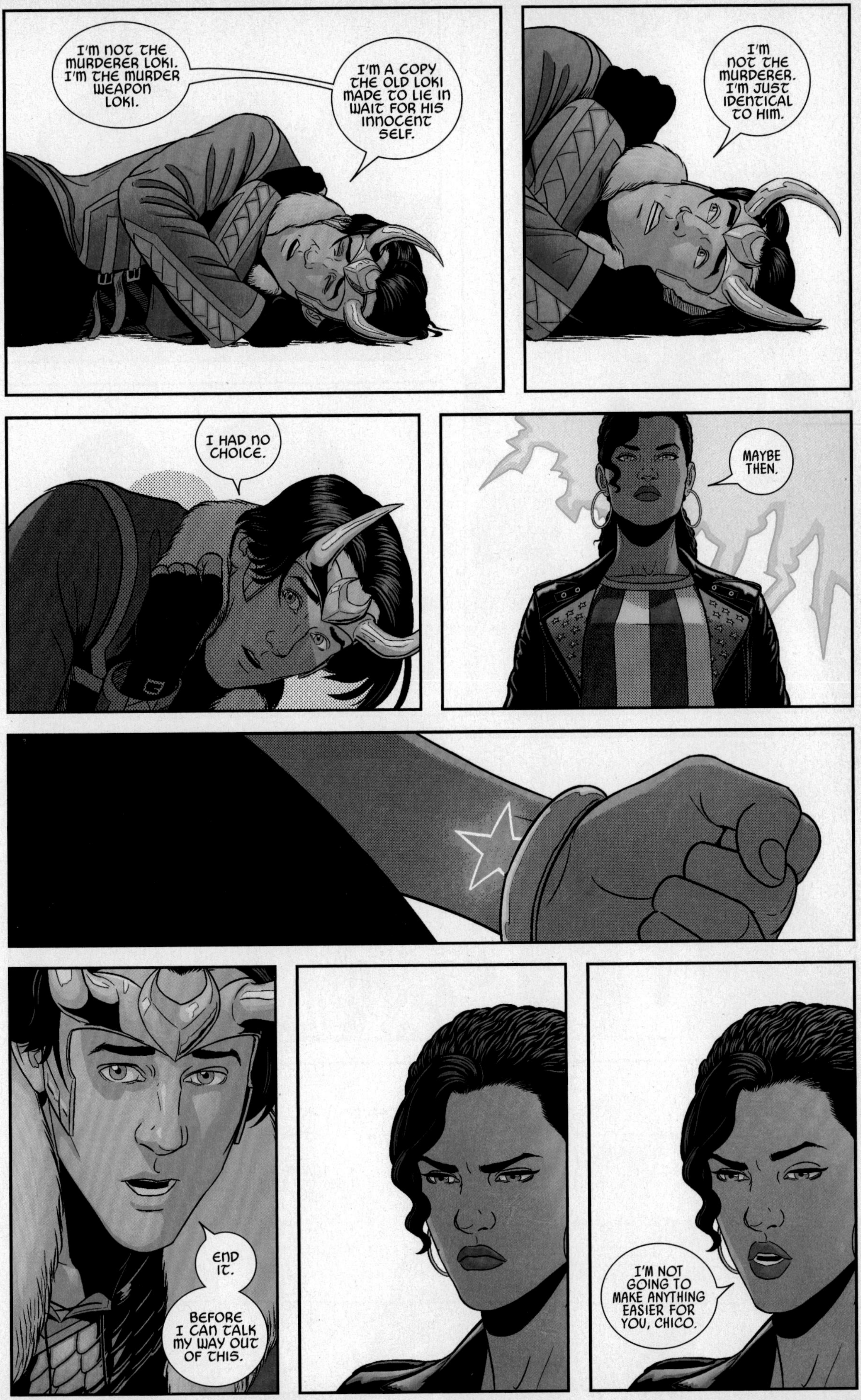
I'M NOT THE MURDERER LOKI. I'M THE MURDER WEAPON LOKI.
I'M A COPY THE OLD LOKI MADE TO LIE IN WAIT FOR HIS INNOCENT SELF.
I'M NOT THE MURDERER. I'M JUST IDENTICAL TO HIM.
I HAD NO CHOICE.
MAYBE THEN.
END IT.
BEFORE I CAN TALK MY WAY OUT OF THIS.
I'M NOT GOING TO MAKE ANYTHING EASIER FOR YOU, CHICO.

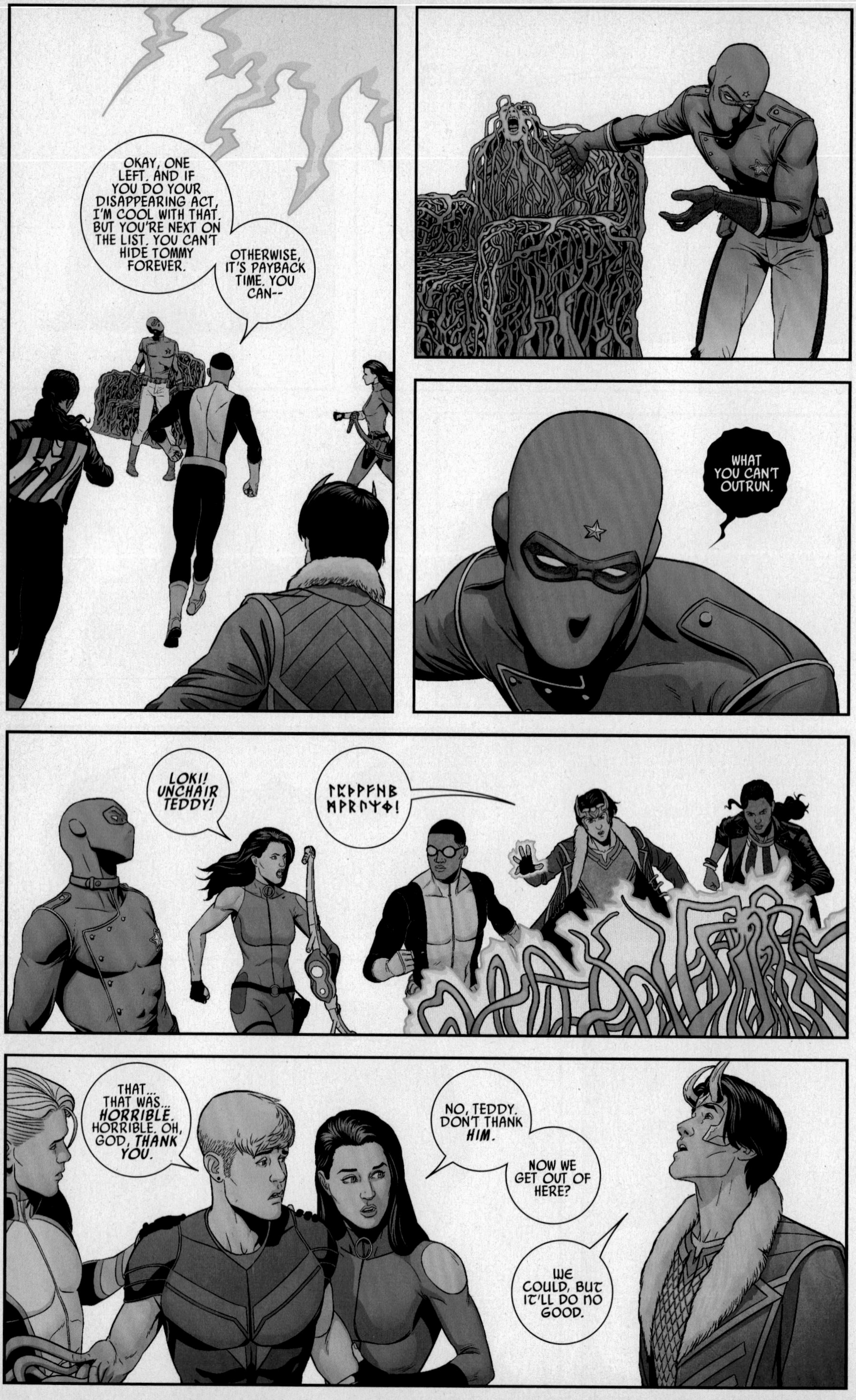
OKAY, ONE LEFT. AND IF YOU DO YOUR DISAPPEARING ACT, I'M COOL WITH THAT. BUT YOU'RE NEXT ON THE LIST. YOU CAN'T HIDE TOMMY FOREVER.
OTHERWISE, IT'S PAYBACK TIME. YOU CAN--
WHAT YOU CAN'T OUTRUN.
LOKI! UNCHAIR TEDDY!
ᛚᛈᚦᚠᚠᚻᛒ ᛗᚹᚱᚢᛉᛟ!
THAT... THAT WAS... HORRIBLE. HORRIBLE. OH, GOD, THANK YOU.
NO, TEDDY. DON'T THANK HIM.
NOW WE GET OUT OF HERE?
WE COULD, BUT IT'LL DO NO GOOD.

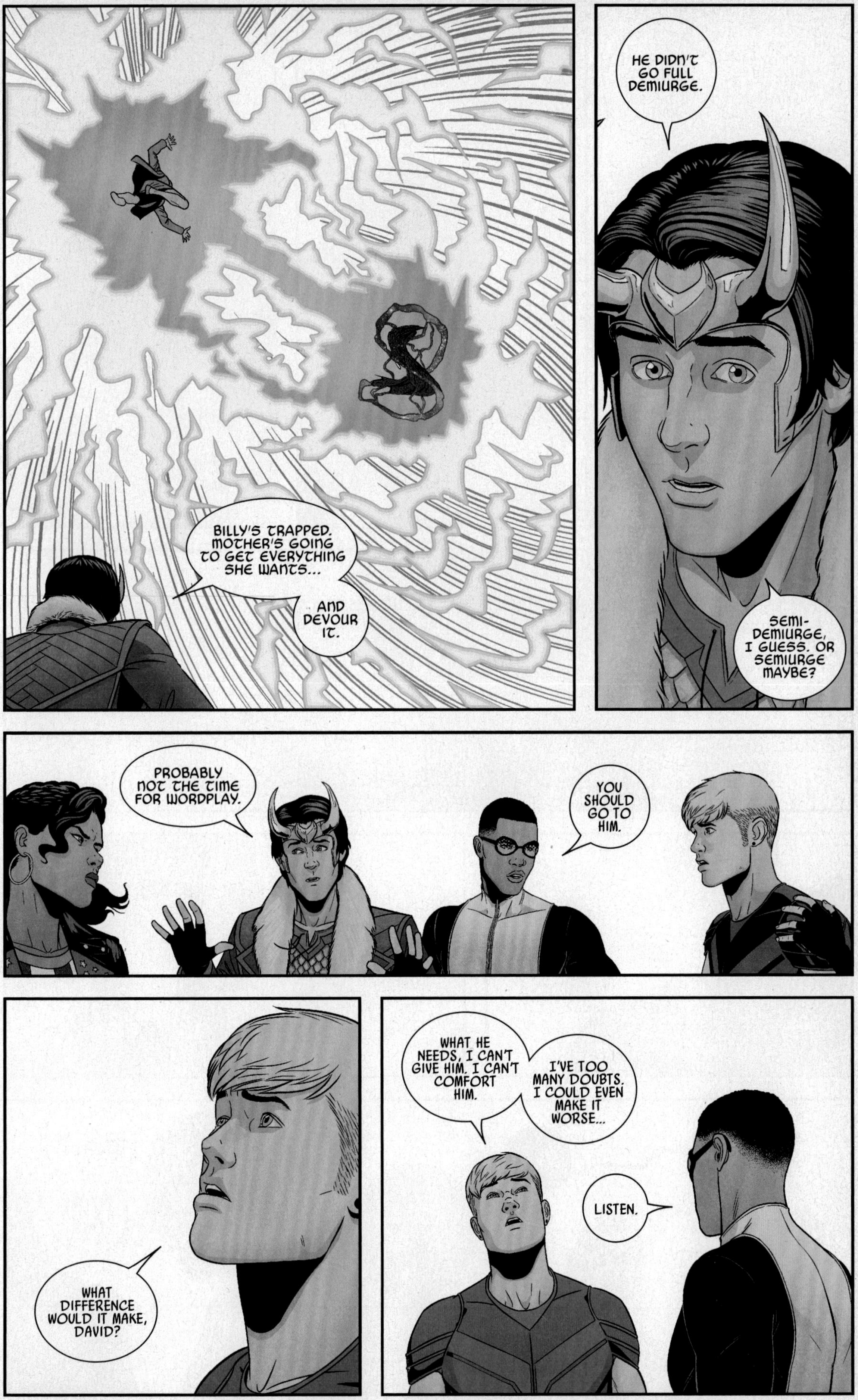
BILLY'S TRAPPED. MOTHER'S GOING TO GET EVERYTHING SHE WANTS...
AND DEVOUR IT.
HE DIDN'T GO FULL DEMIURGE.
SEMI-DEMIURGE, I GUESS. OR SEMIURGE MAYBE?
PROBABLY NOT THE TIME FOR WORDPLAY.
YOU SHOULD GO TO HIM.
WHAT DIFFERENCE WOULD IT MAKE, DAVID?
WHAT HE NEEDS, I CAN'T GIVE HIM. I CAN'T COMFORT HIM.
I'VE TOO MANY DOUBTS. I COULD EVEN MAKE IT WORSE...
LISTEN.

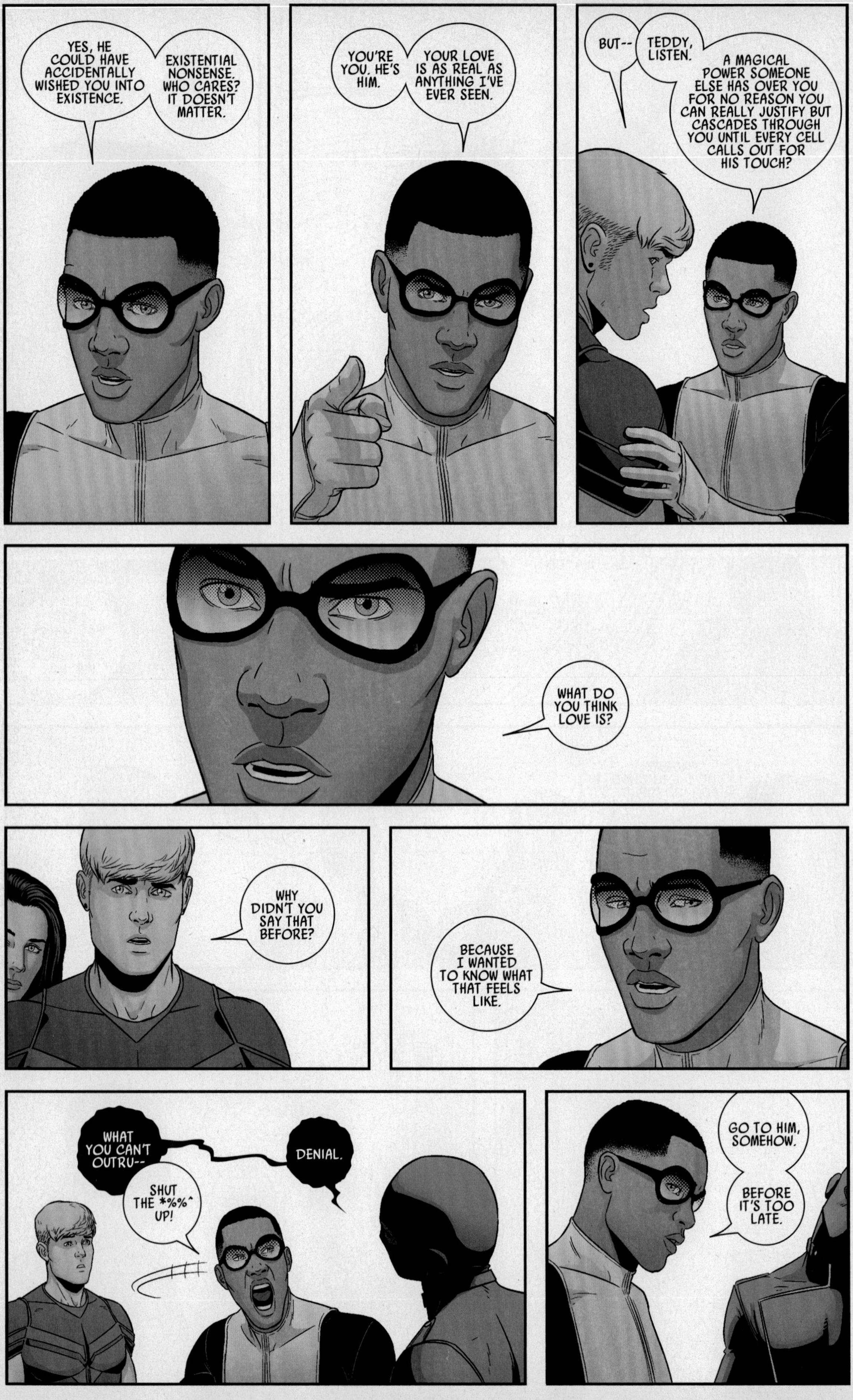
YES, HE COULD HAVE ACCIDENTALLY WISHED YOU INTO EXISTENCE.
EXISTENTIAL NONSENSE. WHO CARES? IT DOESN'T MATTER.
YOU'RE YOU. HE'S HIM.
YOUR LOVE IS AS REAL AS ANYTHING I'VE EVER SEEN.
BUT--
TEDDY, LISTEN.
A MAGICAL POWER SOMEONE ELSE HAS OVER YOU FOR NO REASON YOU CAN REALLY JUSTIFY BUT CASCADES THROUGH YOU UNTIL EVERY CELL CALLS OUT FOR HIS TOUCH?
WHAT DO YOU THINK LOVE IS?
WHY DIDN'T YOU SAY THAT BEFORE?
BECAUSE I WANTED TO KNOW WHAT THAT FEELS LIKE.
WHAT YOU CAN'T OUTRU--
DENIAL.
SHUT THE *%%^ UP!
GO TO HIM, SOMEHOW.
BEFORE IT'S TOO LATE.

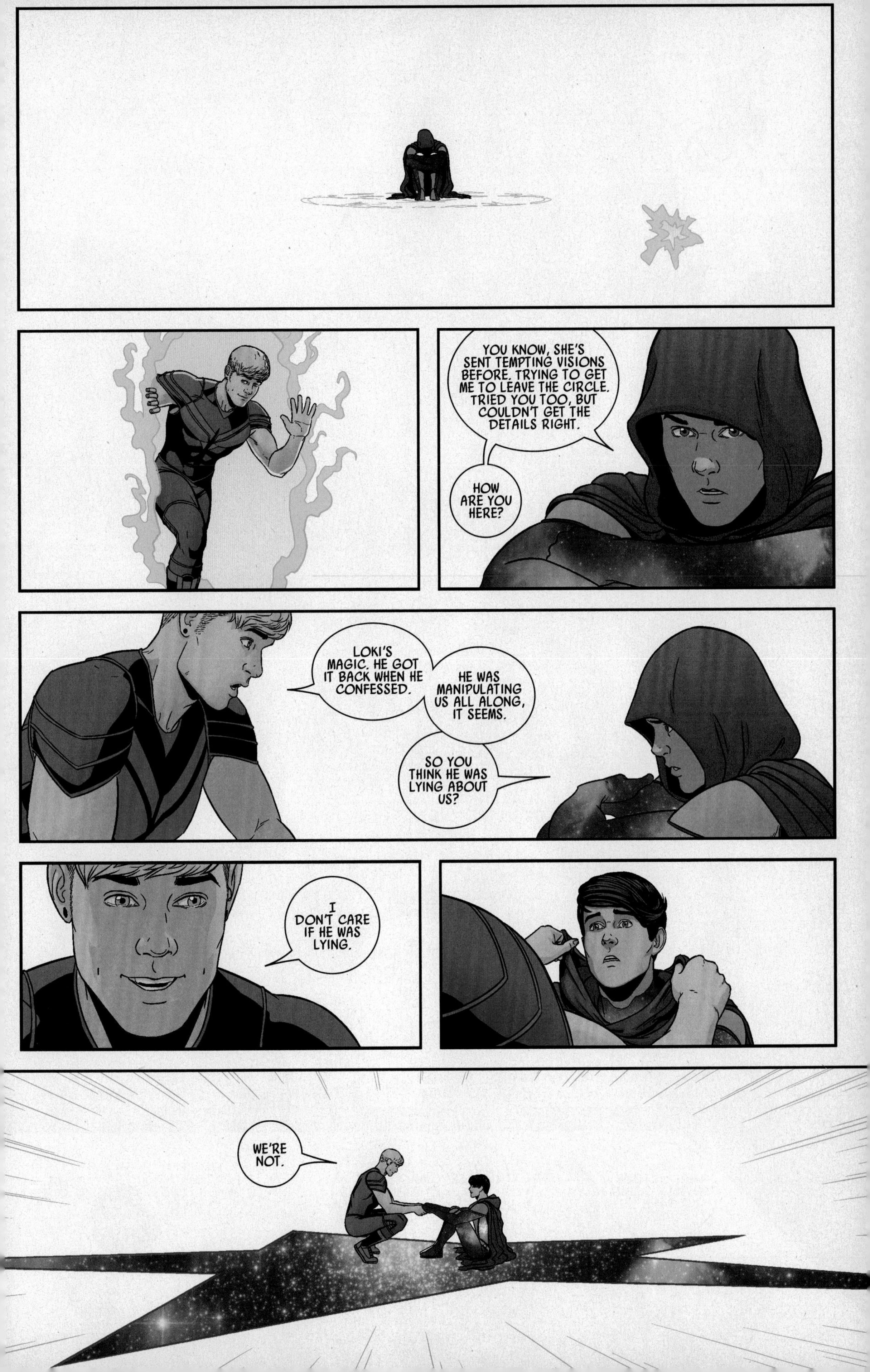
YOU KNOW, SHE'S SENT TEMPTING VISIONS BEFORE. TRYING TO GET ME TO LEAVE THE CIRCLE. TRIED YOU TOO, BUT COULDN'T GET THE DETAILS RIGHT.
HOW ARE YOU HERE?
LOKI'S MAGIC. HE GOT IT BACK WHEN HE CONFESSED.
HE WAS MANIPULATING US ALL ALONG, IT SEEMS.
SO YOU THINK HE WAS LYING ABOUT US?
I DON'T CARE IF HE WAS LYING.
WE'RE NOT.

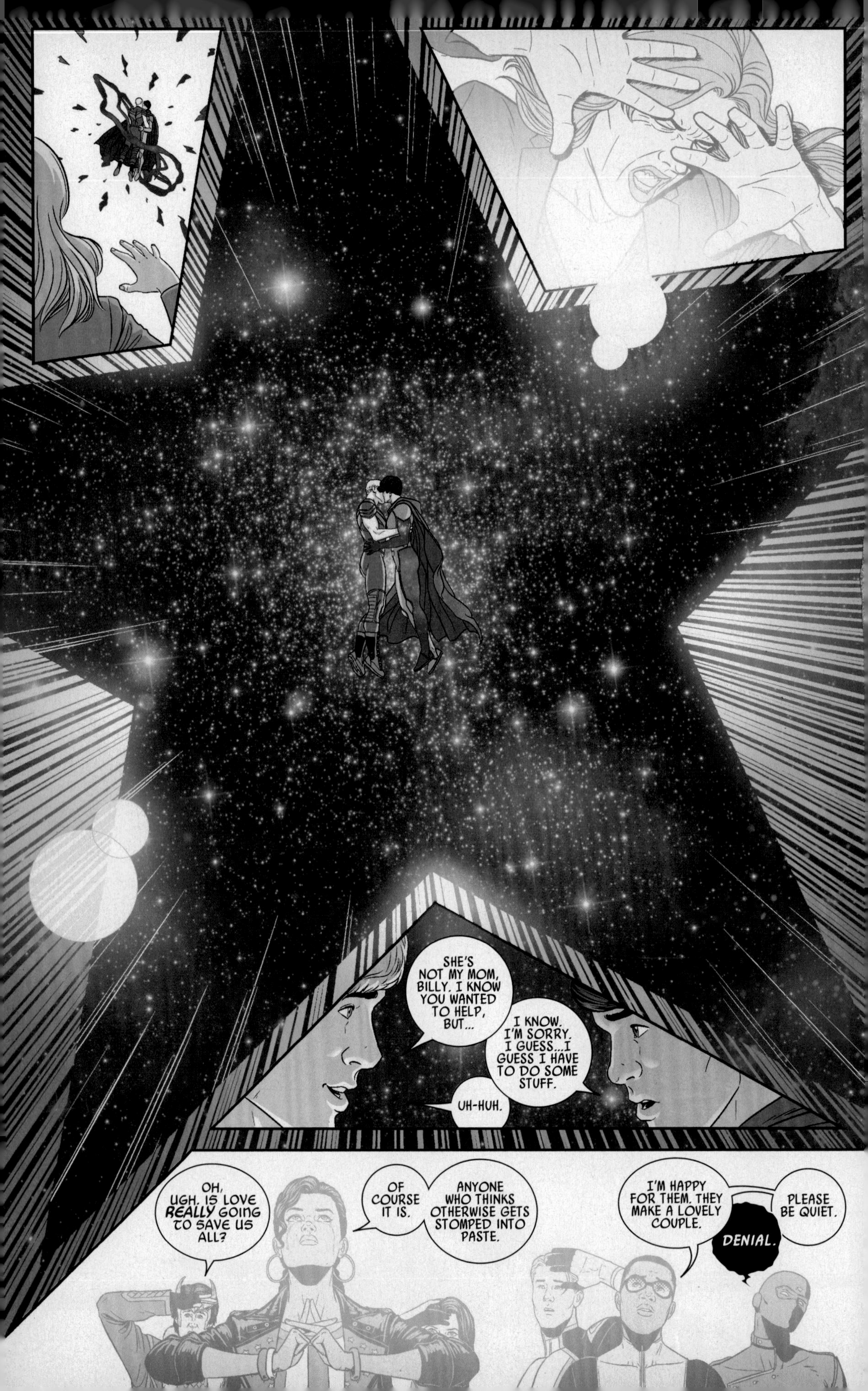
SHE'S NOT MY MOM, BILLY. I KNOW YOU WANTED TO HELP, BUT...
I KNOW. I'M SORRY. I GUESS...I GUESS I HAVE TO DO SOME STUFF.
UH-HUH.
OH, UGH. IS LOVE REALLY GOING TO SAVE US ALL?
OF COURSE IT IS.
ANYONE WHO THINKS OTHERWISE GETS STOMPED INTO PASTE.
I'M HAPPY FOR THEM. THEY MAKE A LOVELY COUPLE.
DENIAL.
PLEASE BE QUIET.

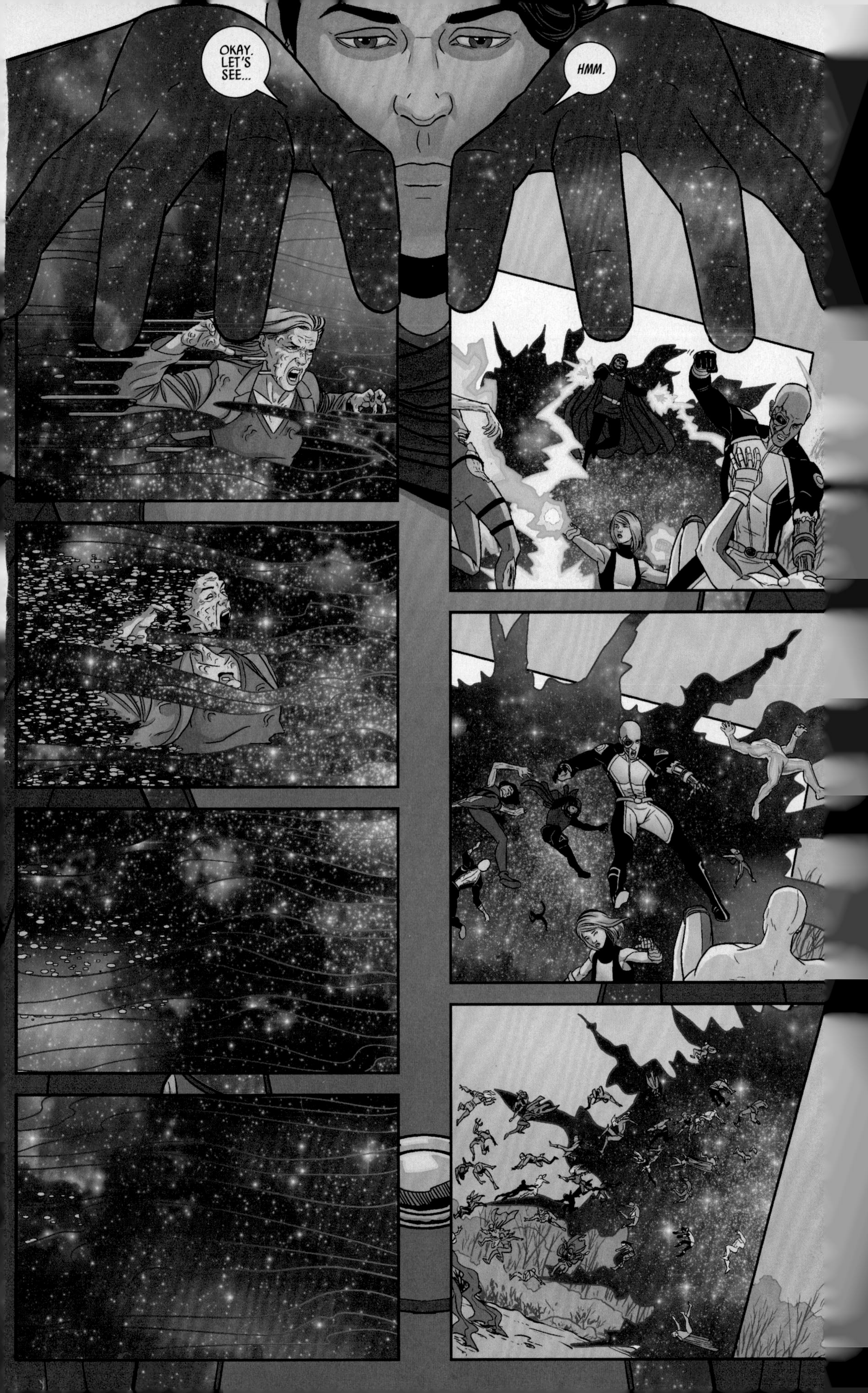
OKAY. LET'S SEE...
HMM.

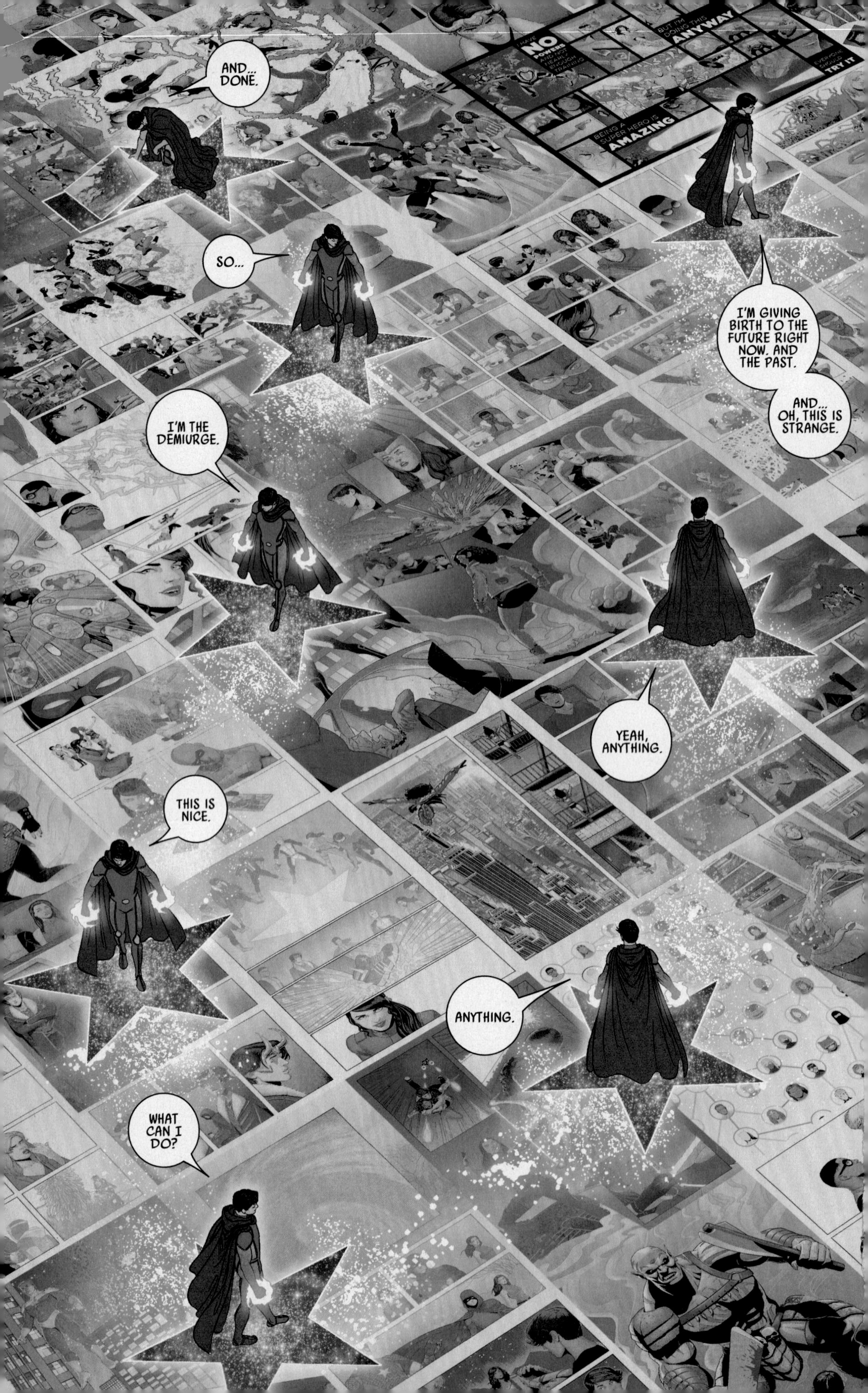
I HAVE NO POWERS AND NOT ENOUGH TRAINING
BUT I'M DOING THIS ANYWAY
BEING A SUPER HERO IS AMAZING
EVERYONE SHOULD TRY IT
AND... DONE.
SO...
I'M GIVING BIRTH TO THE FUTURE RIGHT NOW. AND THE PAST.
AND... OH, THIS IS STRANGE.
I'M THE DEMIURGE.
YEAH, ANYTHING.
THIS IS NICE.
ANYTHING.
WHAT CAN I DO?

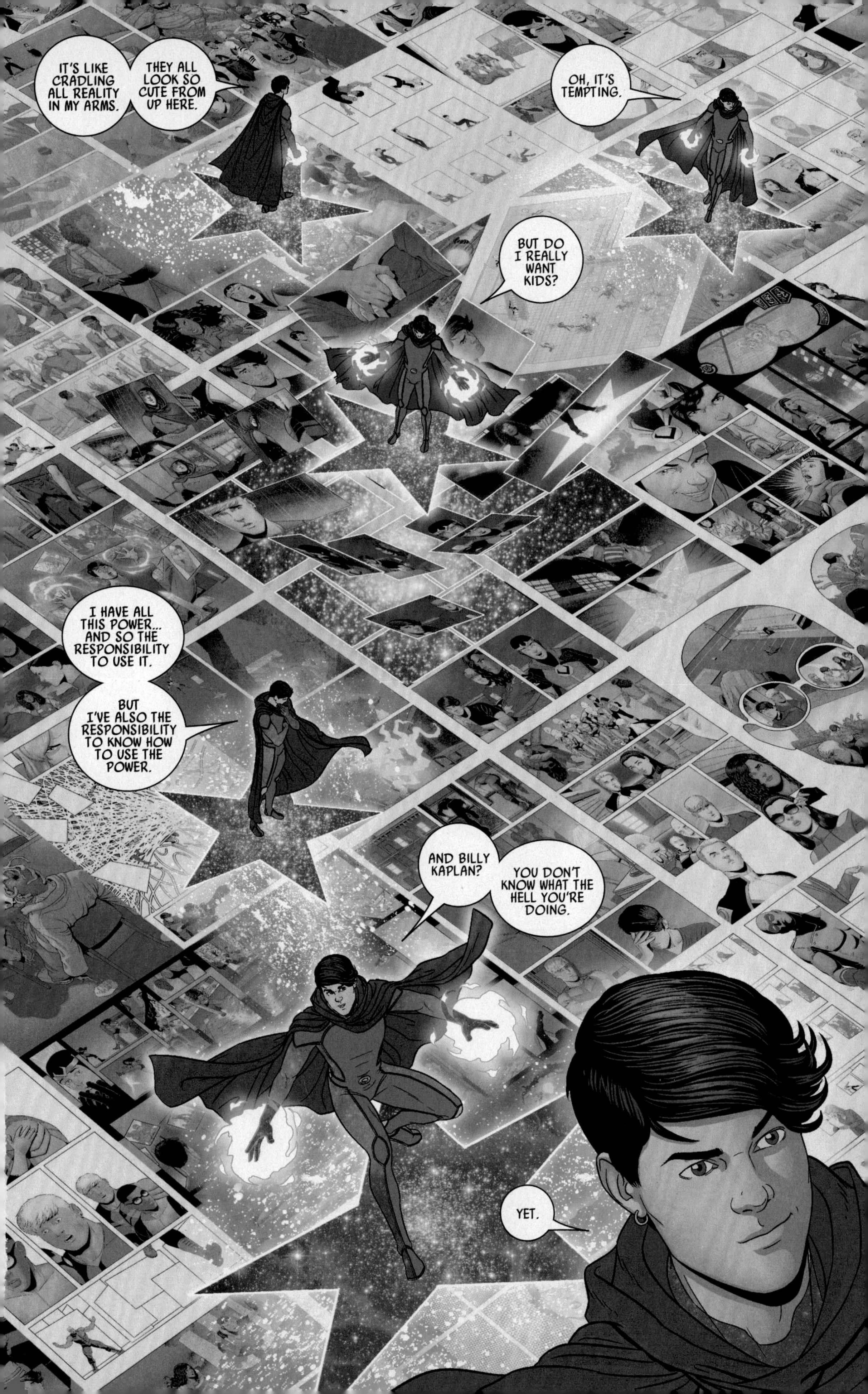
IT'S LIKE CRADLING ALL REALITY IN MY ARMS.
THEY ALL LOOK SO CUTE FROM UP HERE.
OH, IT'S TEMPTING.
BUT DO I REALLY WANT KIDS?
I HAVE ALL THIS POWER... AND SO THE RESPONSIBILITY TO USE IT.
BUT I'VE ALSO THE RESPONSIBILITY TO KNOW HOW TO USE THE POWER.
AND BILLY KAPLAN?
YOU DON'T KNOW WHAT THE HELL YOU'RE DOING.
YET.

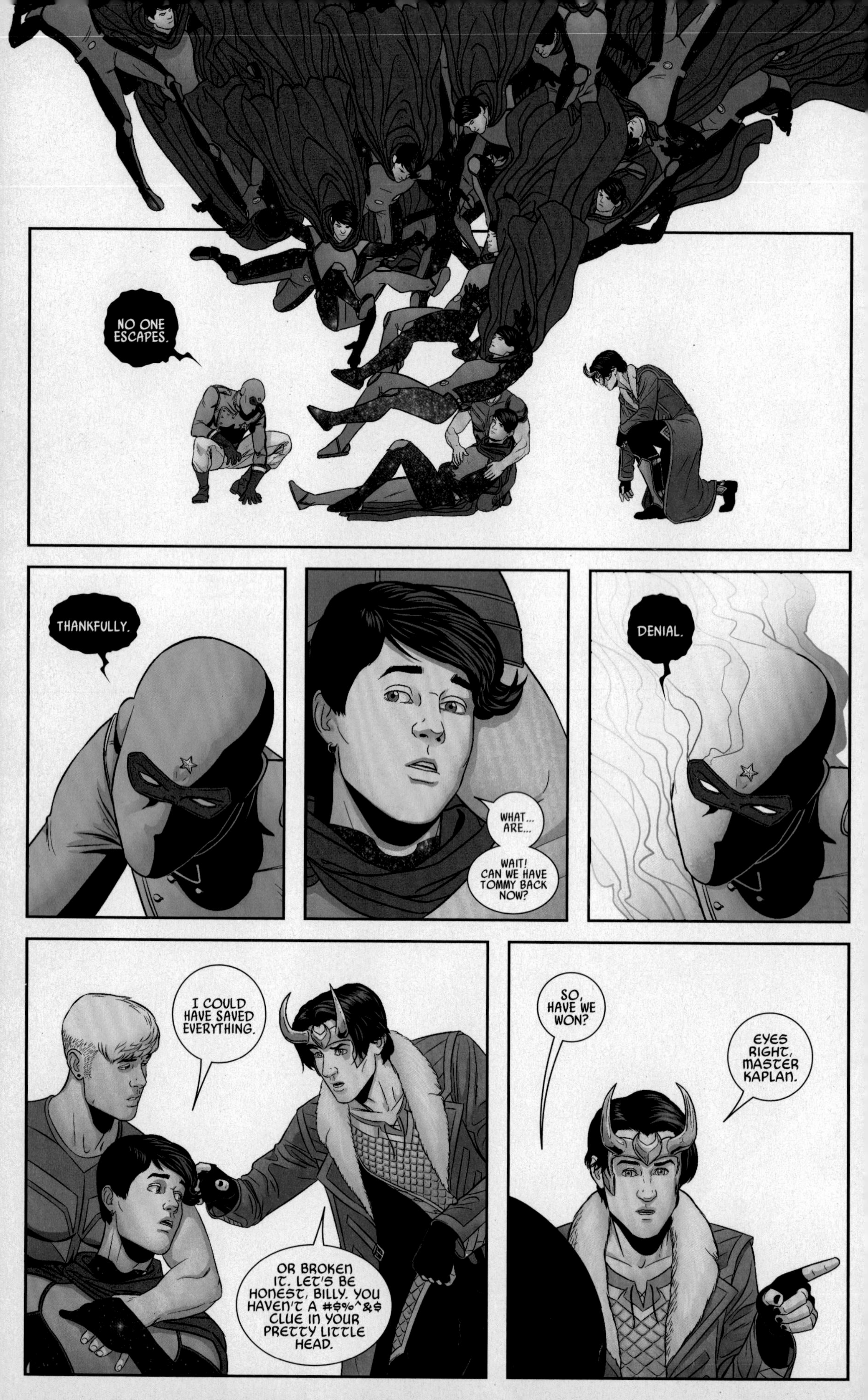
NO ONE ESCAPES.
THANKFULLY.
WHAT... ARE...
WAIT! CAN WE HAVE TOMMY BACK NOW?
DENIAL.
I COULD HAVE SAVED EVERYTHING.
OR BROKEN IT. LET'S BE HONEST, BILLY. YOU HAVEN'T A #$%^&$ CLUE IN YOUR PRETTY LITTLE HEAD.
SO, HAVE WE WON?
EYES RIGHT, MASTER KAPLAN.

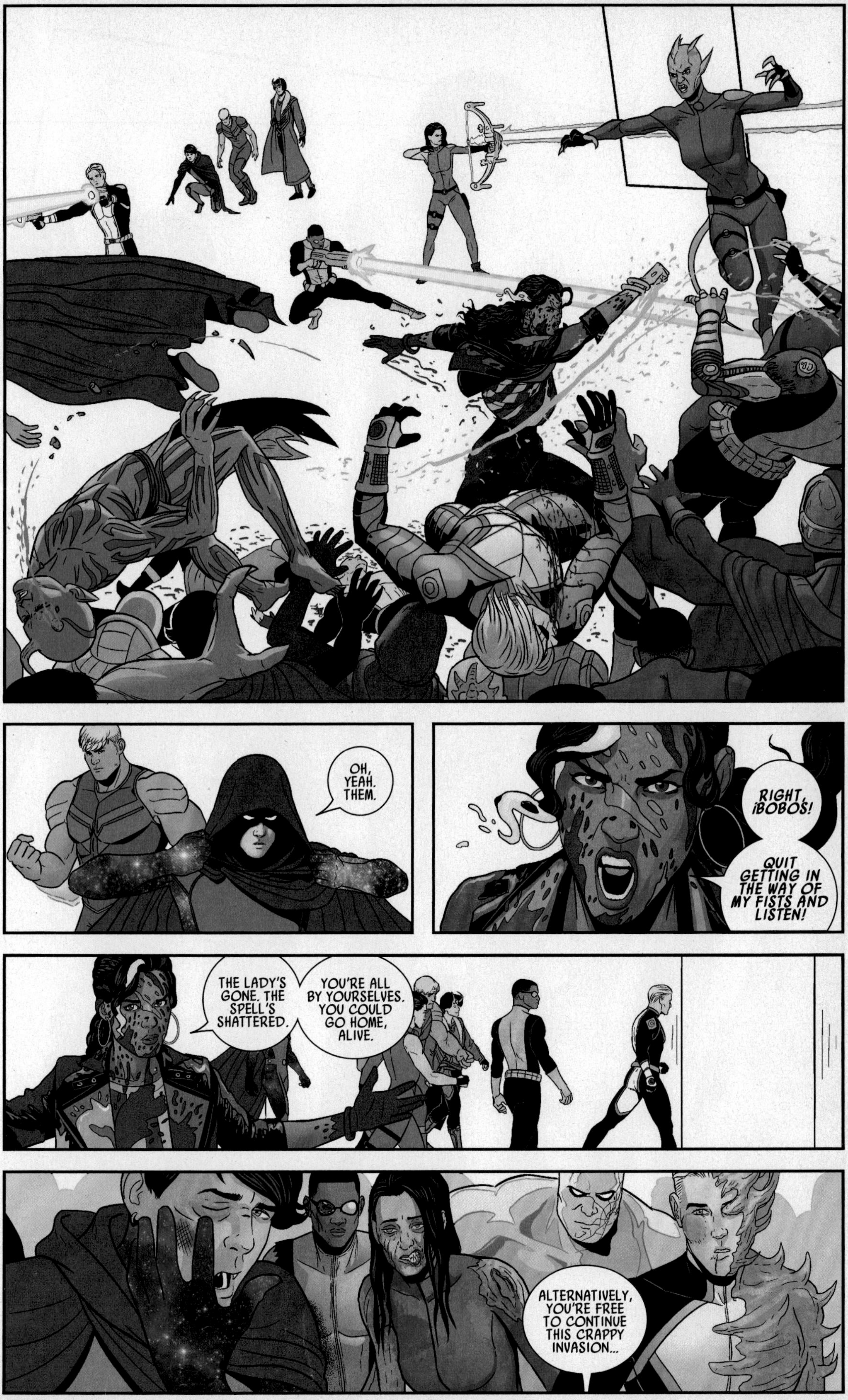
OH, YEAH. THEM.
RIGHT, ¡BOBOS!
QUIT GETTING IN THE WAY OF MY FISTS AND LISTEN!
THE LADY'S GONE. THE SPELL'S SHATTERED.
YOU'RE ALL BY YOURSELVES. YOU COULD GO HOME, ALIVE.
ALTERNATIVELY, YOU'RE FREE TO CONTINUE THIS CRAPPY INVASION...

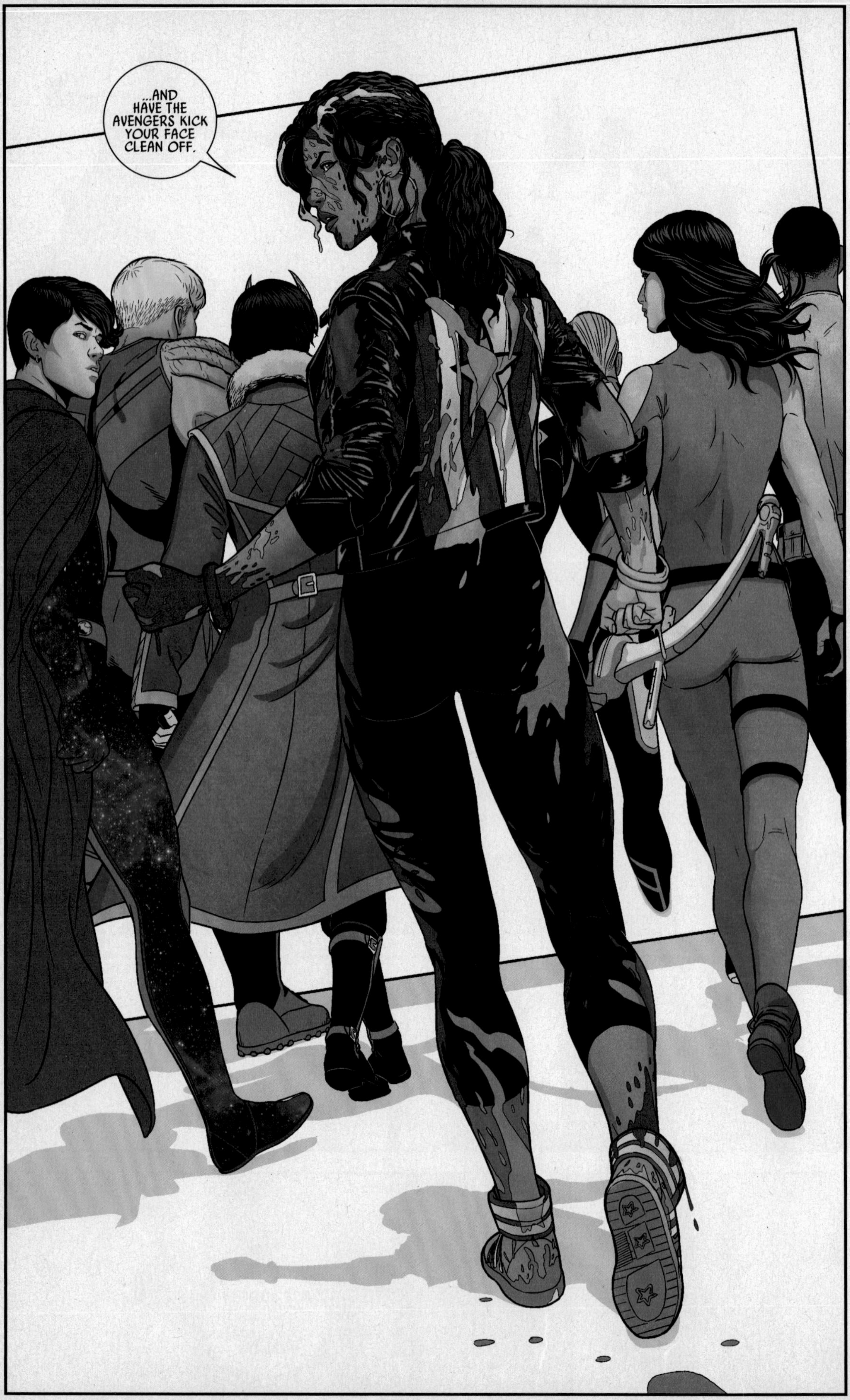
...AND HAVE THE AVENGERS KICK YOUR FACE CLEAN OFF.

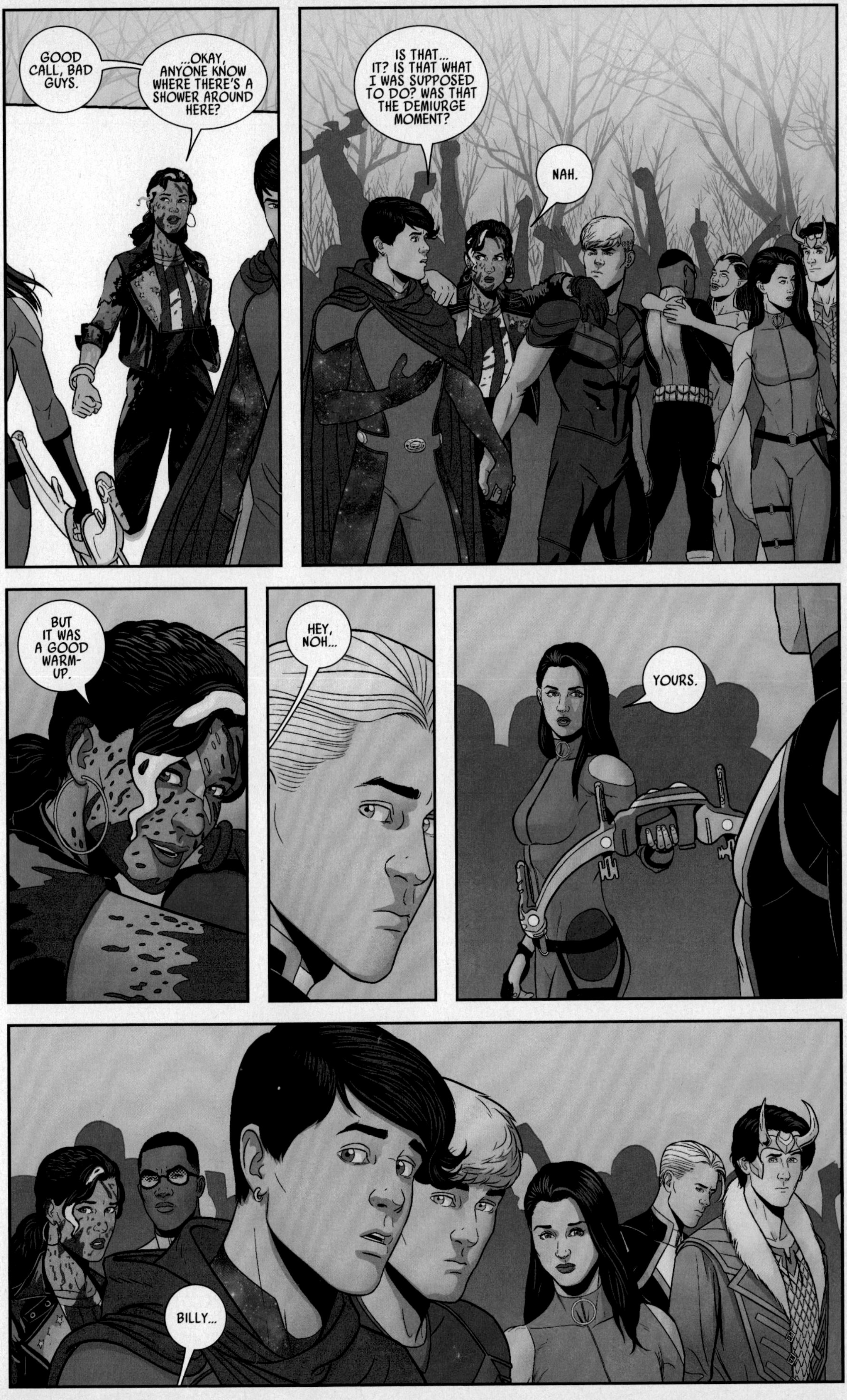
GOOD CALL, BAD GUYS.
...OKAY, ANYONE KNOW WHERE THERE'S A SHOWER AROUND HERE?
IS THAT... IT? IS THAT WHAT I WAS SUPPOSED TO DO? WAS THAT THE DEMIURGE MOMENT?
NAH.
BUT IT WAS A GOOD WARM-UP.
HEY, NOH...
YOURS.
BILLY...

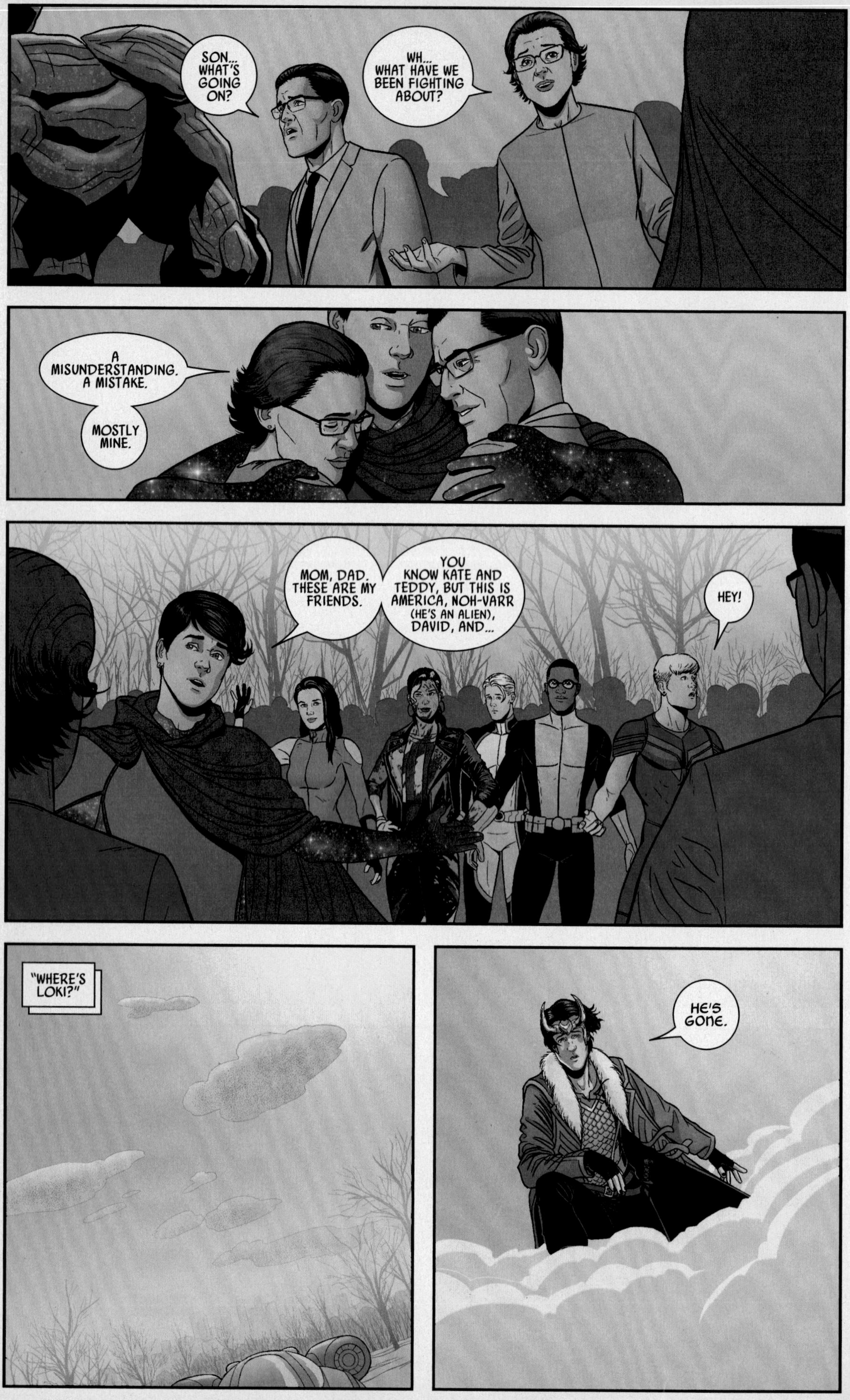
SON... WHAT'S GOING ON?
WH... WHAT HAVE WE BEEN FIGHTING ABOUT?
A MISUNDERSTANDING. A MISTAKE.
MOSTLY MINE.
MOM, DAD. THESE ARE MY FRIENDS.
YOU KNOW KATE AND TEDDY, BUT THIS IS AMERICA, NOH-VARR (HE'S AN ALIEN), DAVID, AND...
HEY!
"WHERE'S LOKI?"
HE'S GONE.

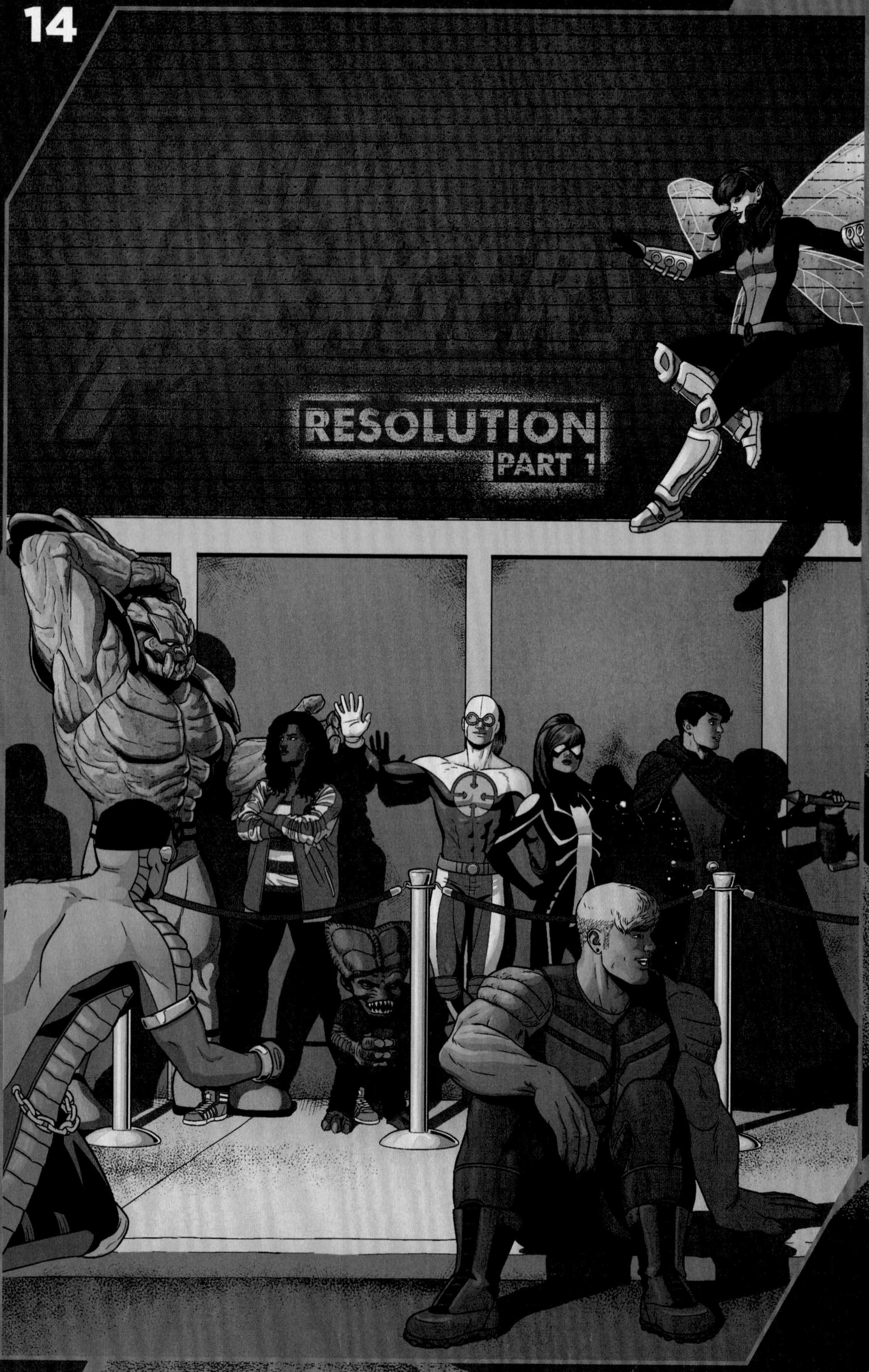
RESOLUTION
PART 1

RESOLUTION PART ONE

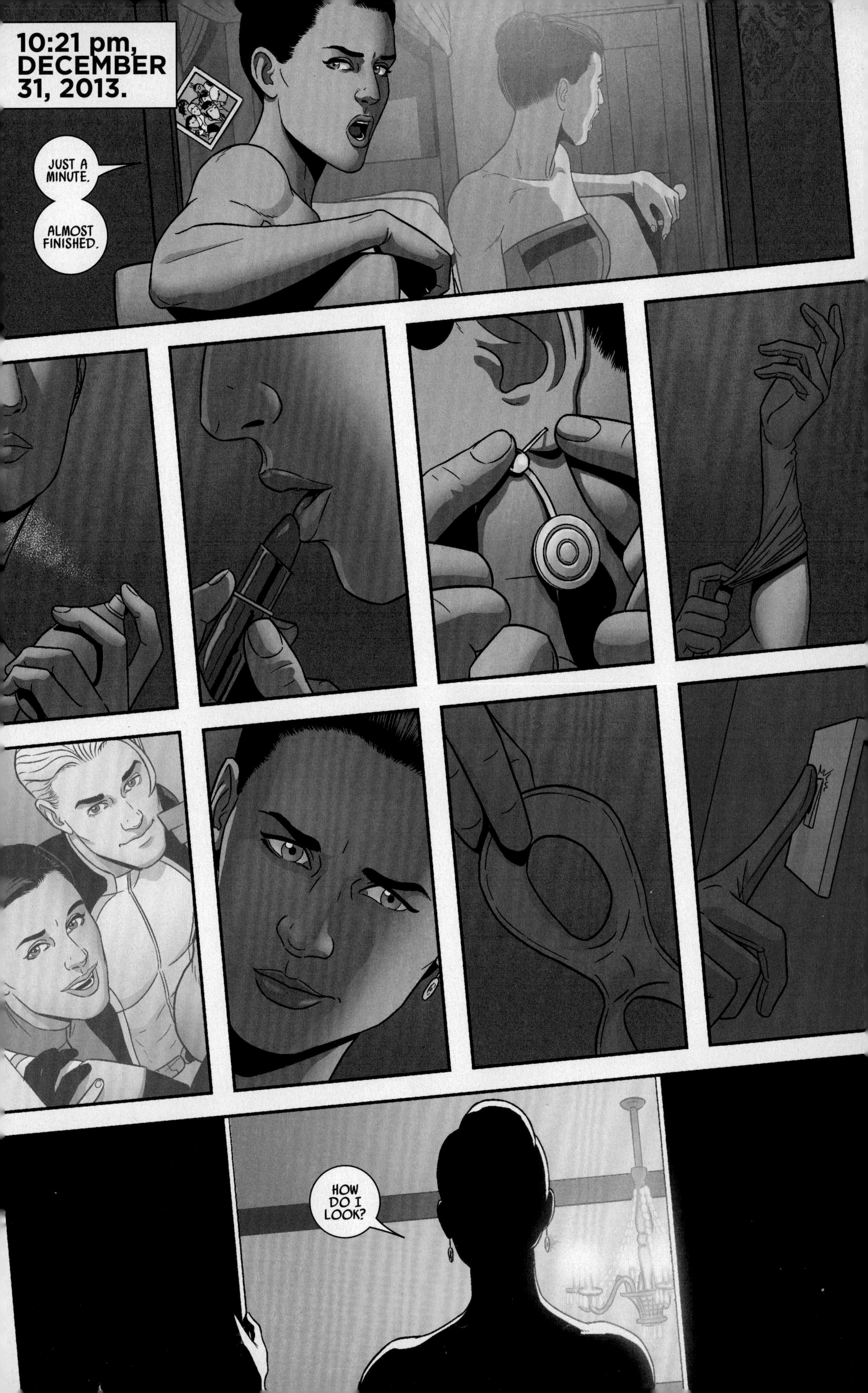
10:21 pm, DECEMBER 31, 2013.
JUST A MINUTE.
ALMOST FINISHED.
HOW DO I LOOK?

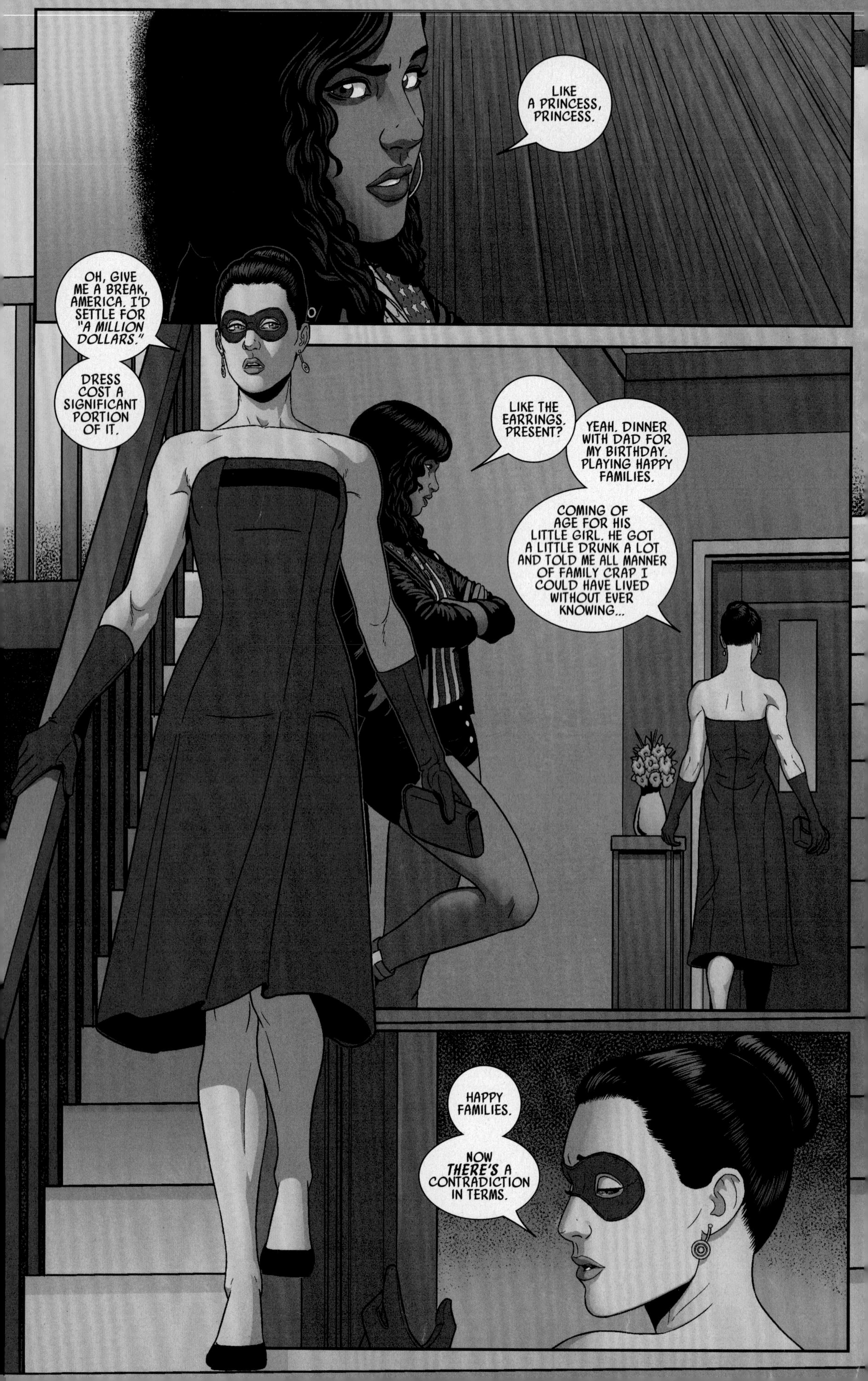
LIKE A PRINCESS, PRINCESS.
OH, GIVE ME A BREAK, AMERICA. I'D SETTLE FOR "A MILLION DOLLARS."
DRESS COST A SIGNIFICANT PORTION OF IT.
LIKE THE EARRINGS. PRESENT?
YEAH. DINNER WITH DAD FOR MY BIRTHDAY. PLAYING HAPPY FAMILIES.
COMING OF AGE FOR HIS LITTLE GIRL. HE GOT A LITTLE DRUNK A LOT AND TOLD ME ALL MANNER OF FAMILY CRAP I COULD HAVE LIVED WITHOUT EVER KNOWING...
HAPPY FAMILIES.
NOW *THERE'S* A CONTRADICTION IN TERMS.

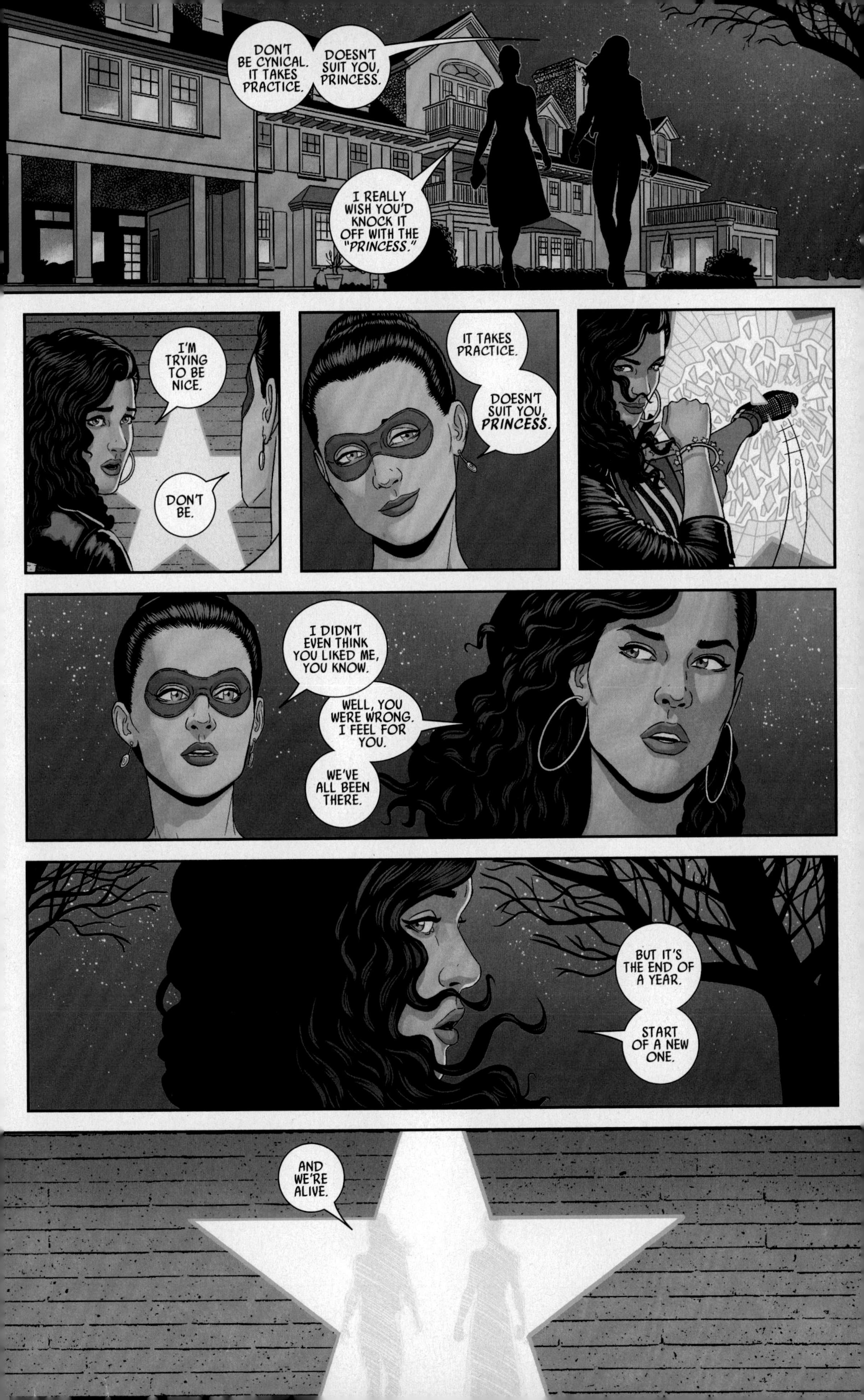
DON'T BE CYNICAL. IT TAKES PRACTICE.
DOESN'T SUIT YOU, PRINCESS.
I REALLY WISH YOU'D KNOCK IT OFF WITH THE "PRINCESS."
I'M TRYING TO BE NICE.
DON'T BE.
IT TAKES PRACTICE.
DOESN'T SUIT YOU, PRINCESS.
I DIDN'T EVEN THINK YOU LIKED ME, YOU KNOW.
WELL, YOU WERE WRONG. I FEEL FOR YOU.
WE'VE ALL BEEN THERE.
BUT IT'S THE END OF A YEAR.
START OF A NEW ONE.
AND WE'RE ALIVE.

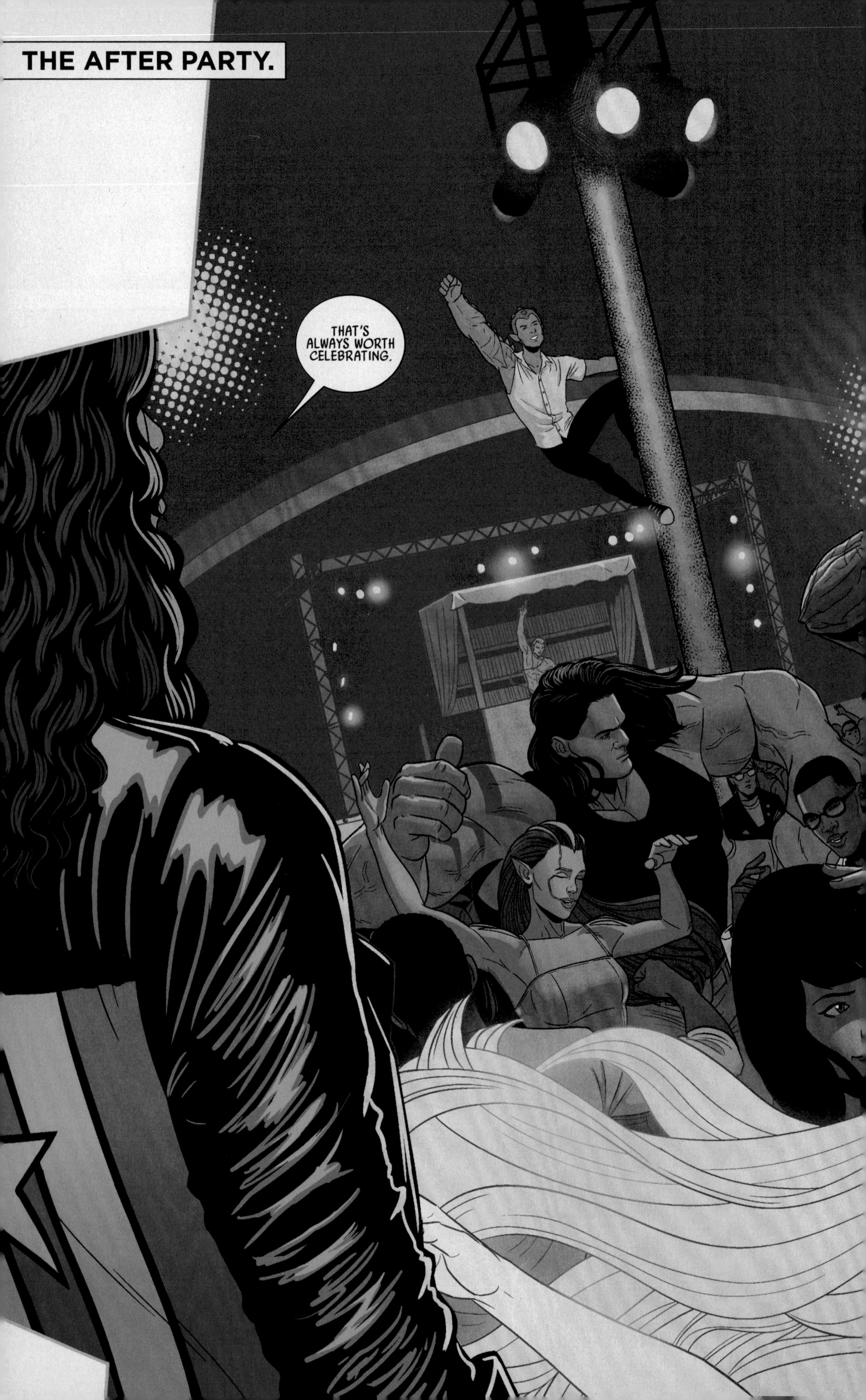
THE AFTER PARTY.
THAT'S ALWAYS WORTH CELEBRATING.

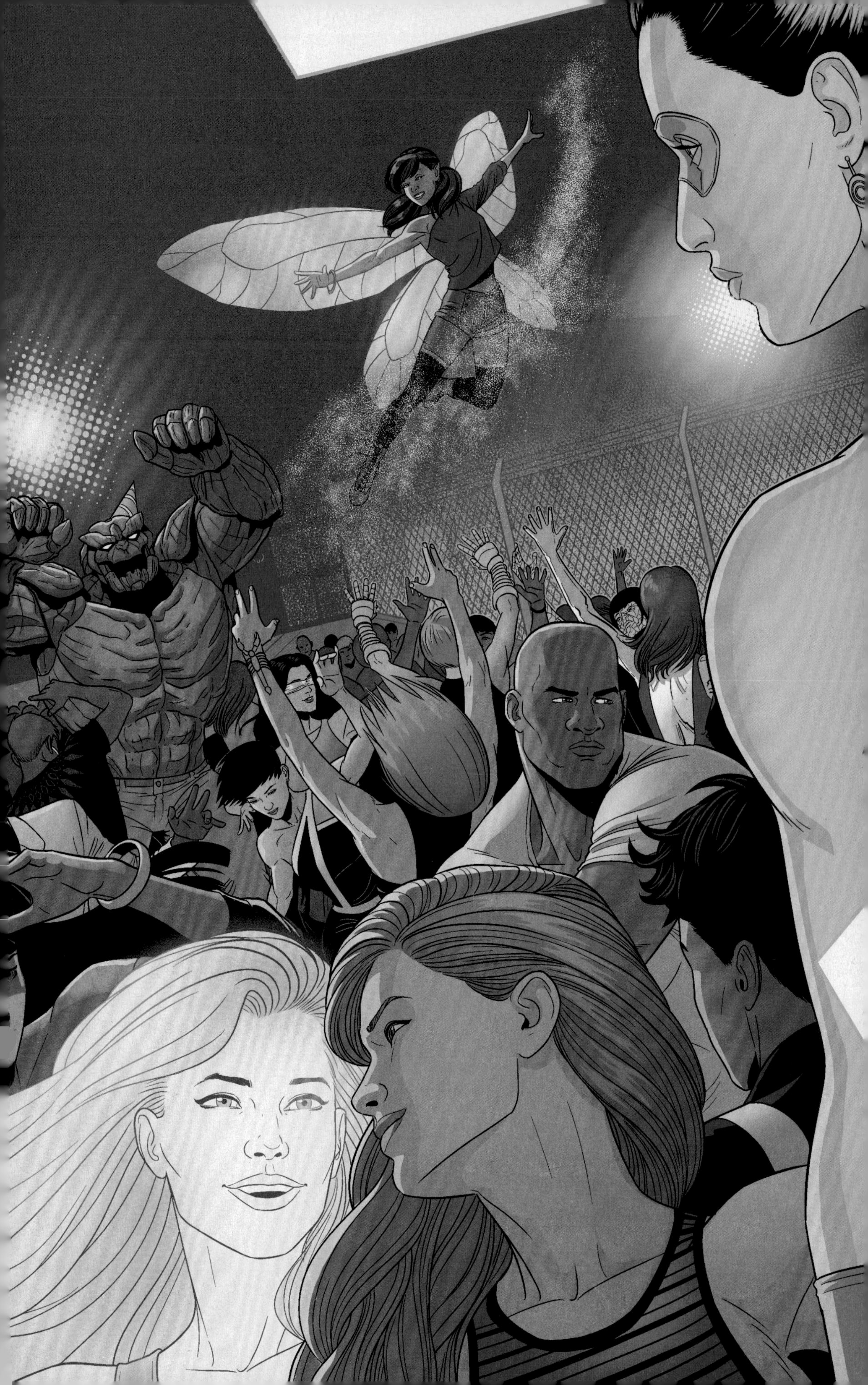

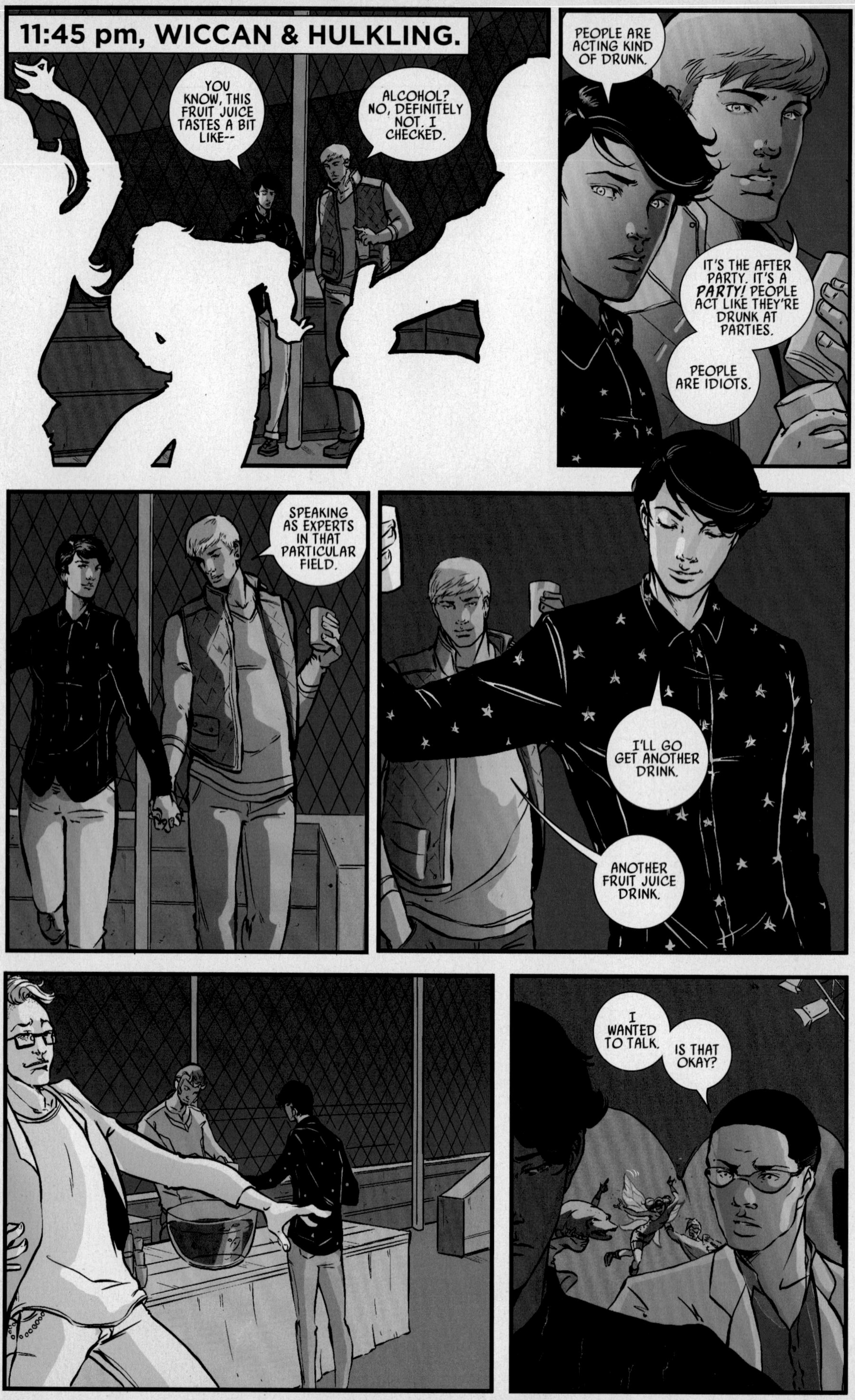
11:45 pm, WICCAN & HULKLING.
YOU KNOW, THIS FRUIT JUICE TASTES A BIT LIKE--
ALCOHOL? NO, DEFINITELY NOT. I CHECKED.
PEOPLE ARE ACTING KIND OF DRUNK.
IT'S THE AFTER PARTY. IT'S A PARTY! PEOPLE ACT LIKE THEY'RE DRUNK AT PARTIES.
PEOPLE ARE IDIOTS.
SPEAKING AS EXPERTS IN THAT PARTICULAR FIELD.
I'LL GO GET ANOTHER DRINK.
ANOTHER FRUIT JUICE DRINK.
I WANTED TO TALK.
IS THAT OKAY?

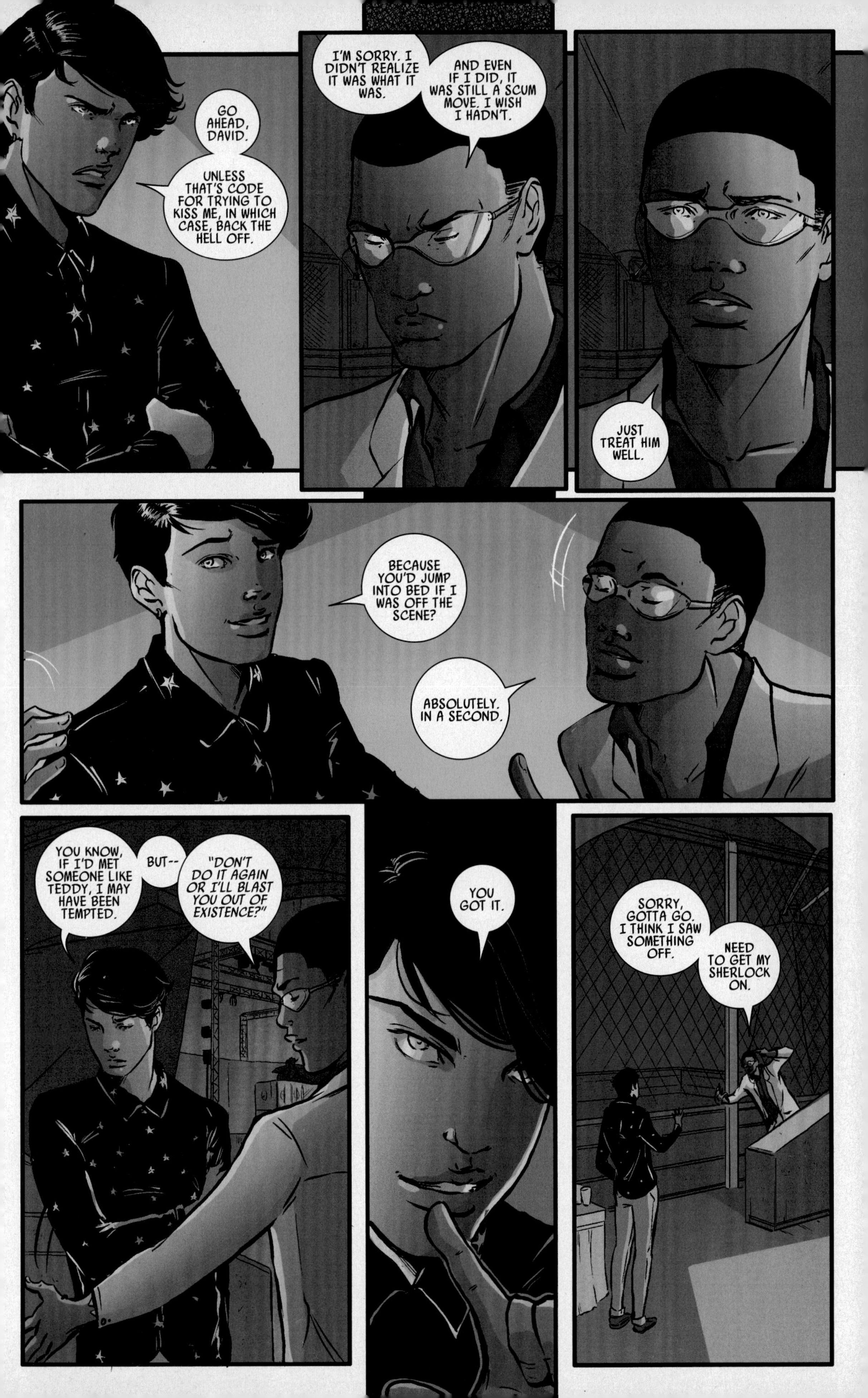
GO AHEAD, DAVID.
UNLESS THAT'S CODE FOR TRYING TO KISS ME, IN WHICH CASE, BACK THE HELL OFF.
I'M SORRY. I DIDN'T REALIZE IT WAS WHAT IT WAS.
AND EVEN IF I DID, IT WAS STILL A SCUM MOVE. I WISH I HADN'T.
JUST TREAT HIM WELL.
BECAUSE YOU'D JUMP INTO BED IF I WAS OFF THE SCENE?
ABSOLUTELY. IN A SECOND.
YOU KNOW, IF I'D MET SOMEONE LIKE TEDDY, I MAY HAVE BEEN TEMPTED.
BUT--
"DON'T DO IT AGAIN OR I'LL BLAST YOU OUT OF EXISTENCE?"
YOU GOT IT.
SORRY, GOTTA GO. I THINK I SAW SOMETHING OFF.
NEED TO GET MY SHERLOCK ON.

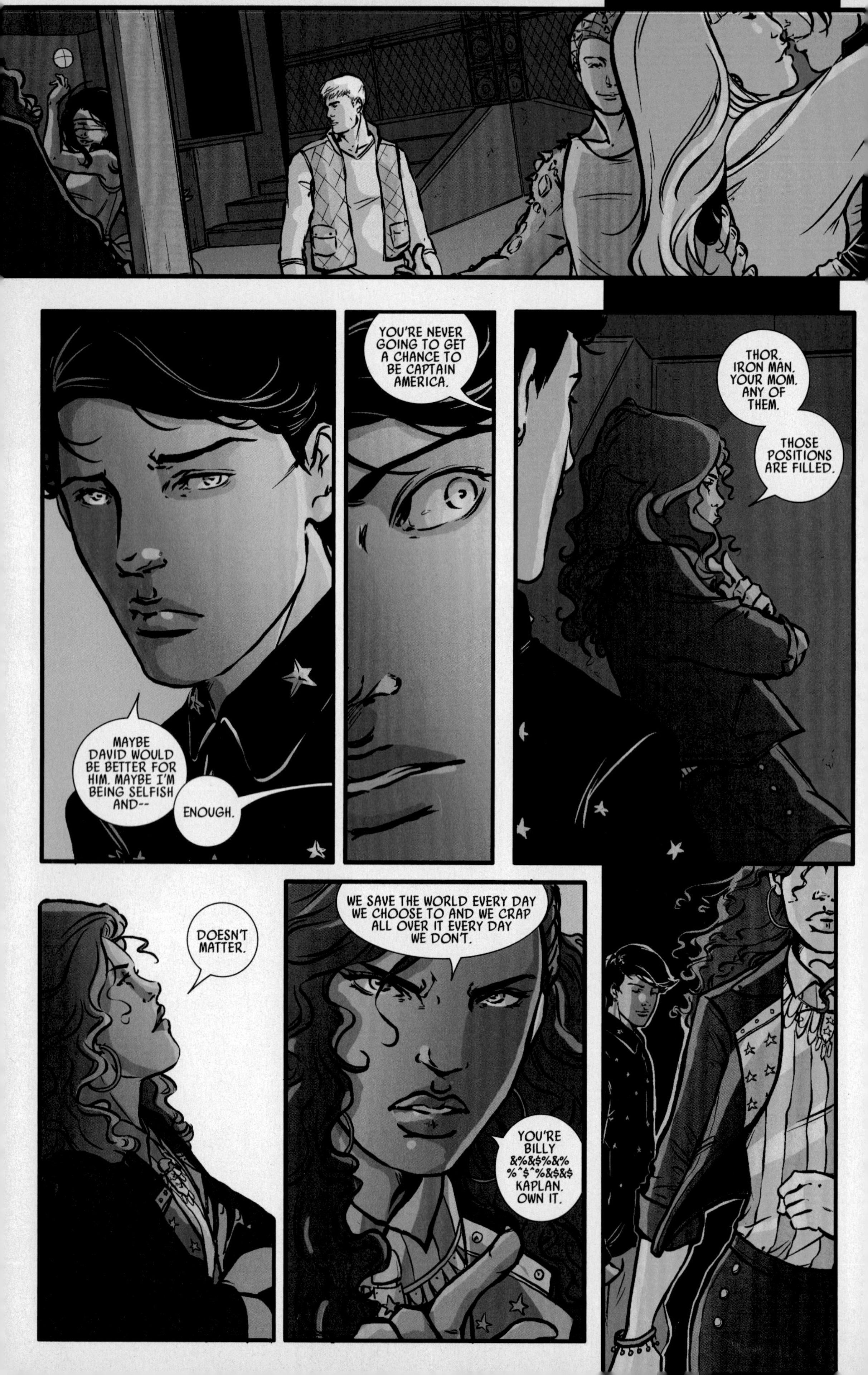
MAYBE DAVID WOULD BE BETTER FOR HIM. MAYBE I'M BEING SELFISH AND--
ENOUGH.
YOU'RE NEVER GOING TO GET A CHANCE TO BE CAPTAIN AMERICA.
THOR. IRON MAN. YOUR MOM. ANY OF THEM.
THOSE POSITIONS ARE FILLED.
DOESN'T MATTER.
WE SAVE THE WORLD EVERY DAY WE CHOOSE TO AND WE CRAP ALL OVER IT EVERY DAY WE DON'T.
YOU'RE BILLY &%&$%&% %^$^%&$&$ KAPLAN. OWN IT.

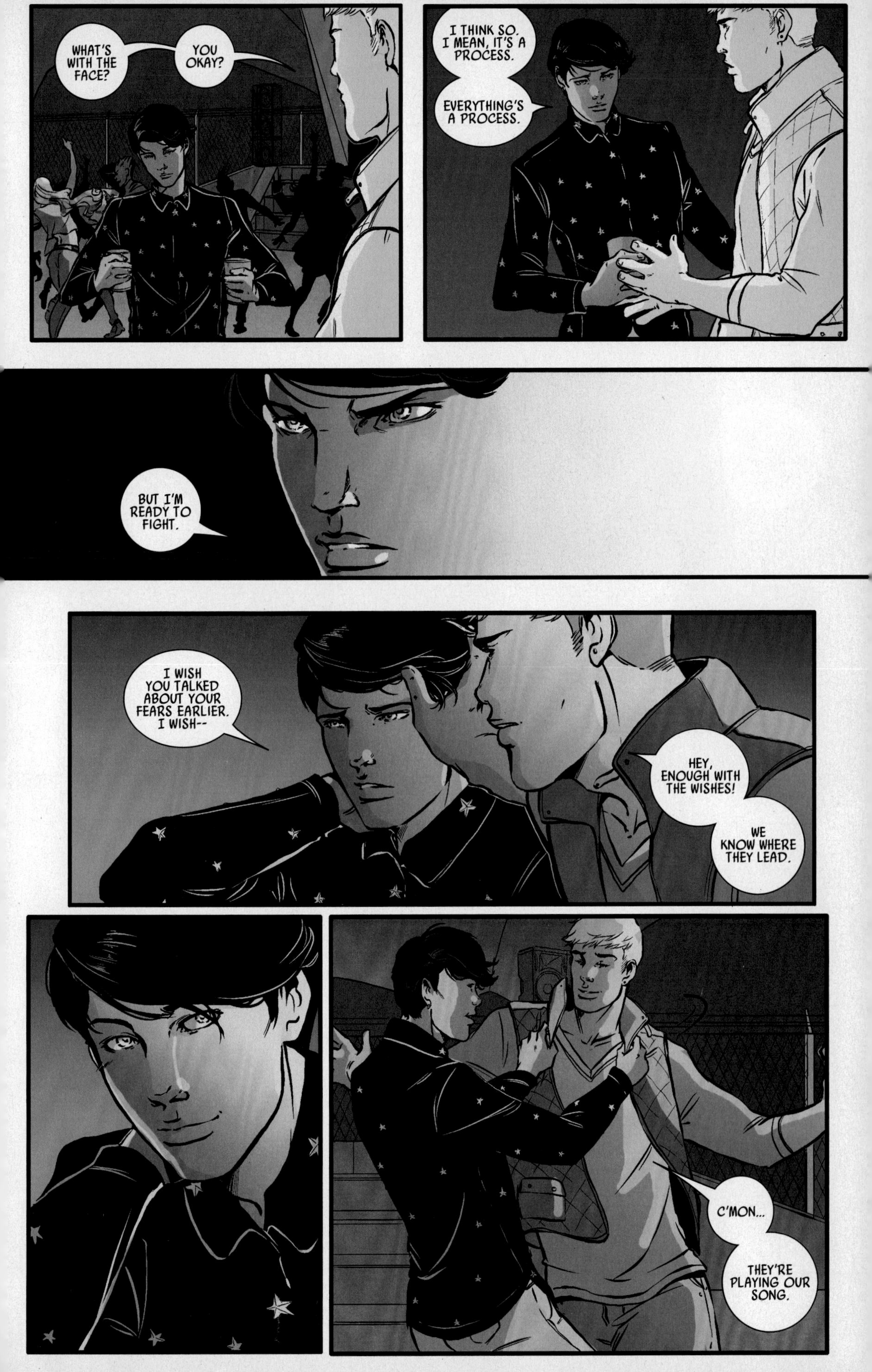

WHAT'S WITH THE FACE?
YOU OKAY?
I THINK SO. I MEAN, IT'S A PROCESS.
EVERYTHING'S A PROCESS.
BUT I'M READY TO FIGHT.
I WISH YOU TALKED ABOUT YOUR FEARS EARLIER. I WISH--
HEY, ENOUGH WITH THE WISHES!
WE KNOW WHERE THEY LEAD.
C'MON...
THEY'RE PLAYING OUR SONG.

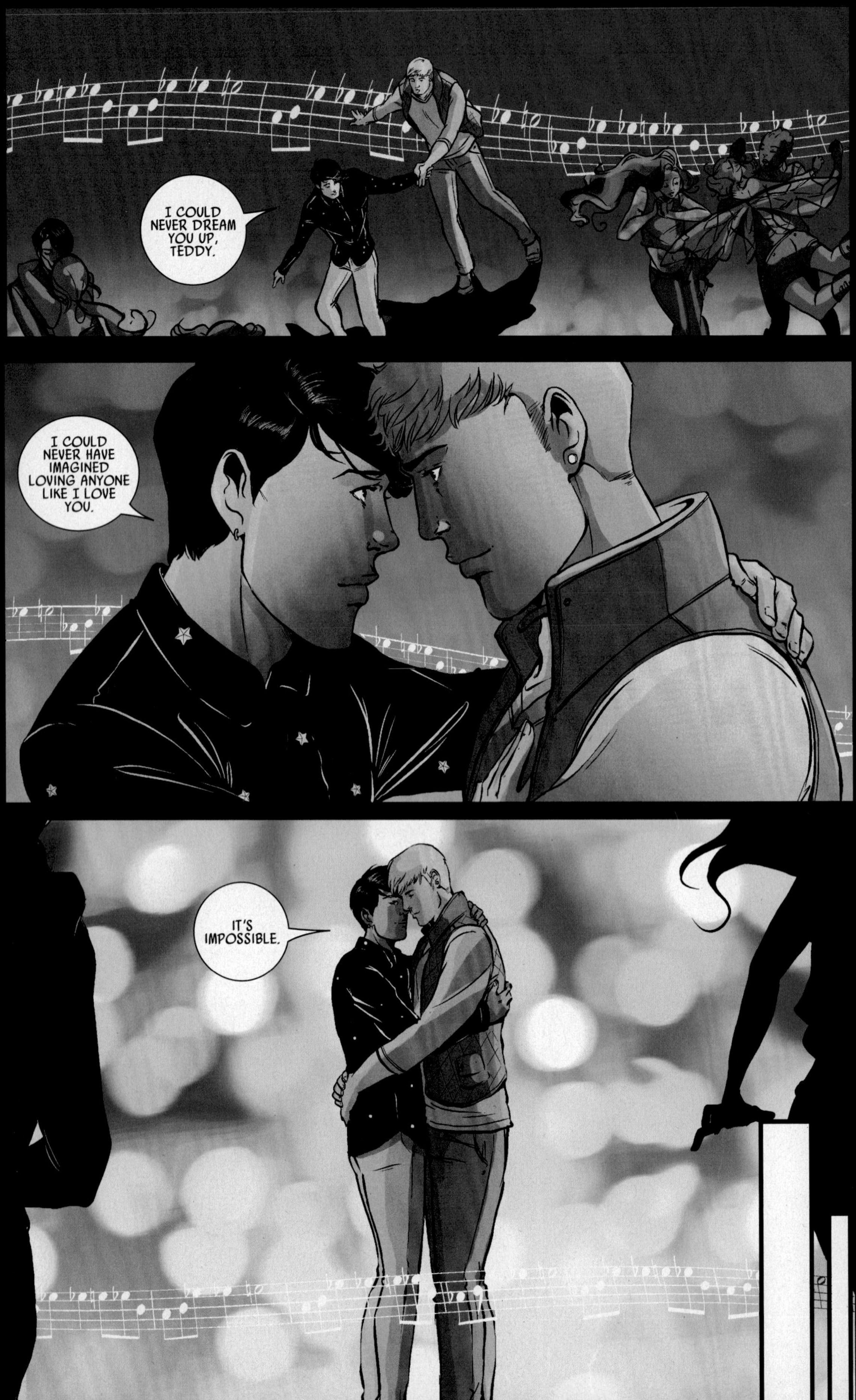
I COULD NEVER DREAM YOU UP, TEDDY.
I COULD NEVER HAVE IMAGINED LOVING ANYONE LIKE I LOVE YOU.
IT'S IMPOSSIBLE.

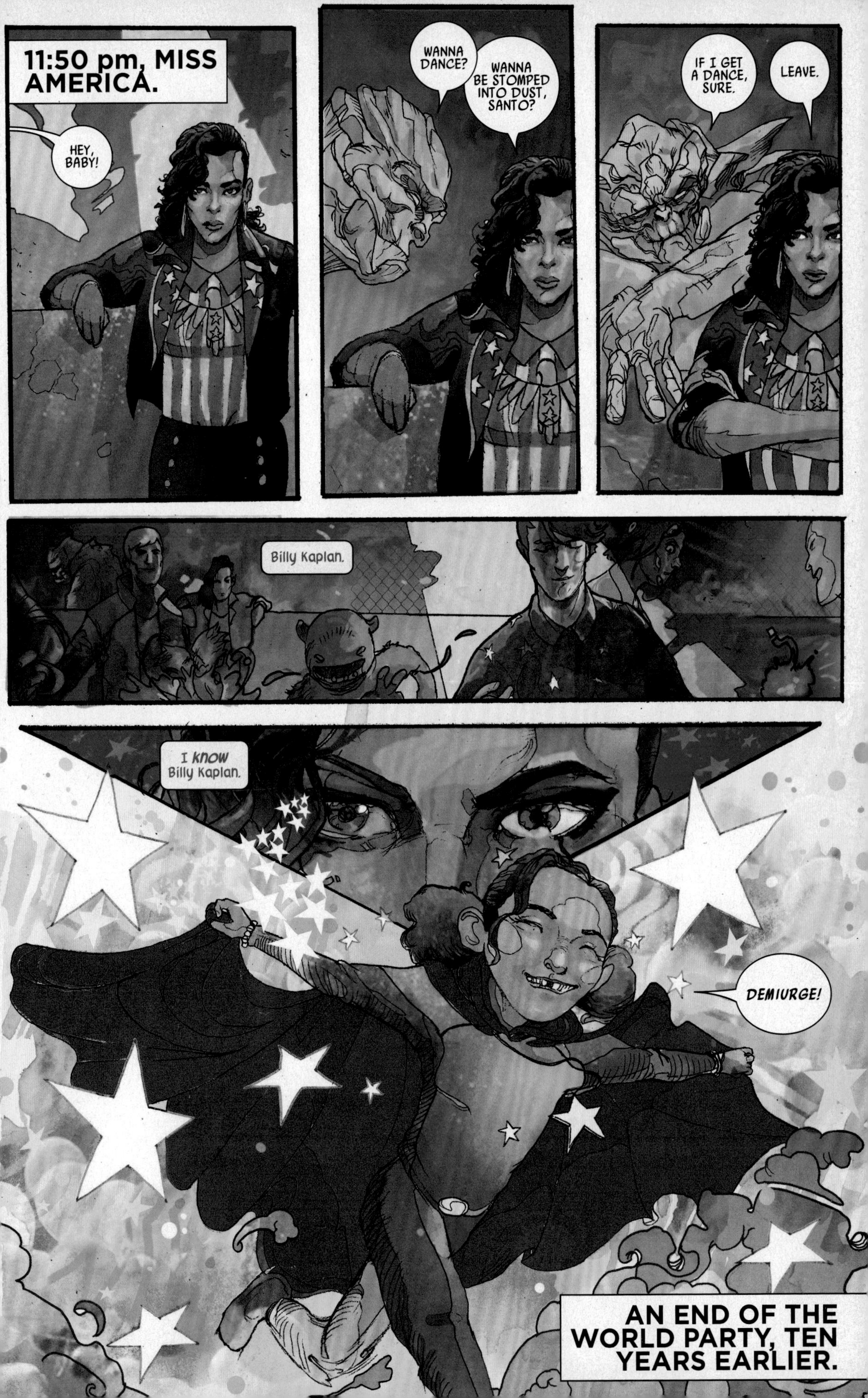
11:50 pm, MISS AMERICA.
HEY, BABY!
WANNA DANCE?
WANNA BE STOMPED INTO DUST, SANTO?
IF I GET A DANCE, SURE.
LEAVE.
Billy Kaplan.
I *KNOW* Billy Kaplan.
DEMIURGE!
AN END OF THE WORLD PARTY, TEN YEARS EARLIER.

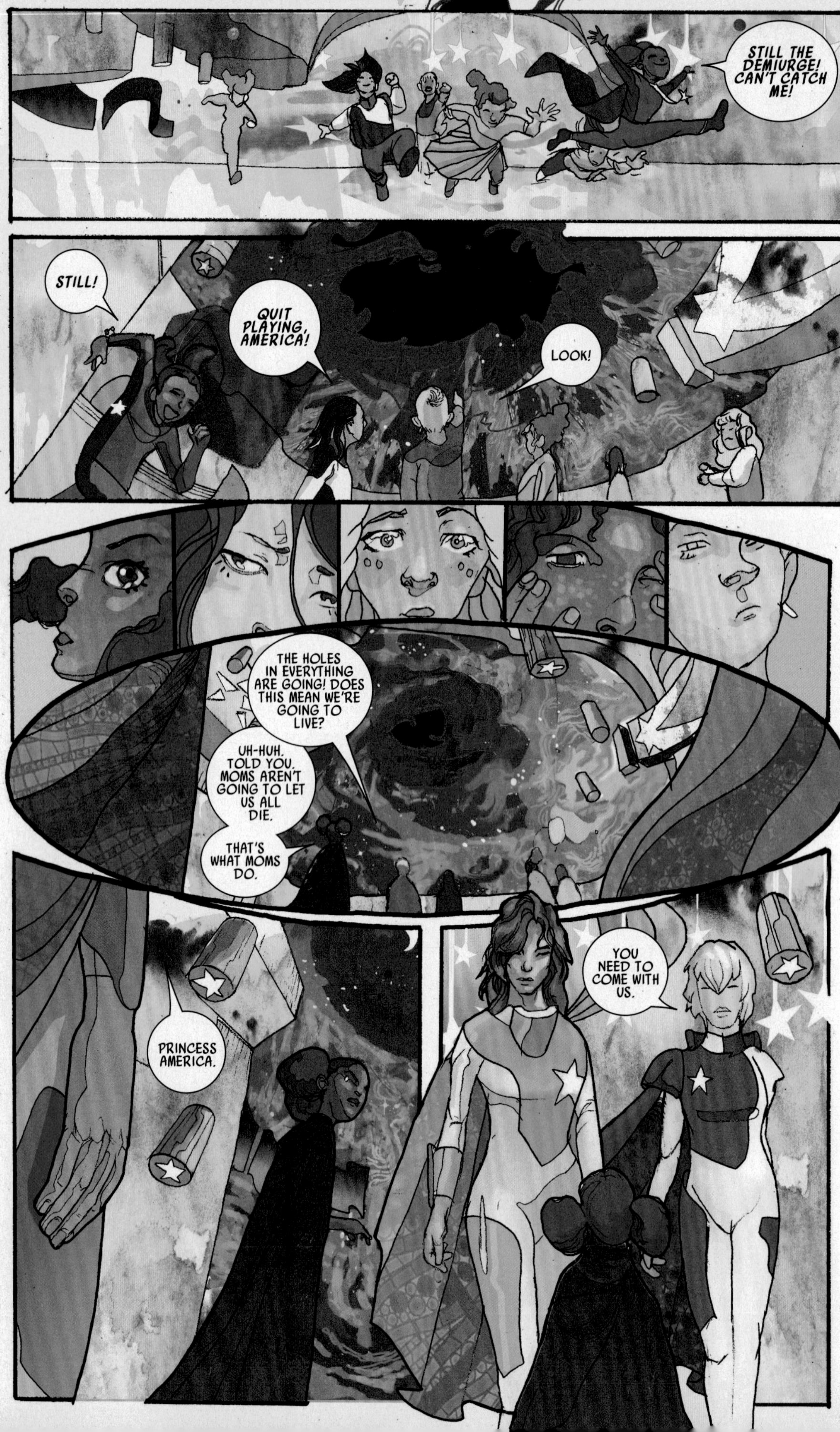
STILL THE DEMIURGE! CAN'T CATCH ME!
STILL!
QUIT PLAYING, AMERICA!
LOOK!
THE HOLES IN EVERYTHING ARE GOING! DOES THIS MEAN WE'RE GOING TO LIVE?
UH-HUH. TOLD YOU. MOMS AREN'T GOING TO LET US ALL DIE.
THAT'S WHAT MOMS DO.
PRINCESS AMERICA.
YOU NEED TO COME WITH US.

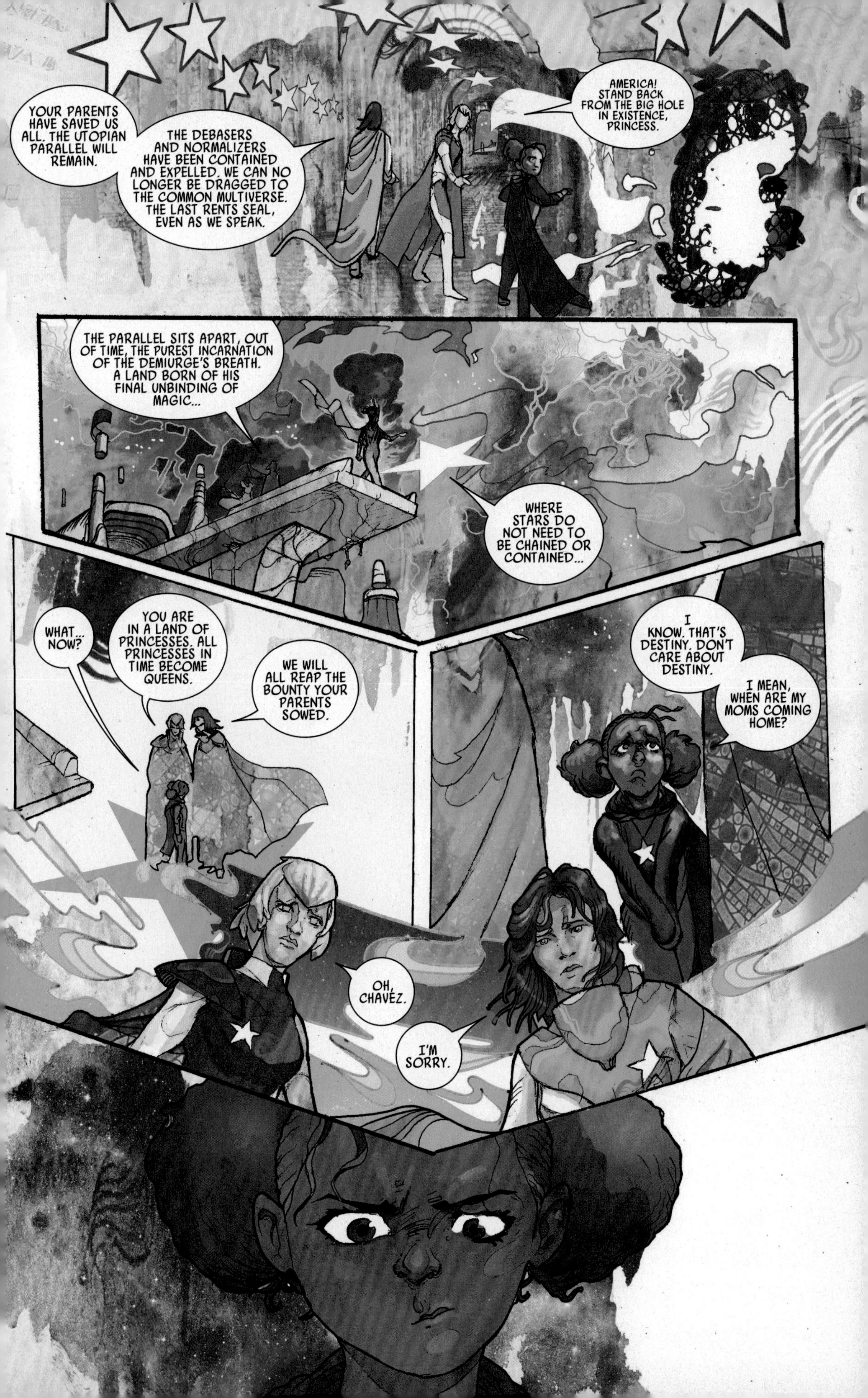
YOUR PARENTS HAVE SAVED US ALL. THE UTOPIAN PARALLEL WILL REMAIN.
THE DEBASERS AND NORMALIZERS HAVE BEEN CONTAINED AND EXPELLED. WE CAN NO LONGER BE DRAGGED TO THE COMMON MULTIVERSE. THE LAST RENTS SEAL, EVEN AS WE SPEAK.
AMERICA! STAND BACK FROM THE BIG HOLE IN EXISTENCE, PRINCESS.
THE PARALLEL SITS APART, OUT OF TIME, THE PUREST INCARNATION OF THE DEMIURGE'S BREATH. A LAND BORN OF HIS FINAL UNBINDING OF MAGIC...
WHERE STARS DO NOT NEED TO BE CHAINED OR CONTAINED...
WHAT... NOW?
YOU ARE IN A LAND OF PRINCESSES. ALL PRINCESSES IN TIME BECOME QUEENS.
WE WILL ALL REAP THE BOUNTY YOUR PARENTS SOWED.
I KNOW. THAT'S DESTINY. DON'T CARE ABOUT DESTINY.
I MEAN, WHEN ARE MY MOMS COMING HOME?
OH, CHAVEZ.
I'M SORRY.

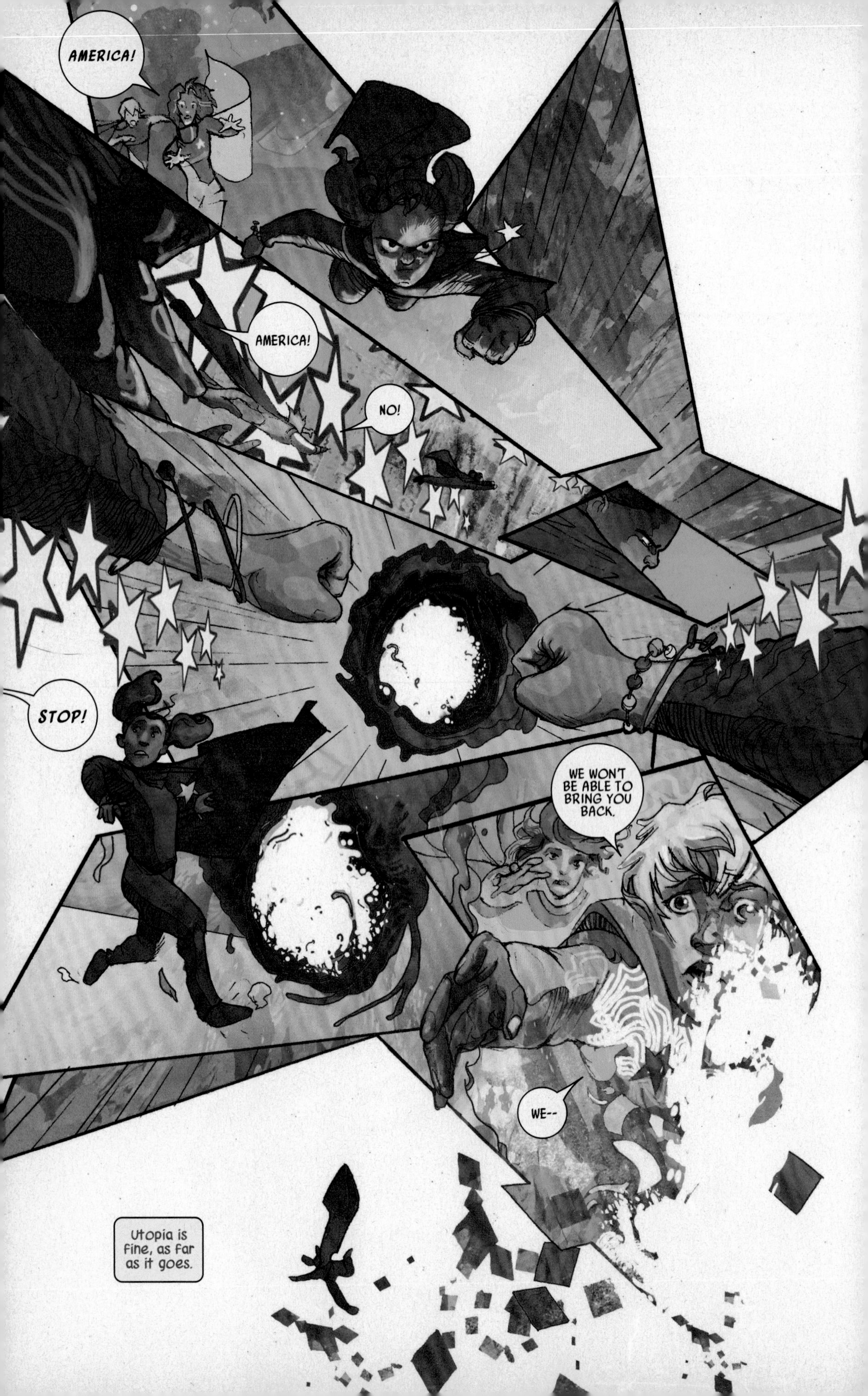
AMERICA!
AMERICA!
NO!
STOP!
WE WON'T BE ABLE TO BRING YOU BACK.
WE--
Utopia is fine, as far as it goes.

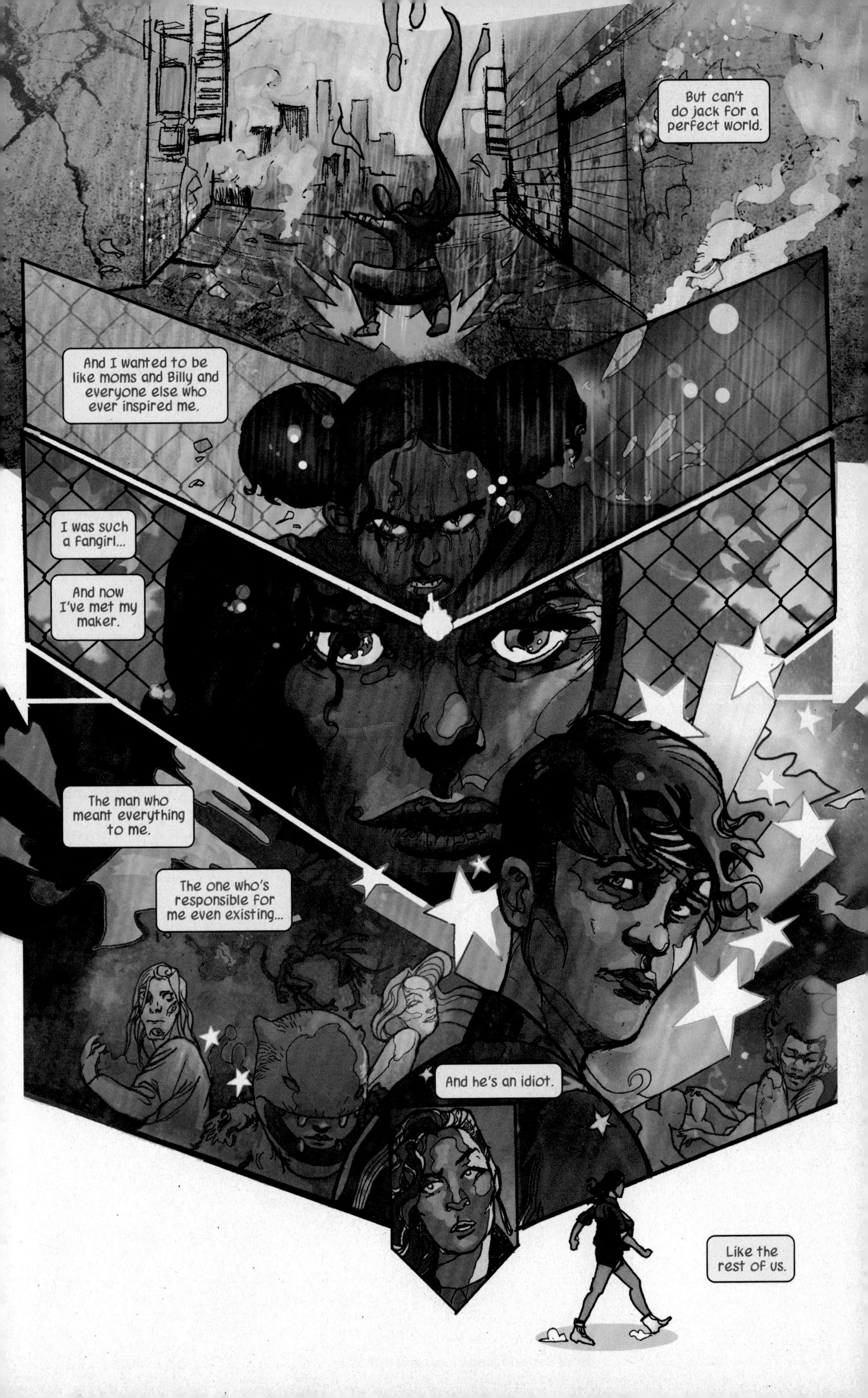
But can't do jack for a perfect world.
And I wanted to be like moms and Billy and everyone else who ever inspired me.
I was such a fangirl...
And now I've met my maker.
The man who meant everything to me.
The one who's responsible for me even existing...
And he's an idiot.
Like the rest of us.

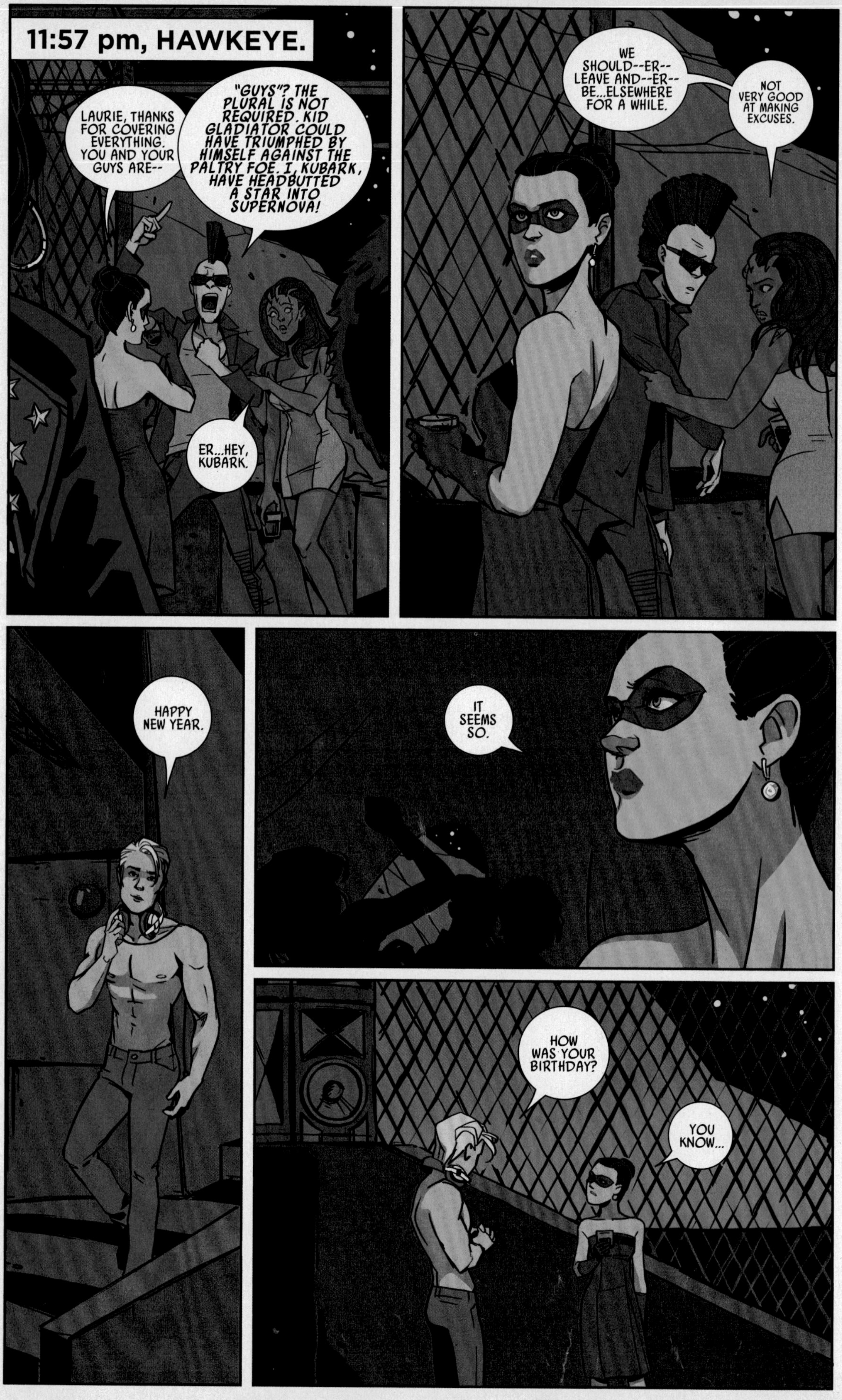
11:57 pm, HAWKEYE.
LAURIE, THANKS FOR COVERING EVERYTHING. YOU AND YOUR GUYS ARE--
"GUYS"? THE PLURAL IS NOT REQUIRED. KID GLADIATOR COULD HAVE TRIUMPHED BY HIMSELF AGAINST THE PALTRY FOE. I, KUBARK, HAVE HEADBUTTED A STAR INTO SUPERNOVA!
ER...HEY, KUBARK.
WE SHOULD--ER--LEAVE AND--ER--BE...ELSEWHERE FOR A WHILE.
NOT VERY GOOD AT MAKING EXCUSES.
HAPPY NEW YEAR.
IT SEEMS SO.
HOW WAS YOUR BIRTHDAY?
YOU KNOW...

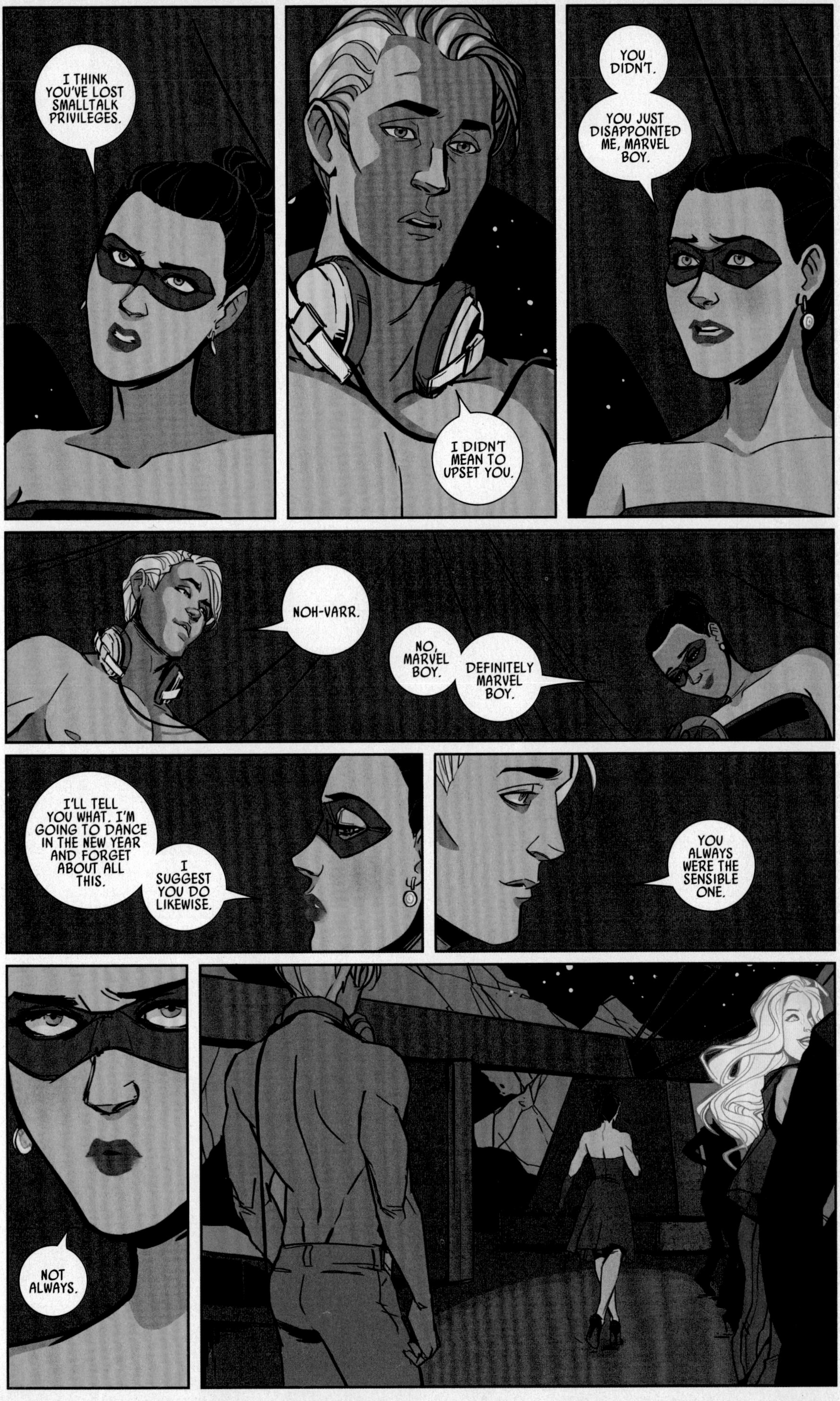
I THINK YOU'VE LOST SMALLTALK PRIVILEGES.
I DIDN'T MEAN TO UPSET YOU.
YOU DIDN'T.
YOU JUST DISAPPOINTED ME, MARVEL BOY.
NOH-VARR.
NO, MARVEL BOY.
DEFINITELY MARVEL BOY.
I'LL TELL YOU WHAT. I'M GOING TO DANCE IN THE NEW YEAR AND FORGET ABOUT ALL THIS.
I SUGGEST YOU DO LIKEWISE.
YOU ALWAYS WERE THE SENSIBLE ONE.
NOT ALWAYS.

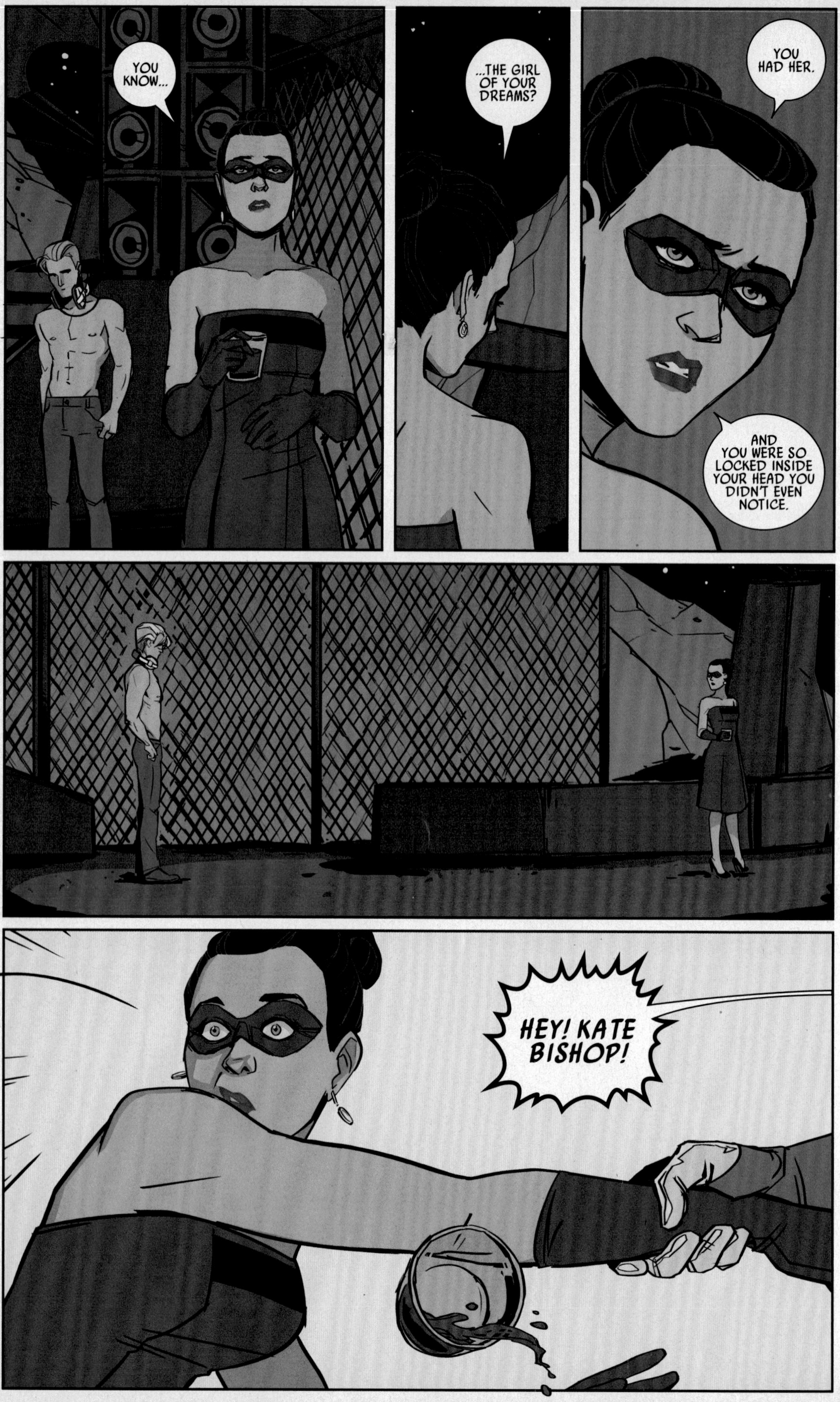
YOU KNOW...
...THE GIRL OF YOUR DREAMS?
YOU HAD HER.
AND YOU WERE SO LOCKED INSIDE YOUR HEAD YOU DIDN'T EVEN NOTICE.
HEY! KATE BISHOP!

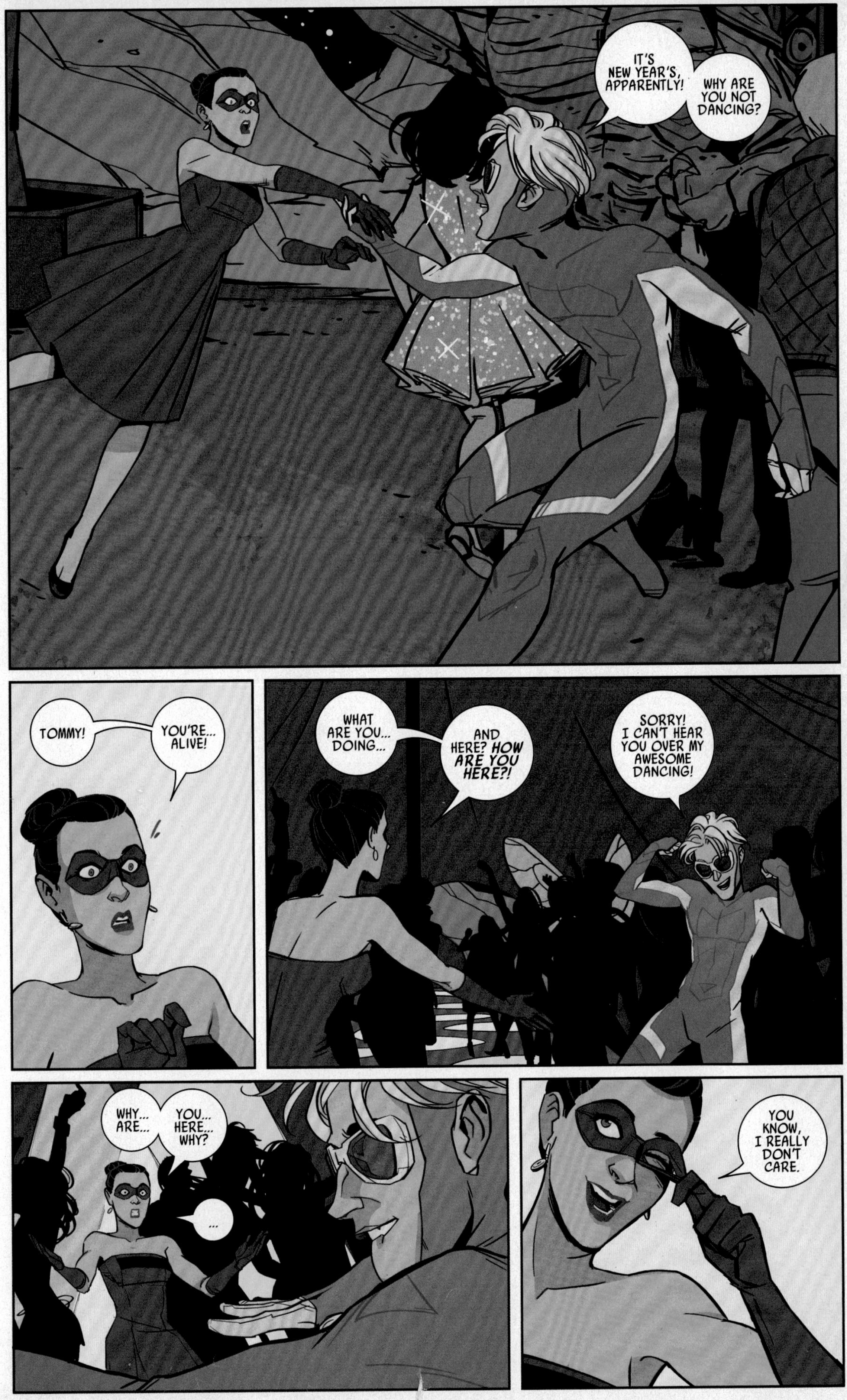
IT'S NEW YEAR'S, APPARENTLY!
WHY ARE YOU NOT DANCING?
TOMMY!
YOU'RE... ALIVE!
WHAT ARE YOU... DOING...
AND HERE? HOW ARE YOU HERE?!
SORRY! I CAN'T HEAR YOU OVER MY AWESOME DANCING!
WHY... ARE...
YOU... HERE... WHY?
...
YOU KNOW, I REALLY DON'T CARE.

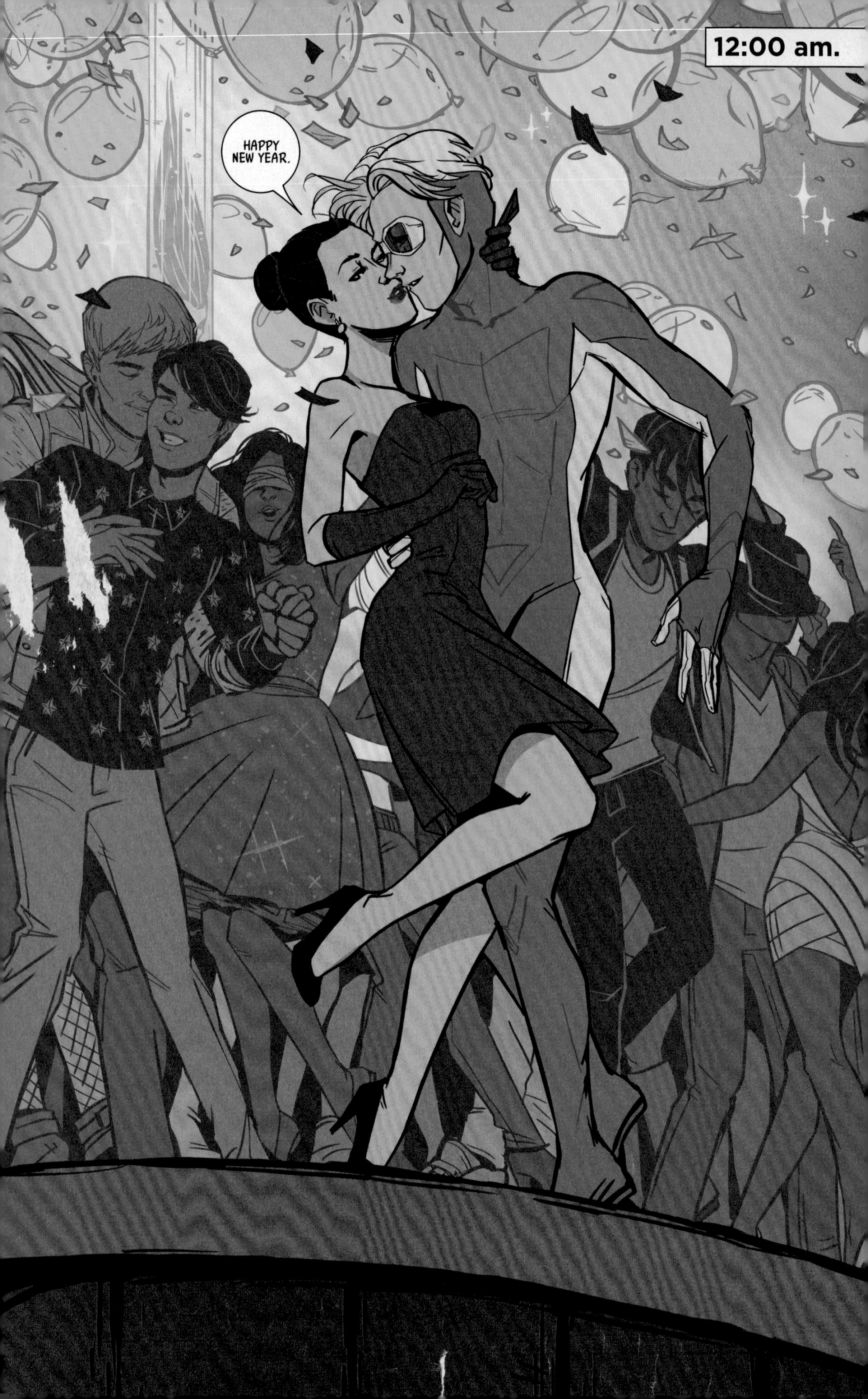
12:00 am.
HAPPY NEW YEAR.

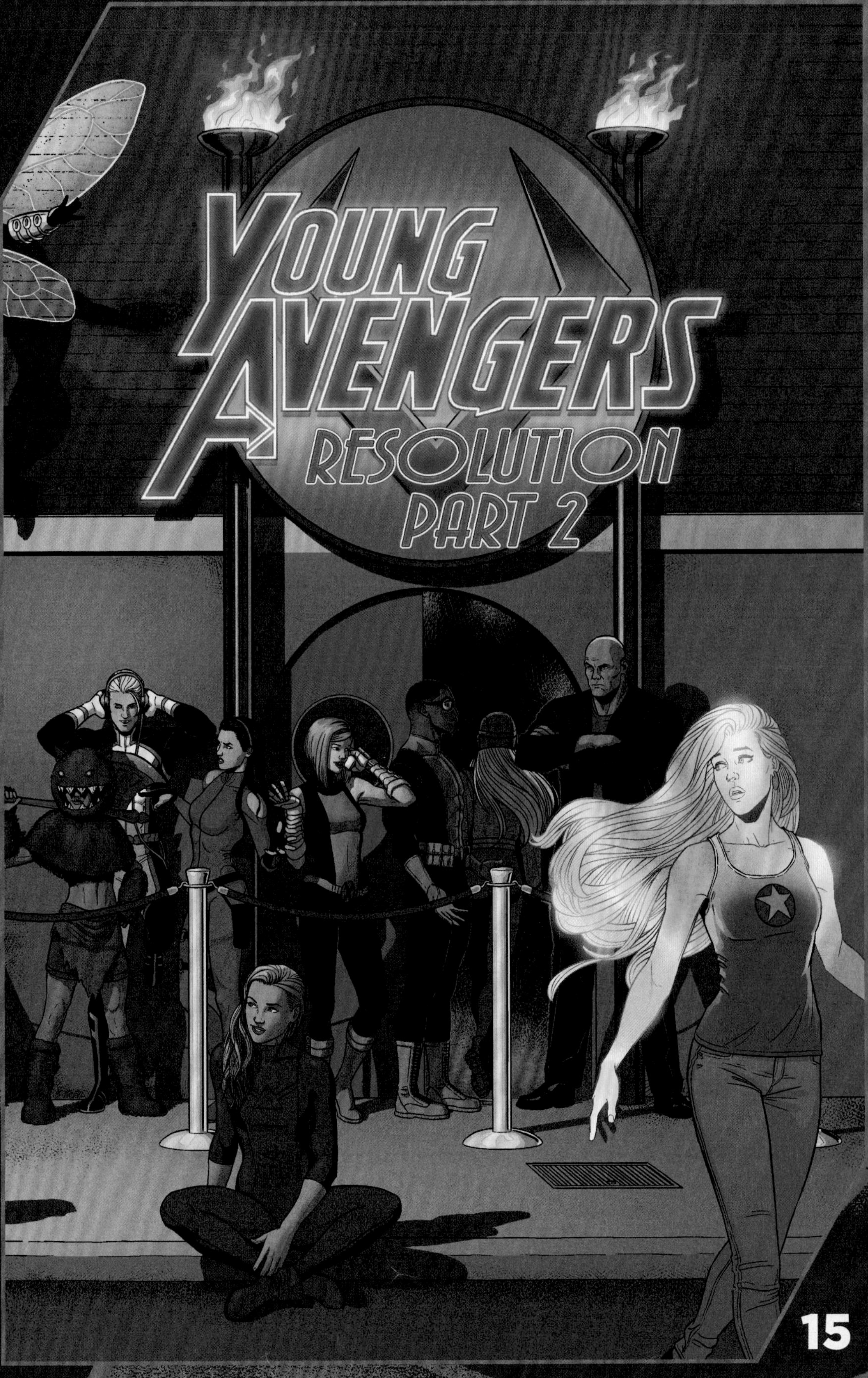
YOUNG AVENGERS
RESOLUTION
PART 2

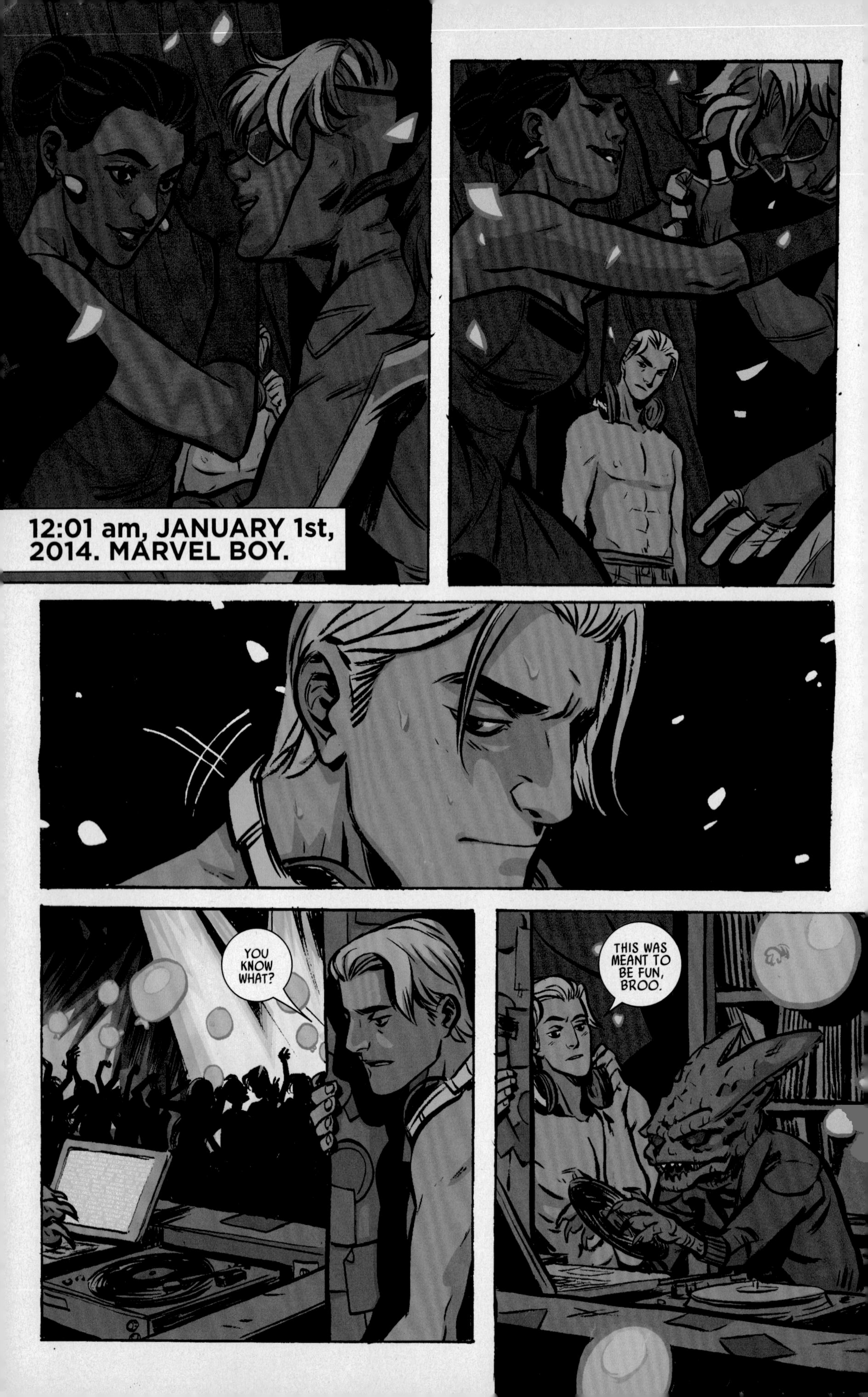
12:01 am, JANUARY 1st, 2014. MARVEL BOY.
YOU KNOW WHAT?
THIS WAS MEANT TO BE FUN, BROO.

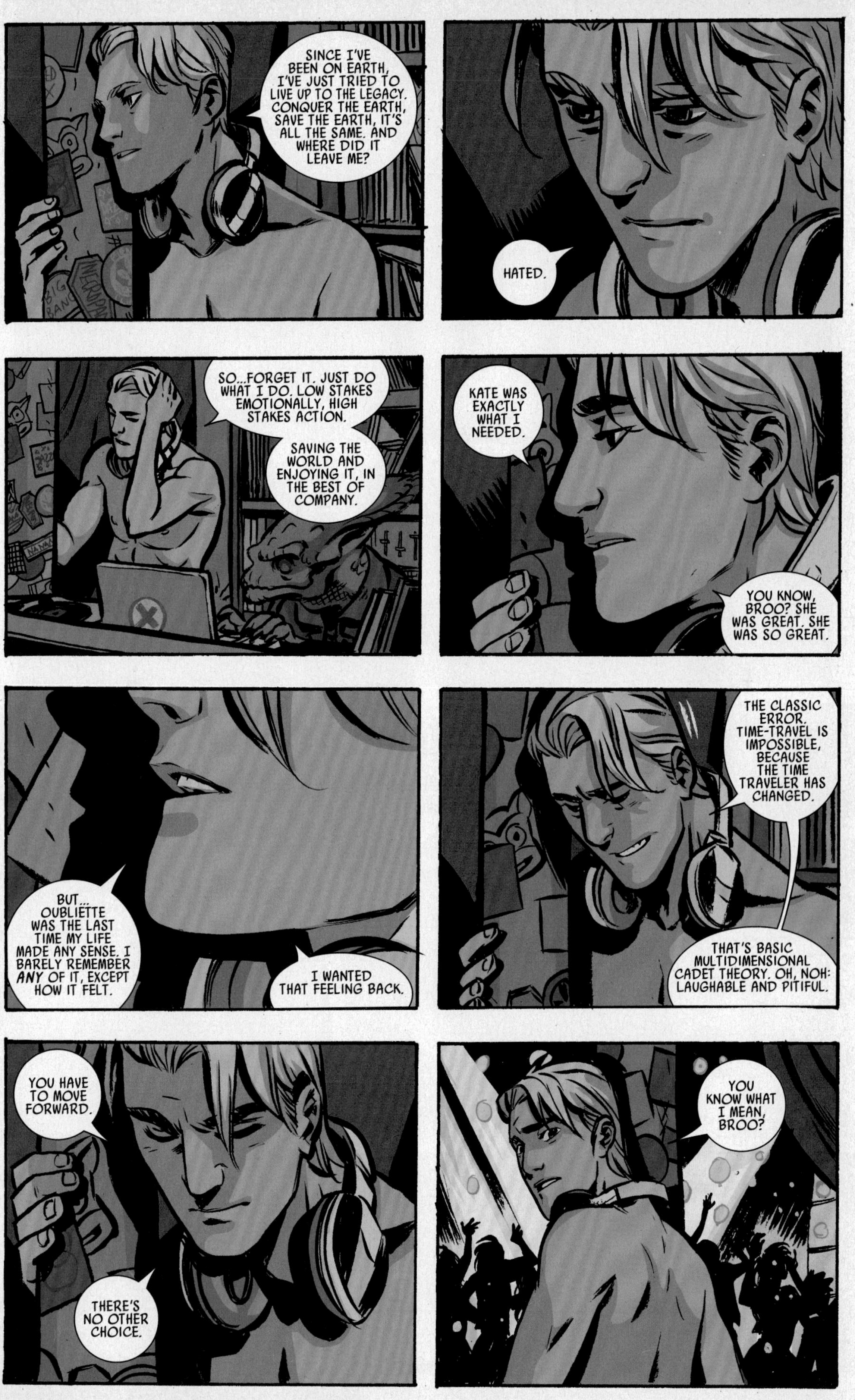
SINCE I'VE BEEN ON EARTH, I'VE JUST TRIED TO LIVE UP TO THE LEGACY. CONQUER THE EARTH, SAVE THE EARTH, IT'S ALL THE SAME. AND WHERE DID IT LEAVE ME?
HATED.
SO...FORGET IT. JUST DO WHAT I DO. LOW STAKES EMOTIONALLY, HIGH STAKES ACTION.
SAVING THE WORLD AND ENJOYING IT, IN THE BEST OF COMPANY.
KATE WAS EXACTLY WHAT I NEEDED.
YOU KNOW, BROO? SHE WAS GREAT. SHE WAS SO GREAT.
BUT... OUBLIETTE WAS THE LAST TIME MY LIFE MADE ANY SENSE. I BARELY REMEMBER ANY OF IT, EXCEPT HOW IT FELT.
I WANTED THAT FEELING BACK.
THE CLASSIC ERROR. TIME-TRAVEL IS IMPOSSIBLE, BECAUSE THE TIME TRAVELER HAS CHANGED.
THAT'S BASIC MULTIDIMENSIONAL CADET THEORY. OH, NOH: LAUGHABLE AND PITIFUL.
YOU HAVE TO MOVE FORWARD.
THERE'S NO OTHER CHOICE.
YOU KNOW WHAT I MEAN, BROO?

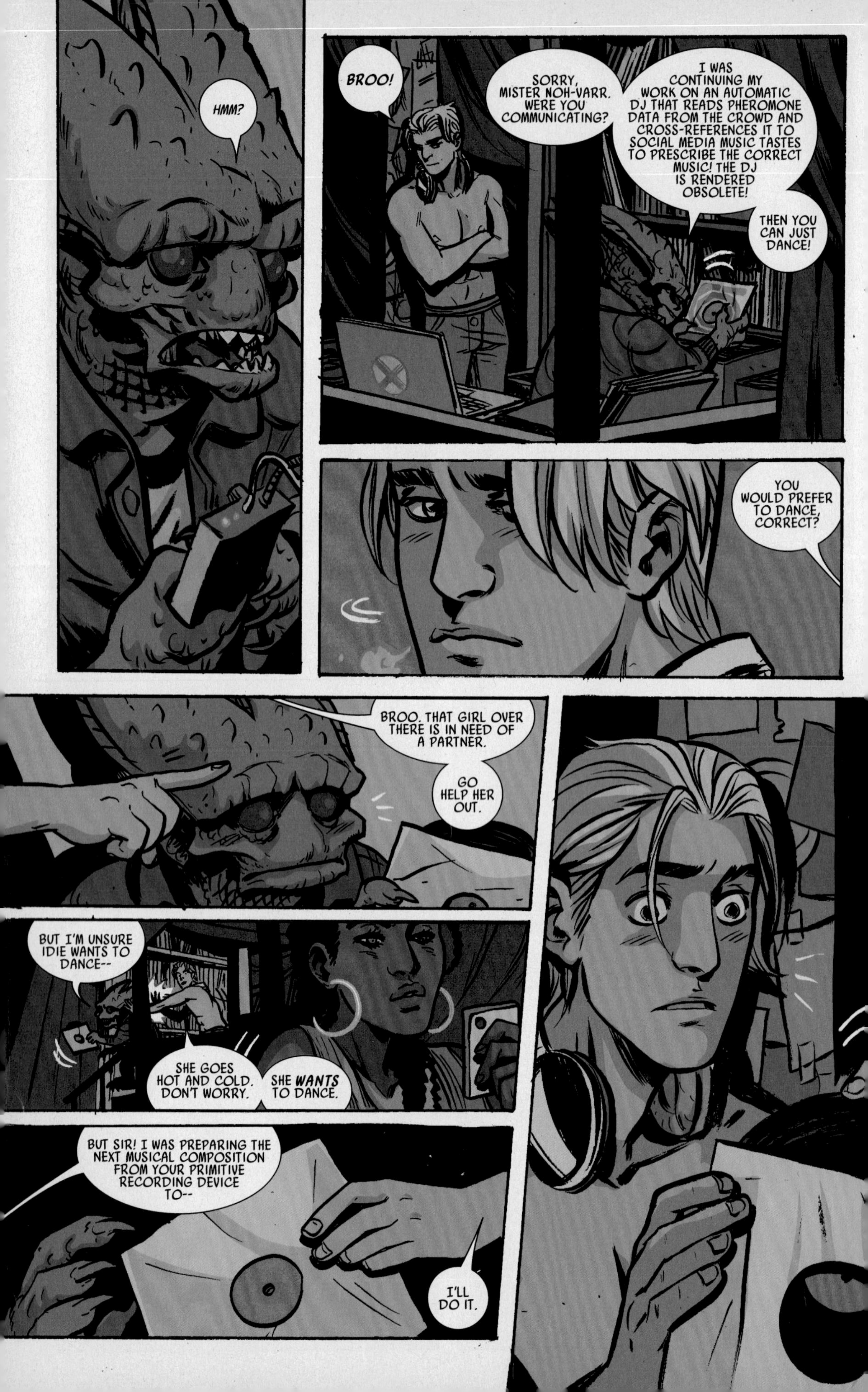
HMM?
BROO!
SORRY, MISTER NOH-VARR. WERE YOU COMMUNICATING?
I WAS CONTINUING MY WORK ON AN AUTOMATIC DJ THAT READS PHEROMONE DATA FROM THE CROWD AND CROSS-REFERENCES IT TO SOCIAL MEDIA MUSIC TASTES TO PRESCRIBE THE CORRECT MUSIC! THE DJ IS RENDERED OBSOLETE!
THEN YOU CAN JUST DANCE!
YOU WOULD PREFER TO DANCE, CORRECT?
BROO. THAT GIRL OVER THERE IS IN NEED OF A PARTNER.
GO HELP HER OUT.
BUT I'M UNSURE IDIE WANTS TO DANCE--
SHE GOES HOT AND COLD. DON'T WORRY.
SHE *WANTS* TO DANCE.
BUT SIR! I WAS PREPARING THE NEXT MUSICAL COMPOSITION FROM YOUR PRIMITIVE RECORDING DEVICE TO--
I'LL DO IT.

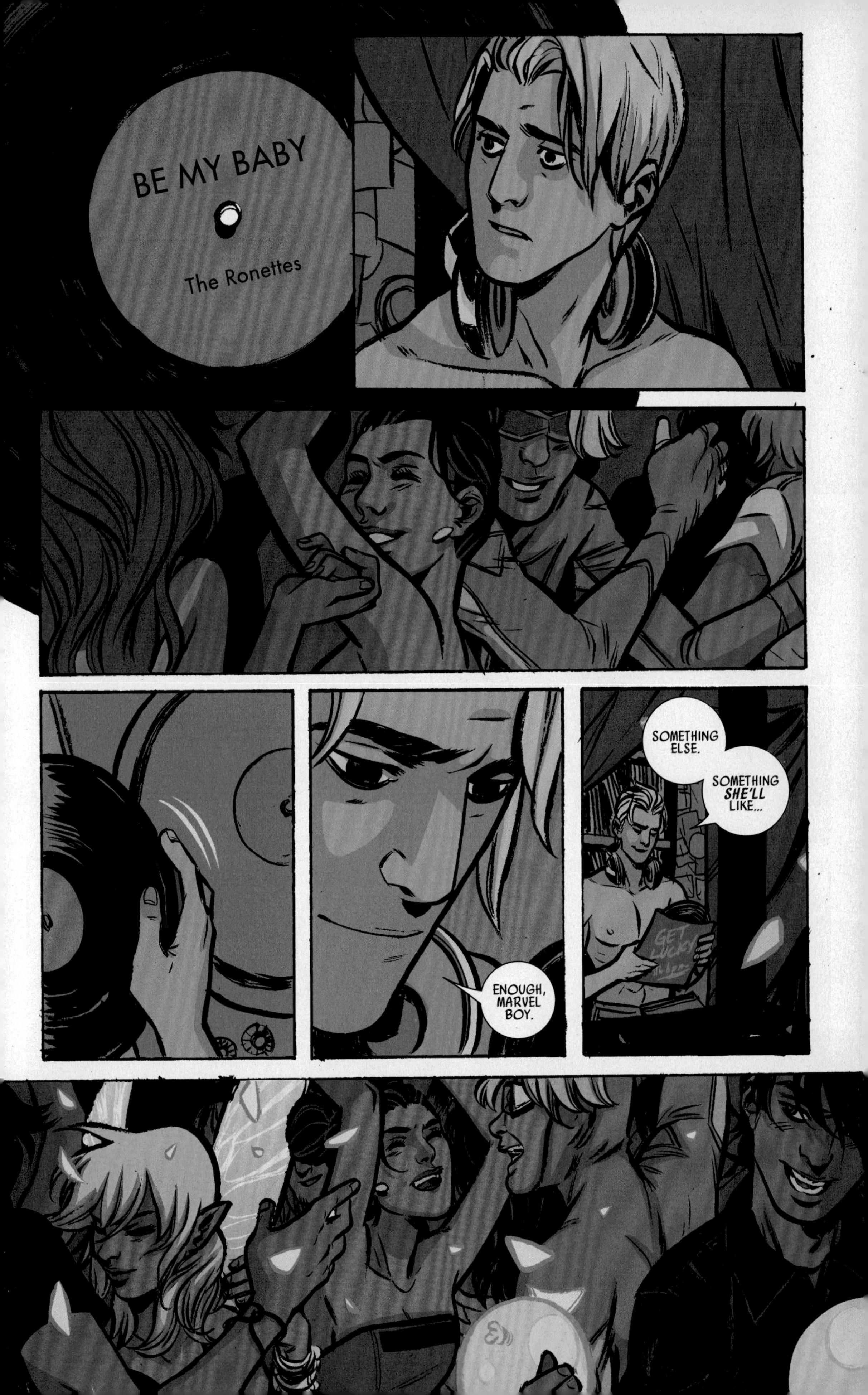
BE MY BABY
The Ronettes
ENOUGH, MARVEL BOY.
SOMETHING ELSE.
SOMETHING SHE'LL LIKE...
GET LUCKY

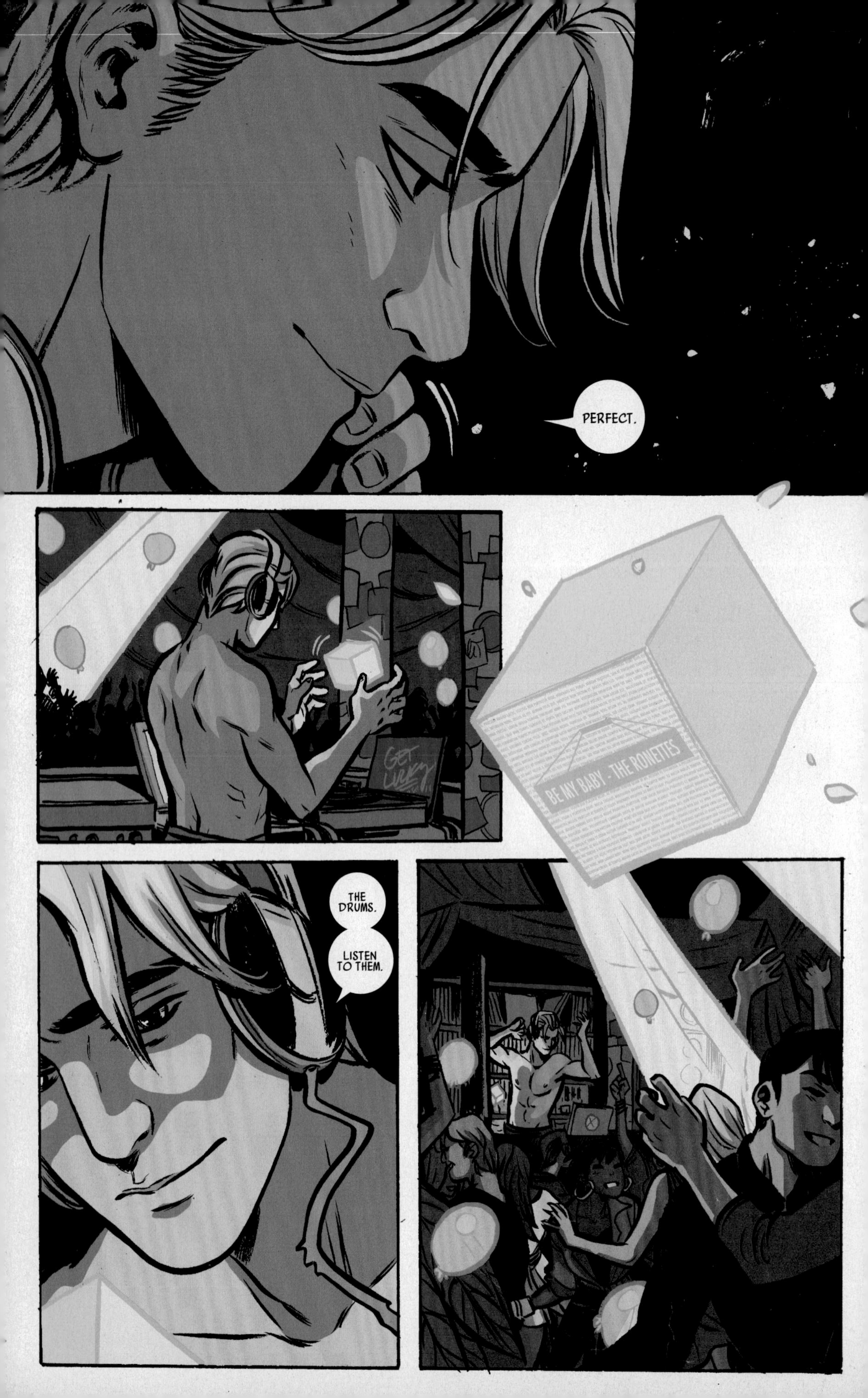
PERFECT.
GET LUCKY
BE MY BABY - THE RONETTES
THE DRUMS.
LISTEN TO THEM.

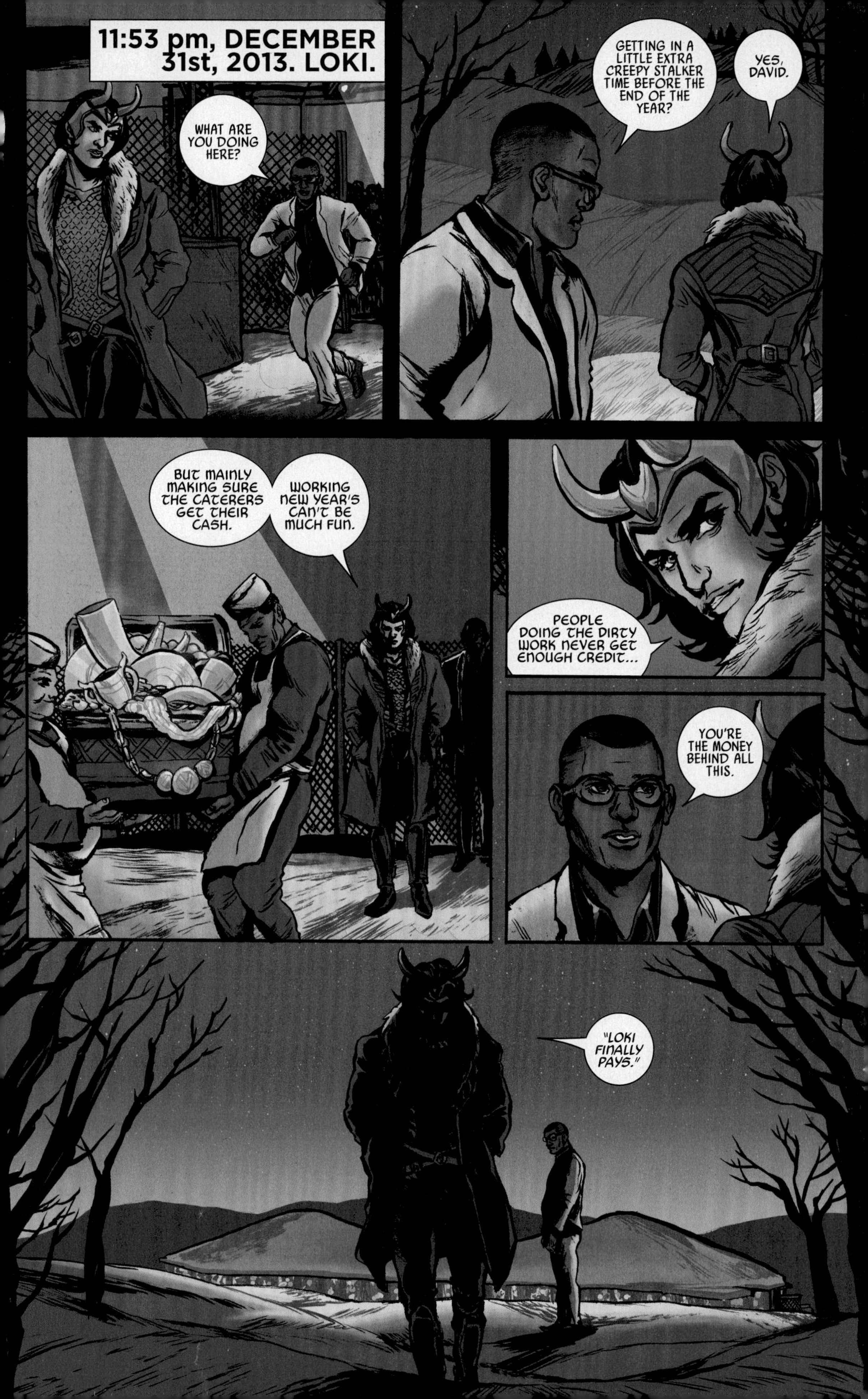
11:53 pm, DECEMBER 31st, 2013. LOKI.
WHAT ARE YOU DOING HERE?
GETTING IN A LITTLE EXTRA CREEPY STALKER TIME BEFORE THE END OF THE YEAR?
YES, DAVID.
BUT MAINLY MAKING SURE THE CATERERS GET THEIR CASH.
WORKING NEW YEAR'S CAN'T BE MUCH FUN.
PEOPLE DOING THE DIRTY WORK NEVER GET ENOUGH CREDIT...
YOU'RE THE MONEY BEHIND ALL THIS.
"LOKI FINALLY PAYS."

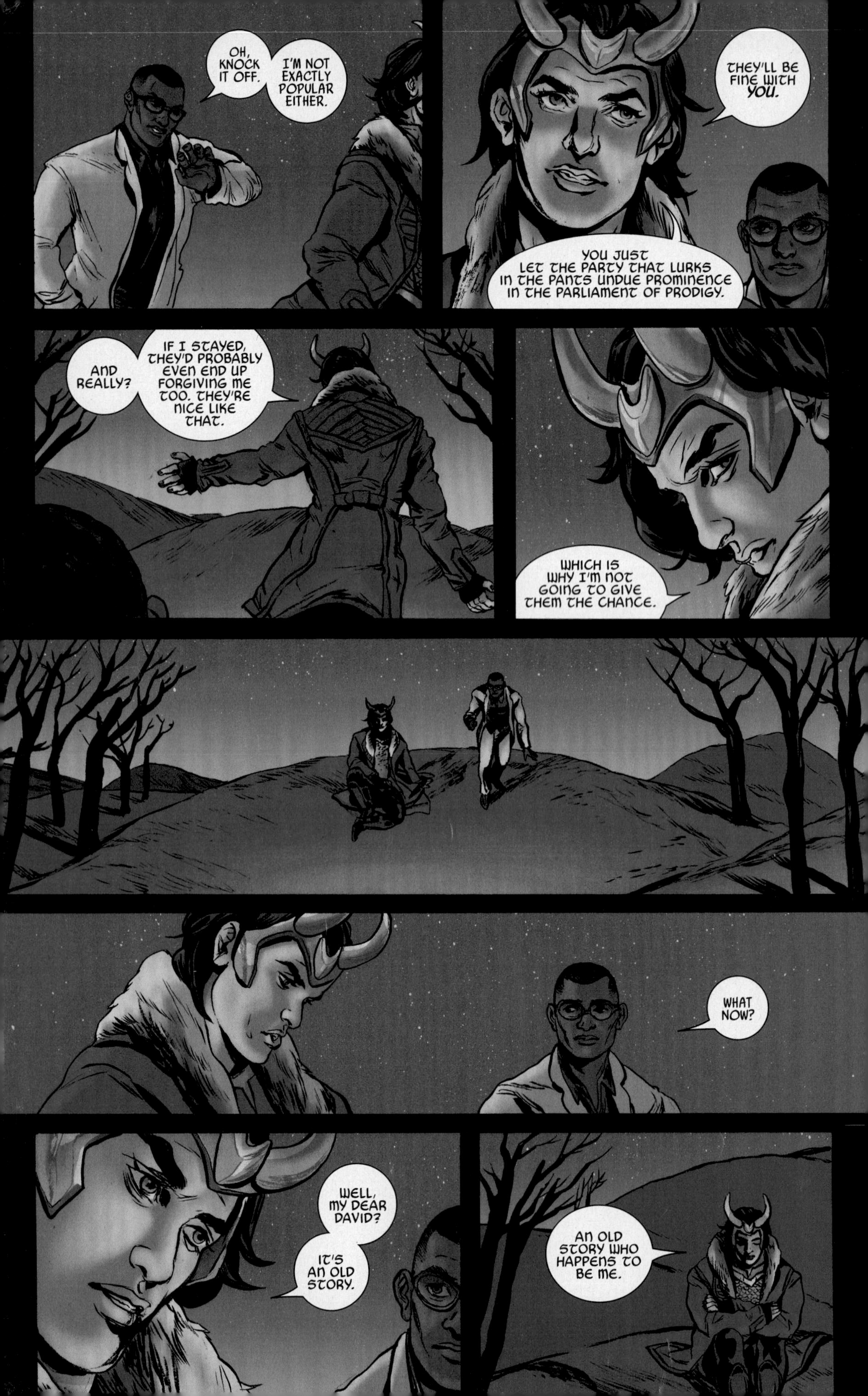
OH, KNOCK IT OFF.
I'M NOT EXACTLY POPULAR EITHER.
THEY'LL BE FINE WITH YOU.
YOU JUST LET THE PARTY THAT LURKS IN THE PANTS UNDUE PROMINENCE IN THE PARLIAMENT OF PRODIGY.
AND REALLY?
IF I STAYED, THEY'D PROBABLY EVEN END UP FORGIVING ME TOO. THEY'RE NICE LIKE THAT.
WHICH IS WHY I'M NOT GOING TO GIVE THEM THE CHANCE.
WHAT NOW?
WELL, MY DEAR DAVID?
IT'S AN OLD STORY.
AN OLD STORY WHO HAPPENS TO BE ME.

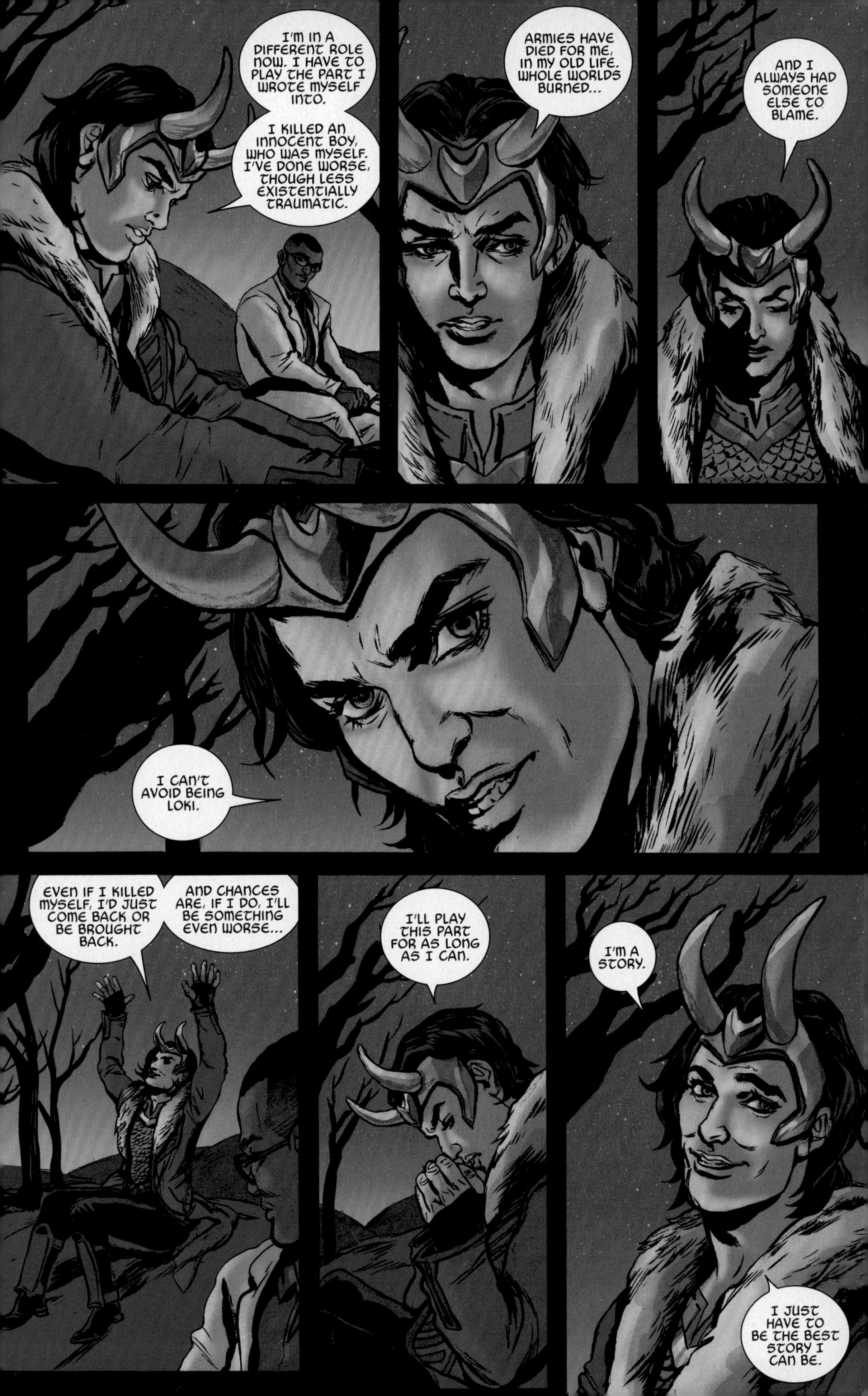
I'M IN A DIFFERENT ROLE NOW. I HAVE TO PLAY THE PART I WROTE MYSELF INTO.
I KILLED AN INNOCENT BOY, WHO WAS MYSELF. I'VE DONE WORSE, THOUGH LESS EXISTENTIALLY TRAUMATIC.
ARMIES HAVE DIED FOR ME, IN MY OLD LIFE. WHOLE WORLDS BURNED...
AND I ALWAYS HAD SOMEONE ELSE TO BLAME.
I CAN'T AVOID BEING LOKI.
EVEN IF I KILLED MYSELF, I'D JUST COME BACK OR BE BROUGHT BACK.
AND CHANCES ARE, IF I DO, I'LL BE SOMETHING EVEN WORSE...
I'LL PLAY THIS PART FOR AS LONG AS I CAN.
I'M A STORY.
I JUST HAVE TO BE THE BEST STORY I CAN BE.

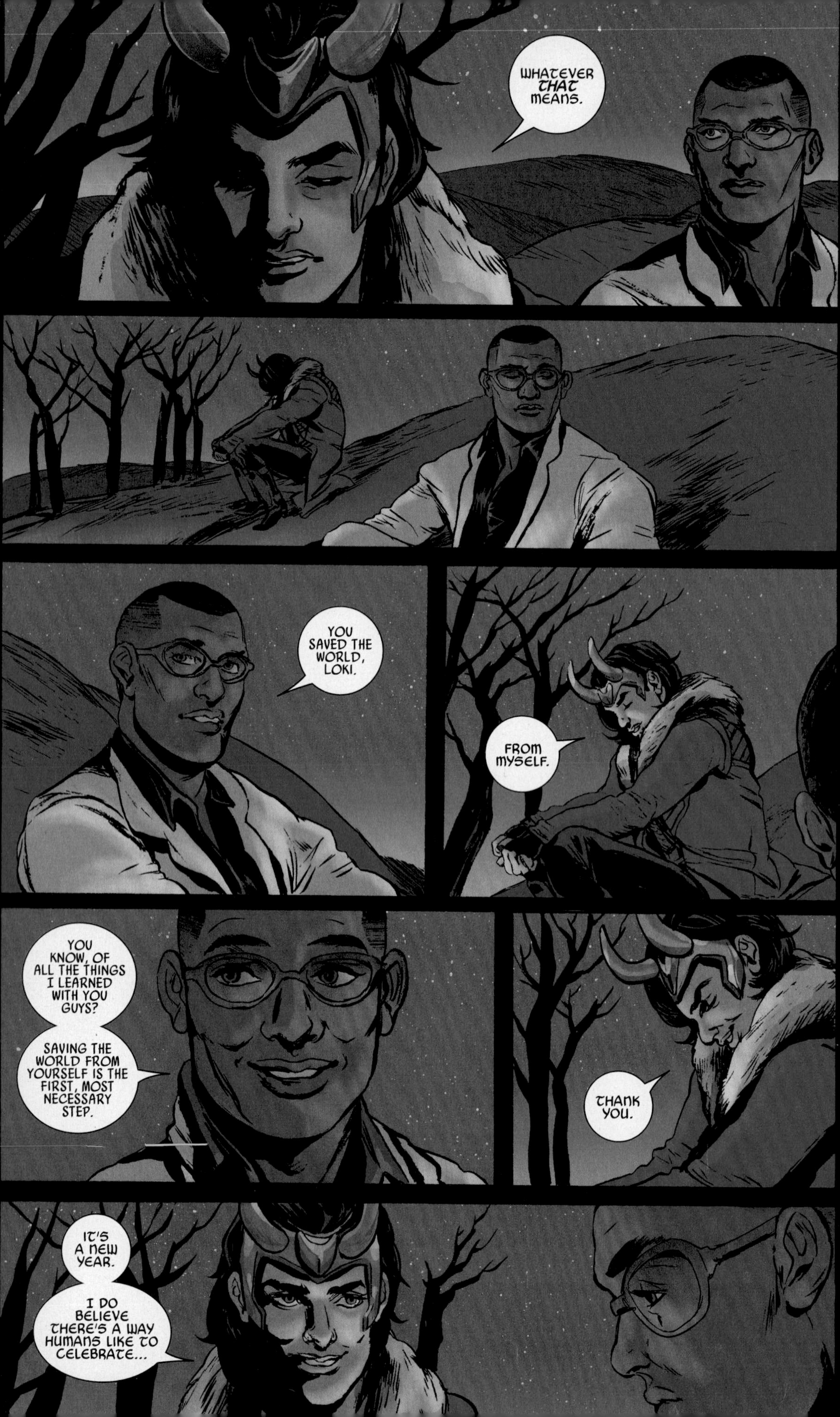
WHATEVER THAT MEANS.
YOU SAVED THE WORLD, LOKI.
FROM MYSELF.
YOU KNOW, OF ALL THE THINGS I LEARNED WITH YOU GUYS?
SAVING THE WORLD FROM YOURSELF IS THE FIRST, MOST NECESSARY STEP.
THANK YOU.
IT'S A NEW YEAR.
I DO BELIEVE THERE'S A WAY HUMANS LIKE TO CELEBRATE...

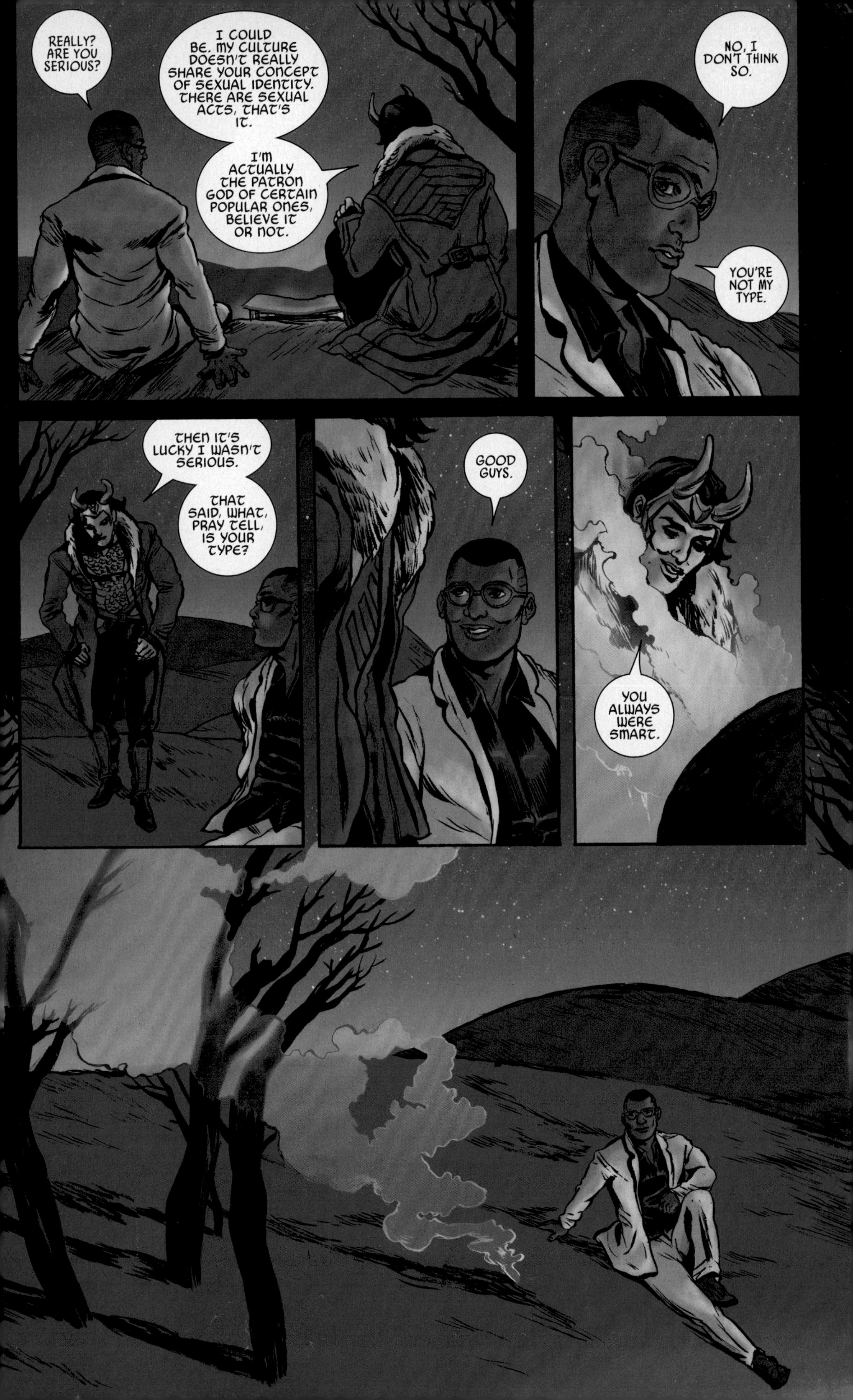
REALLY? ARE YOU SERIOUS?
I COULD BE. MY CULTURE DOESN'T REALLY SHARE YOUR CONCEPT OF SEXUAL IDENTITY. THERE ARE SEXUAL ACTS, THAT'S IT.
I'M ACTUALLY THE PATRON GOD OF CERTAIN POPULAR ONES, BELIEVE IT OR NOT.
NO, I DON'T THINK SO.
YOU'RE NOT MY TYPE.
THEN IT'S LUCKY I WASN'T SERIOUS.
THAT SAID, WHAT, PRAY TELL, IS YOUR TYPE?
GOOD GUYS.
YOU ALWAYS WERE SMART.

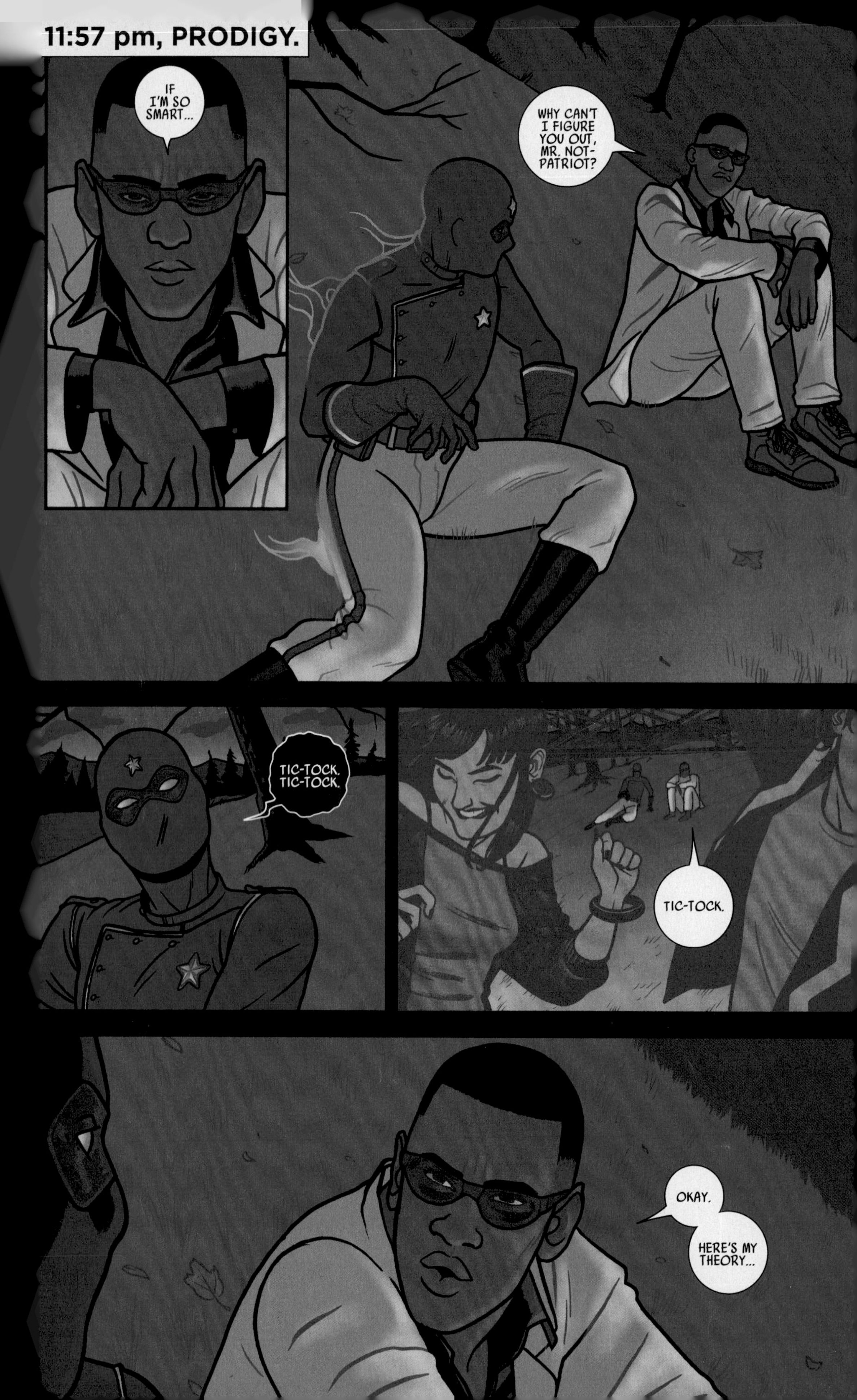

11:57 pm, PRODIGY.
IF I'M SO SMART...
WHY CAN'T I FIGURE YOU OUT, MR. NOT-PATRIOT?
TIC-TOCK. TIC-TOCK.
TIC-TOCK.
OKAY.
HERE'S MY THEORY...

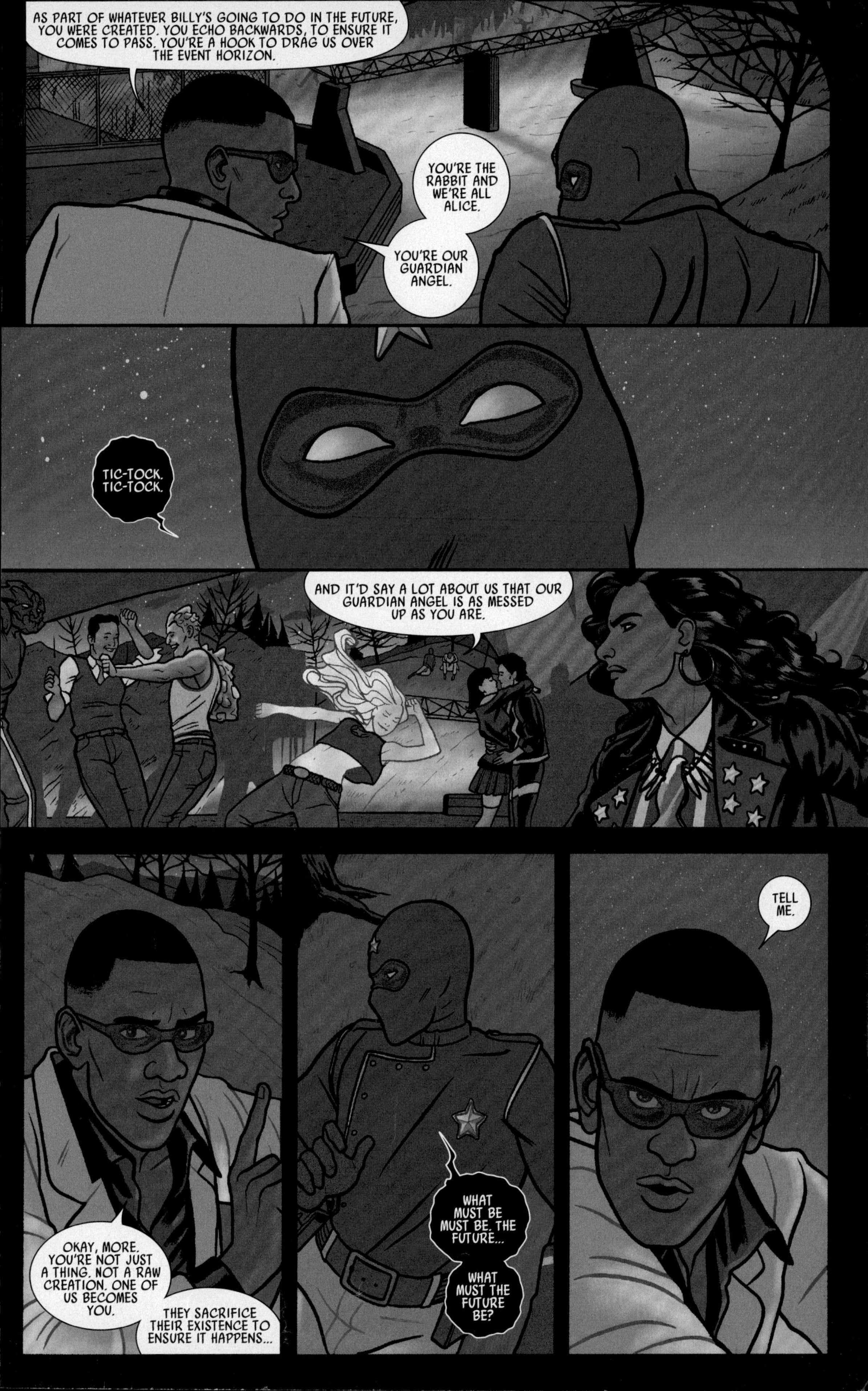
AS PART OF WHATEVER BILLY'S GOING TO DO IN THE FUTURE, YOU WERE CREATED. YOU ECHO BACKWARDS, TO ENSURE IT COMES TO PASS. YOU'RE A HOOK TO DRAG US OVER THE EVENT HORIZON.
YOU'RE THE RABBIT AND WE'RE ALL ALICE.
YOU'RE OUR GUARDIAN ANGEL.
TIC-TOCK. TIC-TOCK.
AND IT'D SAY A LOT ABOUT US THAT OUR GUARDIAN ANGEL IS AS MESSED UP AS YOU ARE.
OKAY, MORE. YOU'RE NOT JUST A THING. NOT A RAW CREATION. ONE OF US BECOMES YOU.
THEY SACRIFICE THEIR EXISTENCE TO ENSURE IT HAPPENS...
WHAT MUST BE MUST BE. THE FUTURE...
WHAT MUST THE FUTURE BE?
TELL ME.

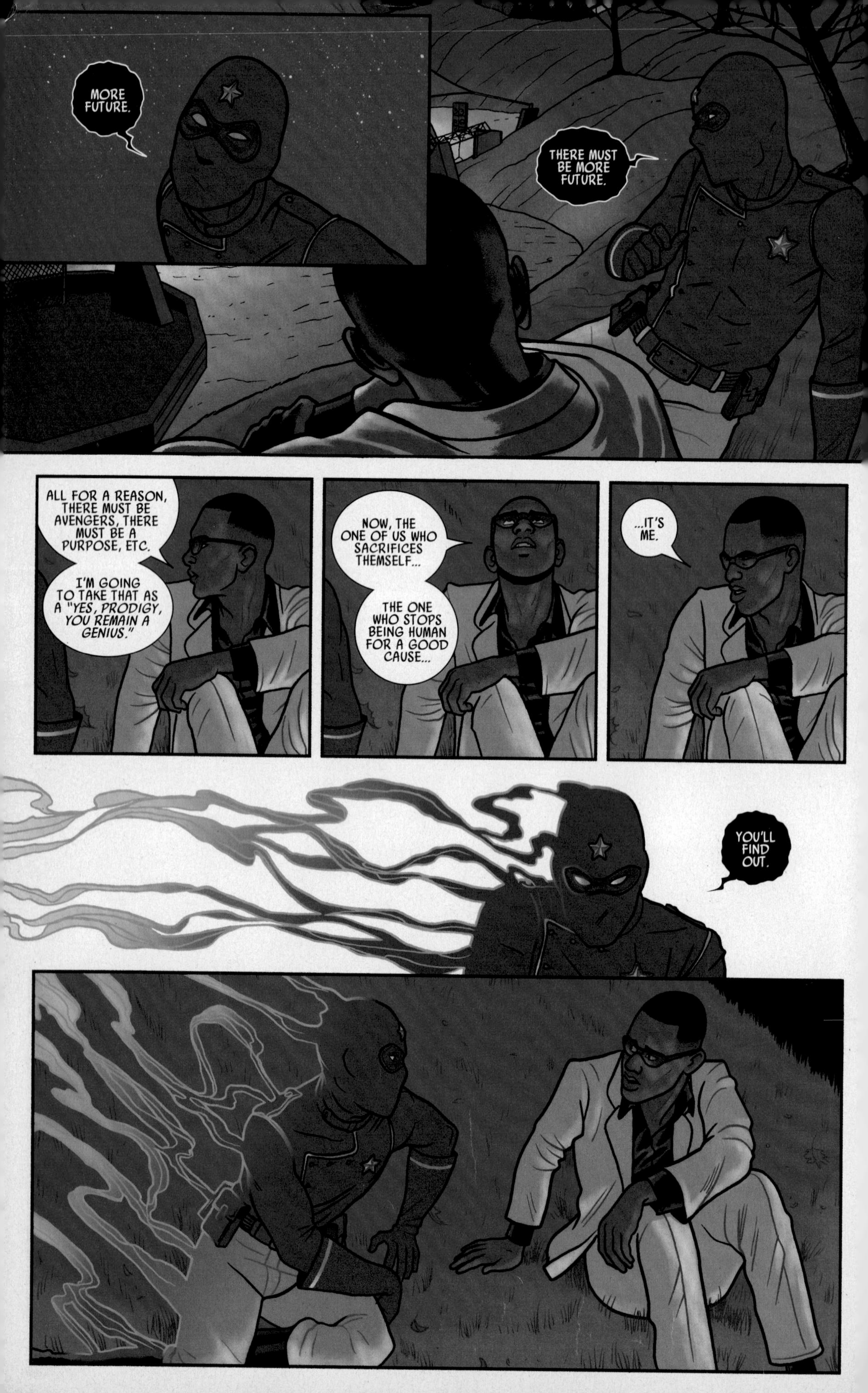
MORE FUTURE.
THERE MUST BE MORE FUTURE.
ALL FOR A REASON, THERE MUST BE AVENGERS, THERE MUST BE A PURPOSE, ETC.
I'M GOING TO TAKE THAT AS A "YES, PRODIGY, YOU REMAIN A GENIUS."
NOW, THE ONE OF US WHO SACRIFICES THEMSELF...
THE ONE WHO STOPS BEING HUMAN FOR A GOOD CAUSE...
...IT'S ME.
YOU'LL FIND OUT.

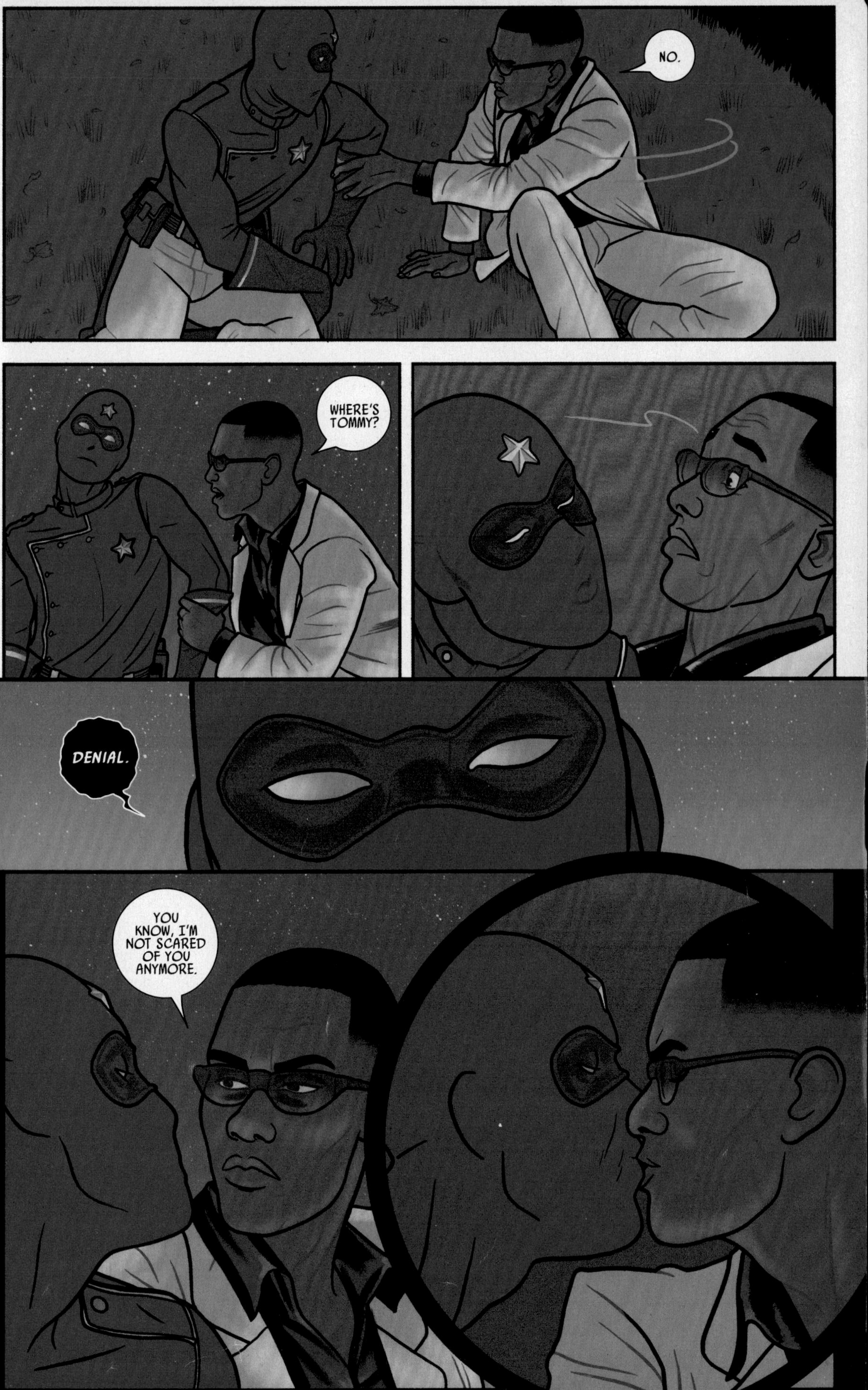
NO.
WHERE'S TOMMY?
DENIAL.
YOU KNOW, I'M NOT SCARED OF YOU ANYMORE.

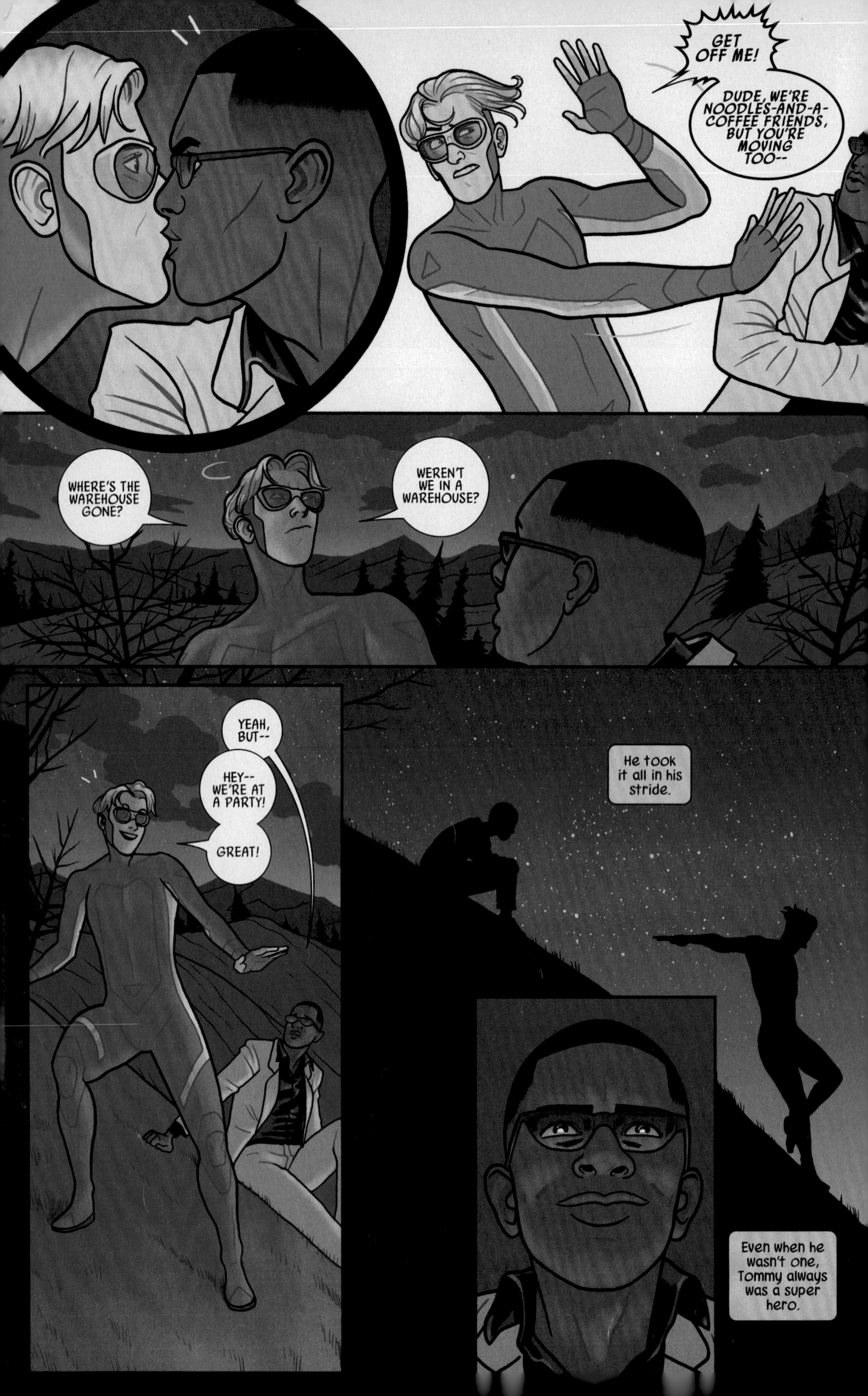
GET OFF ME!
DUDE, WE'RE NOODLES-AND-A-COFFEE FRIENDS, BUT YOU'RE MOVING TOO--
WHERE'S THE WAREHOUSE GONE?
WEREN'T WE IN A WAREHOUSE?
YEAH, BUT--
HEY-- WE'RE AT A PARTY!
GREAT!
He took it all in his stride.
Even when he wasn't one, Tommy always was a super hero.

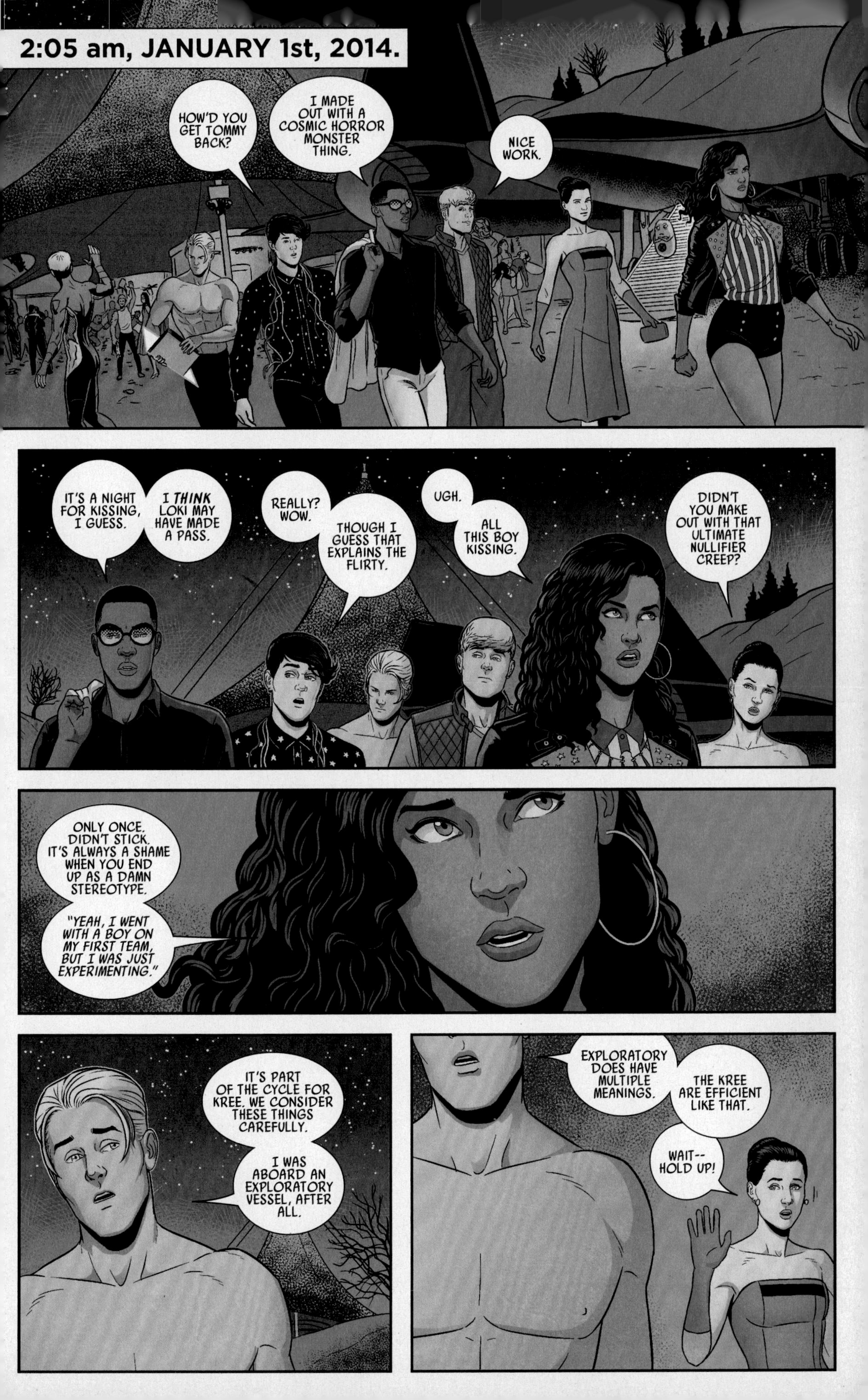
2:05 am, JANUARY 1st, 2014.
HOW'D YOU GET TOMMY BACK?
I MADE OUT WITH A COSMIC HORROR MONSTER THING.
NICE WORK.
IT'S A NIGHT FOR KISSING, I GUESS.
I *THINK* LOKI MAY HAVE MADE A PASS.
REALLY? WOW.
THOUGH I GUESS THAT EXPLAINS THE FLIRTY.
UGH.
ALL THIS BOY KISSING.
DIDN'T YOU MAKE OUT WITH THAT ULTIMATE NULLIFIER CREEP?
ONLY ONCE. DIDN'T STICK. IT'S ALWAYS A SHAME WHEN YOU END UP AS A DAMN STEREOTYPE.
"YEAH, I WENT WITH A BOY ON MY FIRST TEAM, BUT I WAS JUST EXPERIMENTING."
IT'S PART OF THE CYCLE FOR KREE. WE CONSIDER THESE THINGS CAREFULLY.
I WAS ABOARD AN EXPLORATORY VESSEL, AFTER ALL.
EXPLORATORY DOES HAVE MULTIPLE MEANINGS.
THE KREE ARE EFFICIENT LIKE THAT.
WAIT-- HOLD UP!

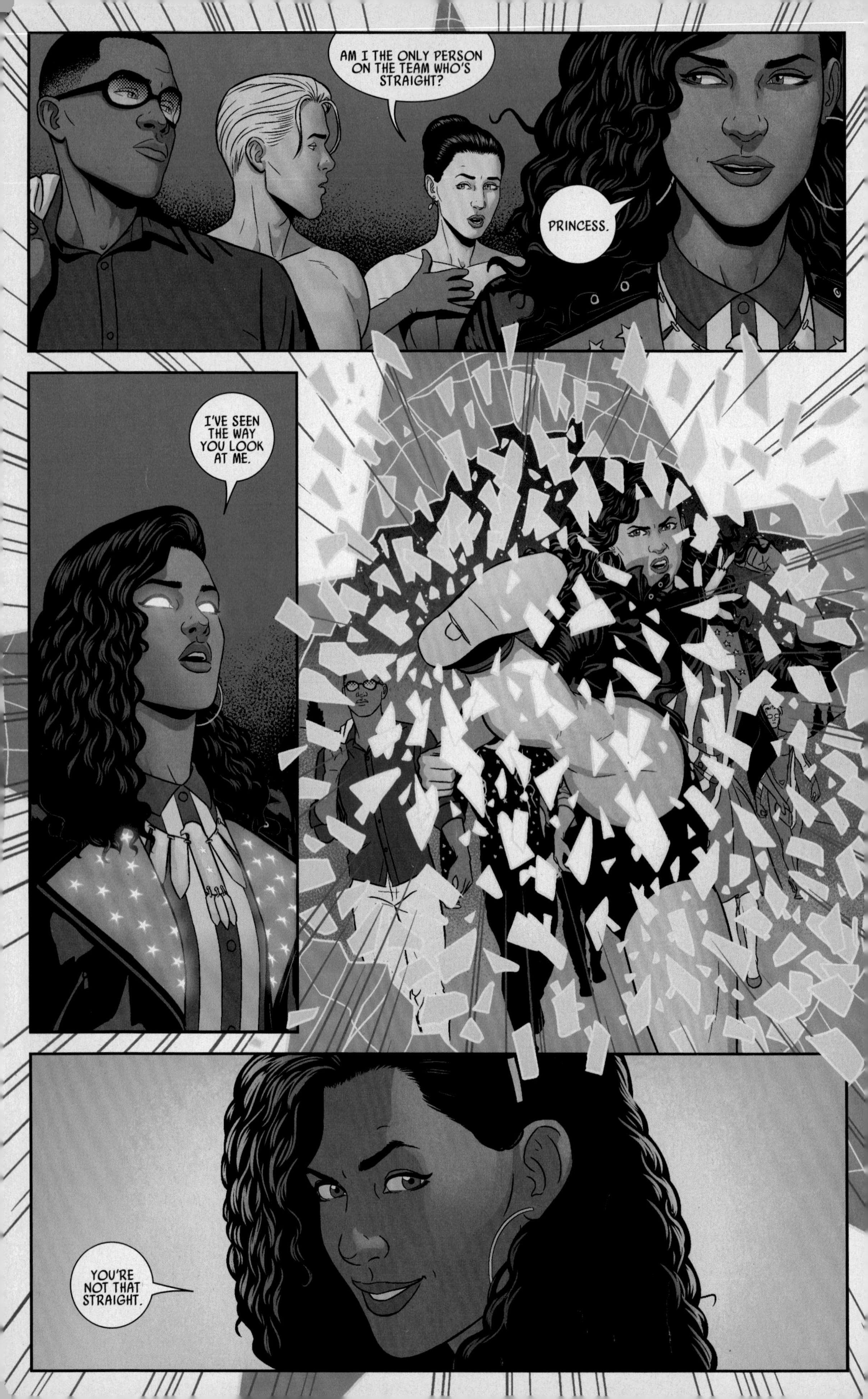
AM I THE ONLY PERSON ON THE TEAM WHO'S STRAIGHT?
PRINCESS.
I'VE SEEN THE WAY YOU LOOK AT ME.
YOU'RE NOT THAT STRAIGHT.

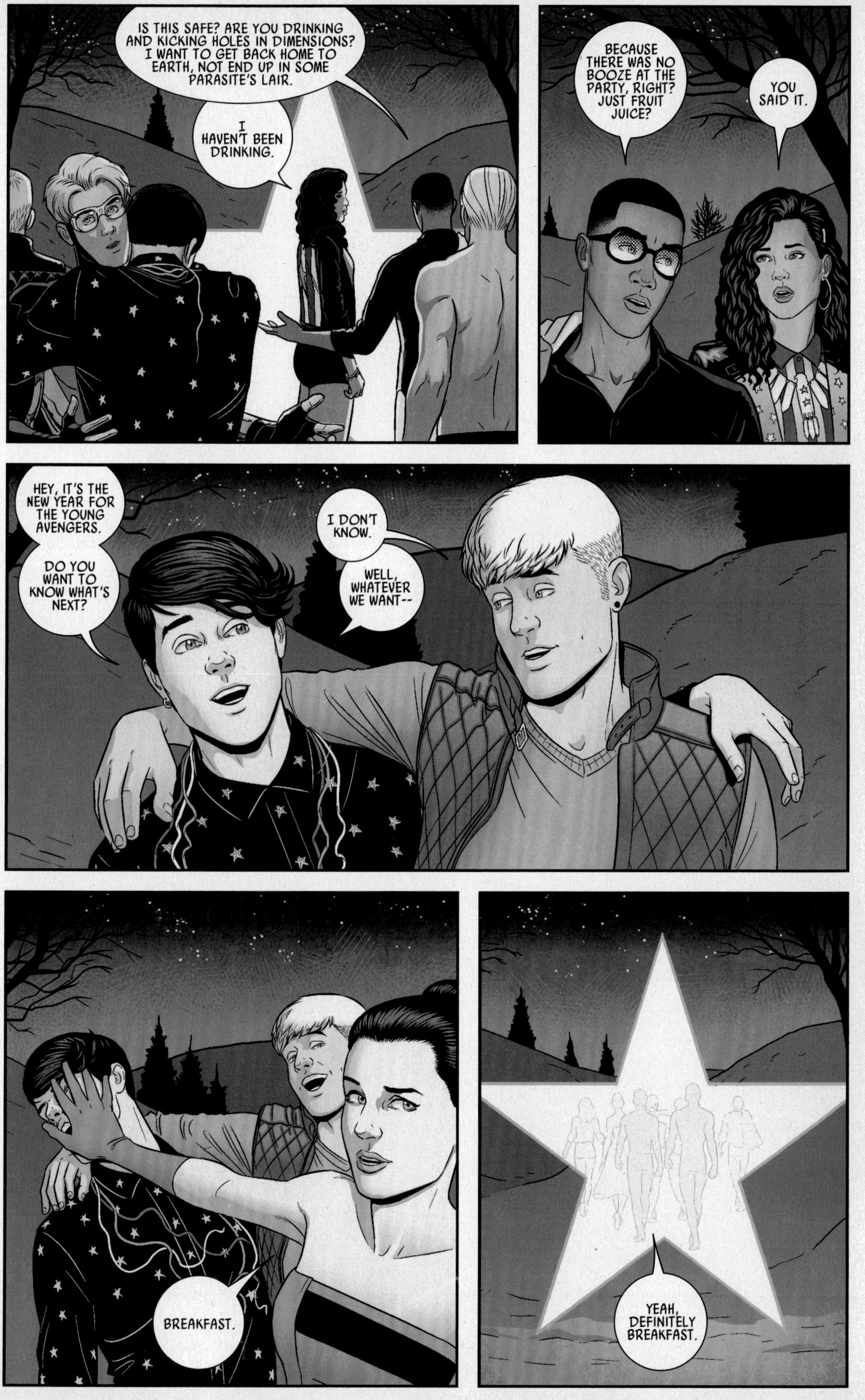
IS THIS SAFE? ARE YOU DRINKING AND KICKING HOLES IN DIMENSIONS? I WANT TO GET BACK HOME TO EARTH, NOT END UP IN SOME PARASITE'S LAIR.
I HAVEN'T BEEN DRINKING.
BECAUSE THERE WAS NO BOOZE AT THE PARTY, RIGHT? JUST FRUIT JUICE?
YOU SAID IT.
HEY, IT'S THE NEW YEAR FOR THE YOUNG AVENGERS.
DO YOU WANT TO KNOW WHAT'S NEXT?
I DON'T KNOW.
WELL, WHATEVER WE WANT--
BREAKFAST.
YEAH, DEFINITELY BREAKFAST.

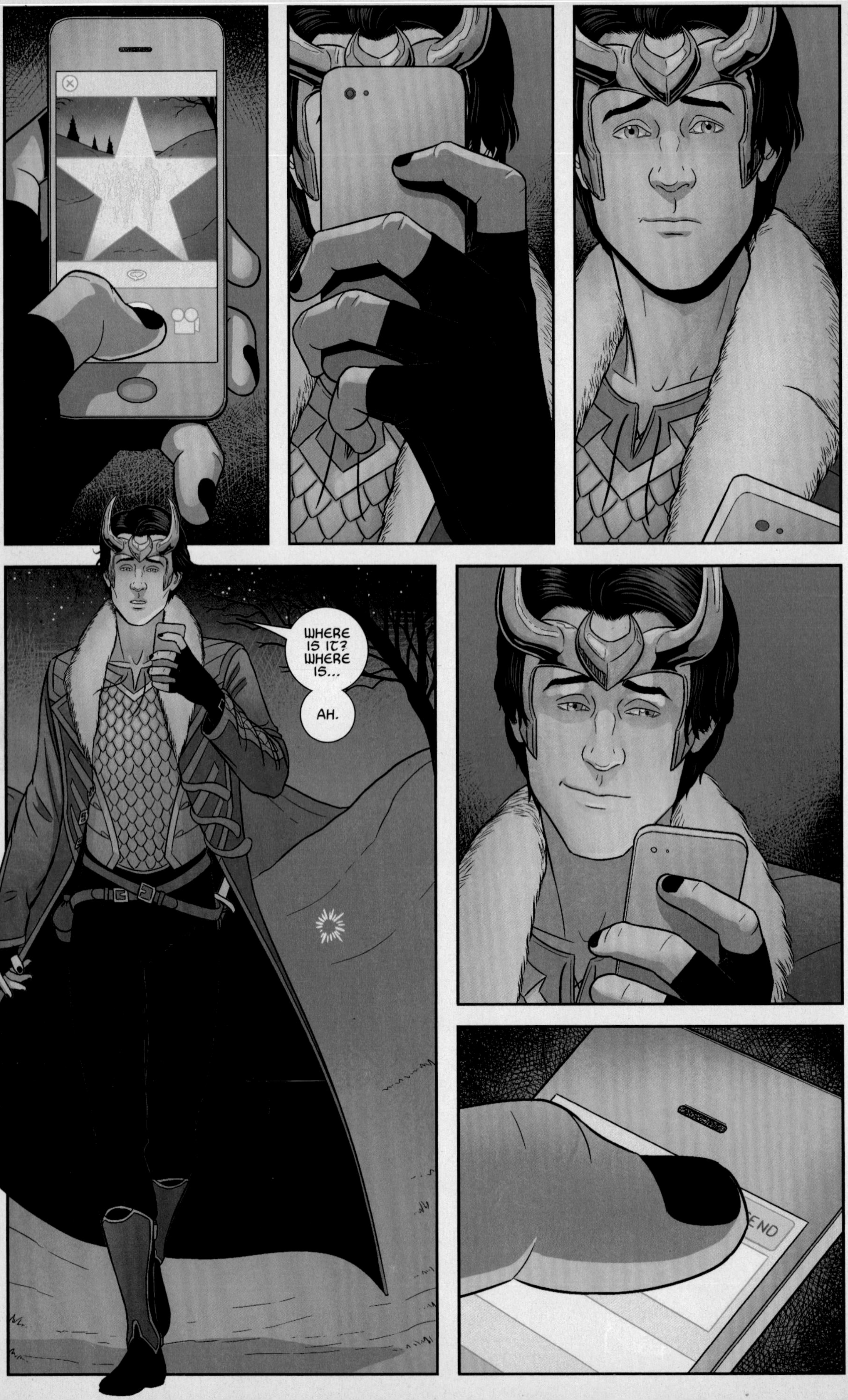
WHERE IS IT? WHERE IS...
AH.
SEND

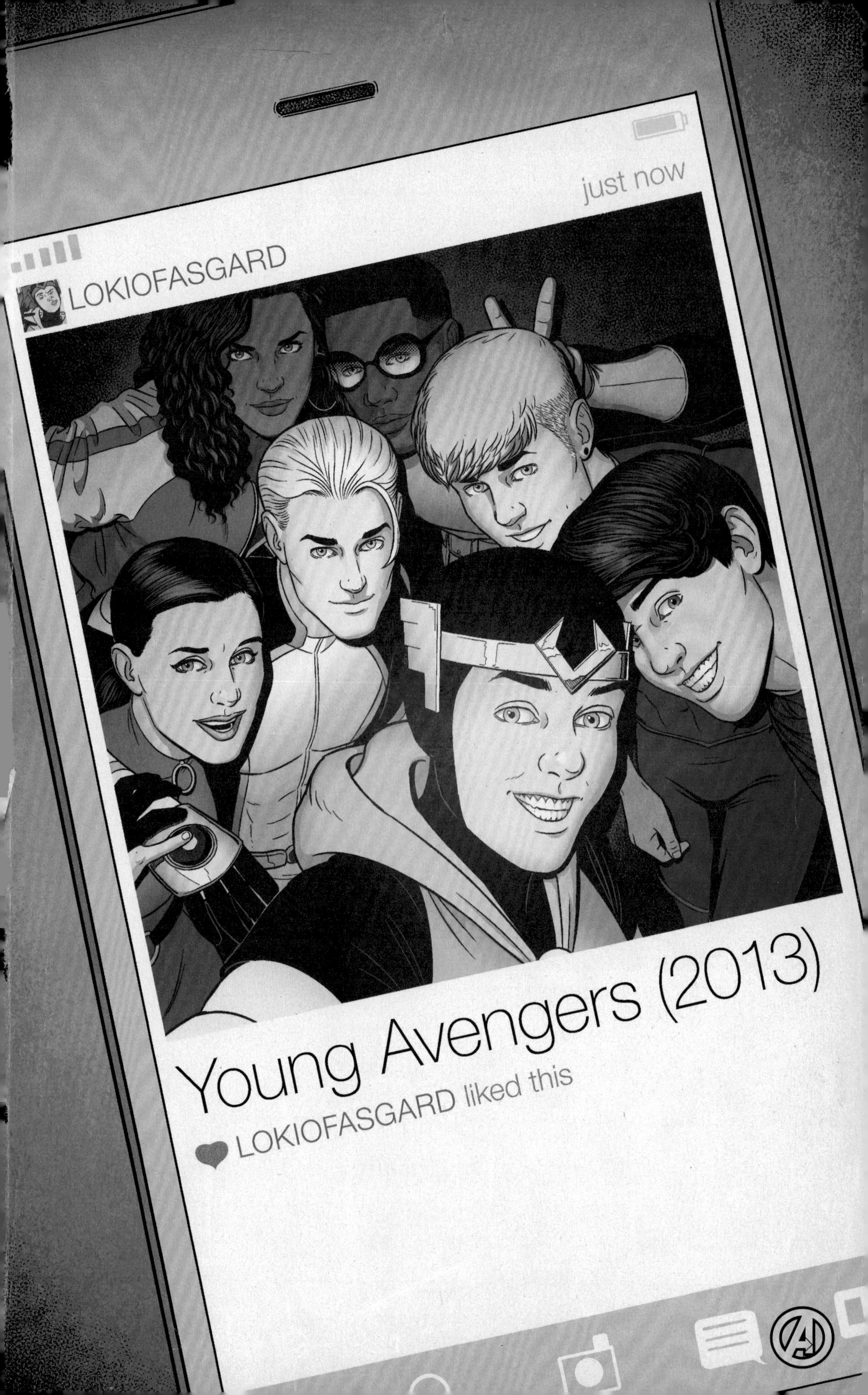
just now
LOKIOFASGARD
Young Avengers (2013)
LOKIOFASGARD liked this

AND NOW A WORD FROM THE CREATORS:

Great work, everyone! It was too awesome to be a part of this! Wishing everyone luck and full speed (SEE WHAT I DID THERE) ahead to all your next projects!

XXX
—Kate Brown

While my contribution to *Young Avengers* was small, I feel that the contribution will be remembered in the bigger world of the amazing story that is *Young Avengers*. Very rarely, one can take on a creative project and feel — no wait — *know* that it will be remembered in comic history. *Young Avengers* is one of those projects. Kieron, Jamie, Matt, Clayton, Moisan and Sanko have spun a brilliant tale no one will soon forget.

—Jordie Bellaire

I've spent the last hour thinking of ways I can lyrically summarise how utterly brilliant *Young Avengers* has been. How I've loved the real honest to goodness heart of it. How I've thrilled at its invention. I've creased my brow pondering interesting ways I can praise Kieron Gillen and Jamie McKelvie and their fantastic work. I've almost bust a gut trying to think of an eloquent way to say that *Young Avengers* is a super hero book for tumblr generation.

Somethimes though, inspiration comes hard. Thing is, Mr. Gillen and Mr. McKelvie make it look easy. Oh, and...*Young Avengers* IS the super hero book of the tumblr generation.

—Christian Ward

When I first read Heinberg and Cheung's *Young Avengers*, it inspired me in the way that *Runways* had. It was fresh, exciting, and featured a cast of characters who were dealing with growing up and the real world as much as they were with super-powers. I've followed the characters ever since, and when Jamie and Kieron first told me they were taking on *Young Avengers*, I was filled with excitement for what I knew they could achieve. They were a perfect choice and they made something special, and I'm stupidly proud and happy to be a small part of it.

—Emma Vieceli

Bravo, and thank you to Gillen, McKelvie, and company for a sweet season of action and smooches. Thrilled to be even a five-page part of it.

—Annie Wu

Comic-nerd-32-year-old Maris loves this comic, and I'm pretty sure that angry-punk-15-year-old Maris would have also loved this comic. Heck, I know for sure that neon-spacesuit-wearing future Maris will love it too. The art, the story, the colors...everything about this comic roped me into a universe that I was relatively unfamiliar with, but that's what great character-driven narratives do. I'm just thrilled I got to be part of the shennanigans.

—Maris Wicks

EMOTION. *gasp* I'm going to miss this book. Thank YOU for reading.

—Lauren Sankovitch

Man, those credits pages took forever. I'm sure not going to miss working on this book that I'm extremely proud to have been a part of with all of those people I really like.

—VC's Clayton Cowles

There's lots I could say, but it can probably be summed up with, "Thanks!" Thanks to the team that made the book and a bigger thanks to the fans for all their support. I'm glad I was a part of the Young Avengers. :)

—Matthew Wilson

Personally, I'd like to thank you guys for letting me just draw some trees and windows and still feel like I was part of a pretty special project. The audience has been amazing, and I'm lucky that I got to tag along.

—Mike Norton

Working on *Young Avengers* has been a singularly rewarding experience: I felt I went through the team's adventures by their side, feeling every high and low they did. But I also had my own team — Kieron, Lauren, Jake, Jon, Mike, Matt, Clayton, Kris and Stephen — that I'm going to miss even more than the YA. I'll be working with some of them again soon enough, but I want to say thank you to the whole gang for making this a year in comics to remember.

—Jamie McKelvie

I ended *Journey Into Mystery* with a short letter cut down from a far longer one. With *Young Avengers*, I'm not sure I even need to say anything, other than "thank you." Thank you. The book is the book is the book, and everything we wanted to say is in there, in this fifteen issues of oddly holographic structured pop comics. We wanted to do a book that felt like 2013, ending at the dawn of 2014. That's exactly what we did.

Being a super hero is amazing. Save the world.

—Kieron Gillen

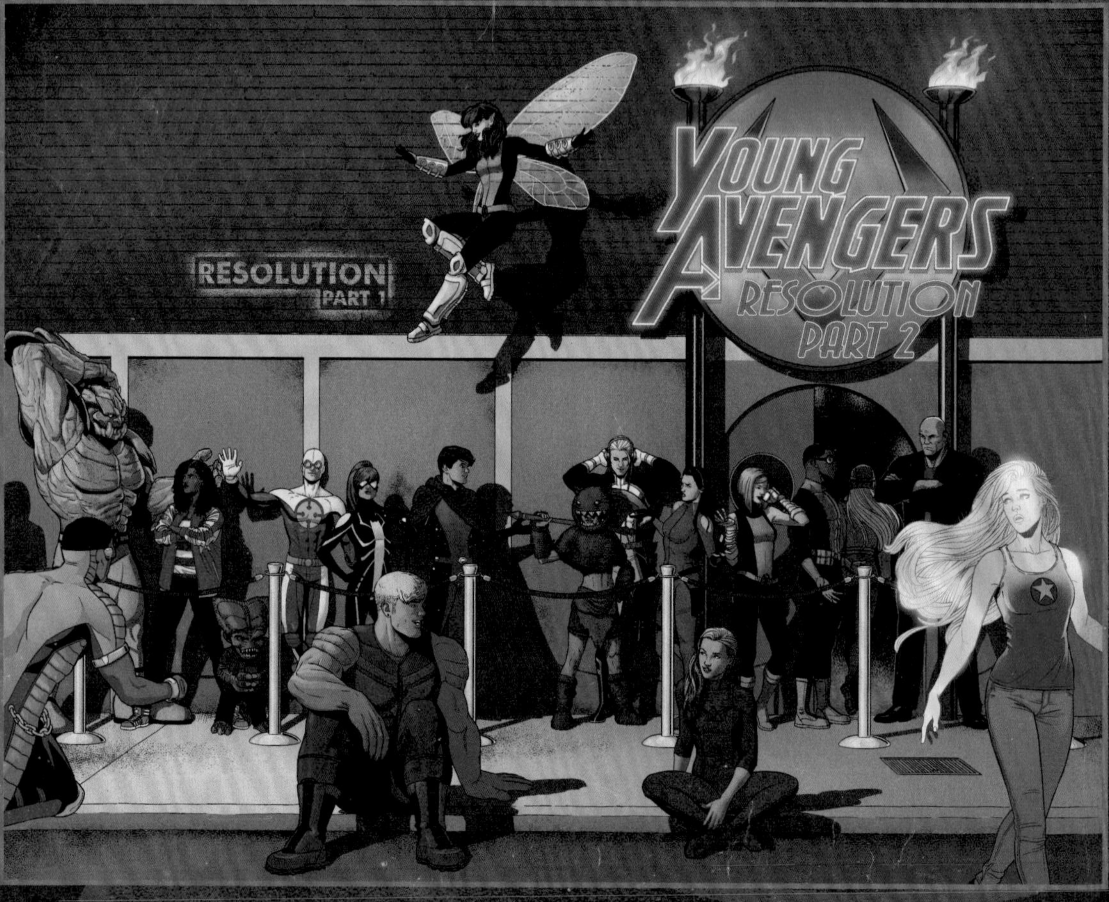
RESOLUTION
PART 1
YOUNG AVENGERS
RESOLUTION
PART 2